ROUTLEDGE LIBRARY EDITIONS:
COLD WAR SECURITY STUDIES

Volume 38

PROBLEMS AND PERSPECTIVES OF CONVENTIONAL DISARMAMENT IN EUROPE

PROBLEMS AND PERSPECTIVES OF CONVENTIONAL DISARMAMENT IN EUROPE

UNITED NATIONS INSTITUTE FOR
DISARMAMENT RESEARCH • UNIDIR

LONDON AND NEW YORK

First published in 1989 by Taylor & Francis Ltd

This edition first published in 2021
by Routledge
2 Park Square, Milton Park, Abingdon, Oxon OX14 4RN

and by Routledge
605 Third Avenue, New York, NY 10017

Routledge is an imprint of the Taylor & Francis Group, an informa business

© 1989 United Nations Institute for Disarmament Research

All rights reserved. No part of this book may be reprinted or reproduced or utilised in any form or by any electronic, mechanical, or other means, now known or hereafter invented, including photocopying and recording, or in any information storage or retrieval system, without permission in writing from the publishers.

Trademark notice: Product or corporate names may be trademarks or registered trademarks, and are used only for identification and explanation without intent to infringe.

British Library Cataloguing in Publication Data
A catalogue record for this book is available from the British Library

ISBN: 978-0-367-56630-2 (Set)
ISBN: 978-0-367-62782-9 (Volume 38) (hbk)

Publisher's Note
The publisher has gone to great lengths to ensure the quality of this reprint but points out that some imperfections in the original copies may be apparent.

Disclaimer
The publisher has made every effort to trace copyright holders and would welcome correspondence from those they have been unable to trace.

PROBLEMS AND PERSPECTIVES OF CONVENTIONAL DISARMAMENT IN EUROPE

United Nations Institute for Disarmament Research • UNIDIR

Taylor & Francis
New York • Bristol, PA • Washington D.C. • London

USA	Publishing Office:	Taylor & Francis New York Inc. 79 Madison Avenue, New York, NY 10016-7892
	Sales Office:	Taylor & Francis Inc. 1900 Frost Road, Bristol, PA 19007
UK		Taylor & Francis Ltd. 4 John Street, London WC1N 2ET

Problems and Perspectives of Conventional Disarmament in Europe

Copyright © 1989 United Nations Institute for Disarmament Research

All rights reserved. No part of this publication may be reproduced, stored in a retrieval system, or transmitted, in any form or by any means, electronic, electrostatic, magnetic tape, mechanical, photocopying, recording or otherwise, without the prior permission of the copyright owner.

First published 1989
Printed in the United States of America

Library of Congress Cataloging in Publication Data

Problems and perspectives of conventional disarmament in Europe.

   1. Disarmament—Congresses. 2. Europe—Military relations—Congresses. I. United Nations Institute for Disarmament Research.
JX1974.P684 1989   337.1′74′094   89-20421
ISBN 0-8448-1652-3

Contents

Preface	vi
UNIDIR	vii
Opening Address I	viii
Opening Address II	x
Keynote Address	xii
Introduction	xvi

Part I: Conventional Forces in Europe: Present State and Strategic Doctrines

Chapter 1.	Reduction of Conventional Forces in Europe – Problems and Perspectives *Victor Karpov*	3
Chapter 2.	Factual Groundwork *Arne Olav Brundtland*	7
Chapter 3.	Responses	
	First Response *William Hopkinson*	16
	Second Response *Manfred Müller*	18
	Third Response *Théodore Winkler*	20

Part II: Problems of Comparison between Different Conventional Armament Systems

Chapter 4.	Problems and Perspectives of Conventional Disarmament *Jon Gundersen*	25
Chapter 5.	Problems of Comparison *Gyula Horn*	30

Chapter 6.	Responses	
	First Response	35
	Joachim Krause	
	Second Response	37
	Kari Möttölä	
	Third Response	38
	Hans-Peter Neuhold	

Part III: Objectives and Methods of Reduction, Limitation, and Stabilization

Chapter 7.	Limitation and Reduction of Conventional Arms: Objectives and Methods	45
	Nikolai Chervov	
Chapter 8.	Future Negotiations on Conventional Stability	49
	Jerome Paolini	
Chapter 9.	Responses	
	First Response	54
	Benoit d'Aboville	
	Second Response	56
	Rolf Ekéus	
	Third Response	57
	John van Oudenaren	
	Fourth Response	60
	Zdeněk Pagáč	

Part IV: Confidence-Building Measures and Verification

Chapter 10.	CSBMs in Europe: A Future-Oriented Concept	65
	Adam-Daniel Rotfeld	
Chapter 11.	Verification of Confidence- and Security-Building Measures	80
	Joseph Schärli	
Chapter 12.	Responses	
	First Response	88
	Jean Desazars de Montgailhard	
	Second Response	93
	Ignac Golob	
	Third Response	98
	Roger J. Hill	
	Fourth Response	100
	Victor-Yves Ghebali	

Part V: Conventional Disarmament in Europe and Its Impact on the Rest of the World

Chapter 13. The Prospect of Conventional Disarmament 105
              Oluyemi Adeniji

Chapter 14. Super Power Relations as a Key 114
              Rikhi Jaipal

Chapter 15. Responses
              First Response 123
                Marcos Castrioto de Azambuja
              Second Response 126
                Fan Guoxiang
              Third Response 129
                Pierre Morel
              Fourth Response 132
                John Edwin Mroz
              Fifth Response 135
                Hennig Wegener

List of Conference Participants 139

UNIDIR Publications 141

Preface

In paragraphs 81 and 82 of the Final Document of the Tenth Special Session of the General Assembly, the most comprehensive consensus statement on disarmament formulated to date by the international community—the provisions of which, according to the statute of UNIDIR forms the basis of its work—it was considered that "Together with the negotiations on nuclear disarmament measures, the limitation and gradual reduction of armed forces and conventional weapons should be resolutely pursued within the framework of progress towards general and complete disarmament." States with larger military arsenals were especially urged to pursue endeavors and Europe was specifically singled out as a priority region of the globe where agreement on mutual reductions and limitations of military potential could greatly contribute to the enhancement of international peace and security.

The Washington Treaty between the USA and USSR on the Elimination of their Intermediate-range and Shorter-range Nuclear Missiles has given new momentum to discussions for further disarmament measures between the two main military alliances in both the nuclear and conventional fields and brought to the fore the controversial issue of the correlation between nuclear and conventional weapons in securing military stability in Europe.

Situated as they are in the most densely armed region in the world, and having experienced two devastating wars in the century, the European States are the first to acknowledge the fundamental importance of reducing military tensions among themselves. However, divergences remain as to the concrete ways and means for the attainment of their security objectives on the basis of mutually acceptable reductions of their respective forces.

During January 23-25, 1989, the United Nations Institute for Disarmament Research (UNIDIR), with the cooperation of the Institut Français des Relations Internationales, held a Conference on Problems and Perspectives of Conventional Disarmament in Europe, in Geneva, Switzerland, shortly before the opening of the CFE talks in Vienna. Its purpose was to explore the ideas and discuss proposals and counterproposals concerning the issue. This book contains the discussions of the meeting.

The book is divided into five parts, containing the five sessions of the Conference. Each part has three chapters. The first two chapters in each part contain the reports of the main speakers at each session. The third chapter in each part contains the responses of speakers to the respective reports.

UNIDIR is glad to publish different perspectives on Conventional Disarmament in Europe in the conviction this will contribute to a better understanding and evaluation of the concerns and expectations of all concerned thereby assisting in the search for an acceptable outcome at the negotiations.

I would like to acknowledge the special grants made to UNIDIR by the Government of Switzerland and the Canadian Institute for International Peace and Security to defray the costs of the Conference held in January 1989.

Jayantha Dhanapala
Director, UNIDIR

UNIDIR

United Nations Institute for Disarmament Research
Institut des Nations Unies pour la Recherche sur le Désarmement

UNIDIR is an autonomous institution within the framework of the United Nations. It was established in 1980 by the General Assembly for the purpose of undertaking independent research on disarmament and related problems, particularly international security issues.

The work of the Institute aims at:

1. Providing the international community with more diversified and complete data on problems relating to international security, the armaments race, and disarmament in all fields, particularly in the nuclear field, so as to facilitate progress, through negotiations, toward greater security for all States and toward the economic and social development of all peoples;

2. Promoting informed participation by all States in disarmament efforts;

3. Assisting ongoing negotiations in disarmament and continuing efforts to ensure greater international security at a progressively lower level of armaments; particularly nuclear armaments, by means of objective and factual studies and analyses;

4. Carrying out more in-depth, forward looking, and long-term research on disarmament, so as to provide a general insight into the problems involved, and stimulating new initiatives for new negotiations.

The contents of UNIDIR publications are the responsibility of the authors and not of UNIDIR. Although UNIDIR takes no position on the view and conclusions expressed by the authors of its research reports, it does assume responsibility for determining whether they merit publication.

UNIDIR

Palais des Nations
CH-1211 Geneva 10
Tel. (022) 34 60 11

Opening Address I

This conference on Problems and Perspectives of Conventional Disarmament in Europe is organized by the United Nations Institute for Disarmament Research with the cooperation of the Institut Français des Relations Internationales. UNIDIR is an autonomous institution within the United Nations system with a statute approved by the General Assembly and containing a specific mandate for the task of undertaking independent research on disarmament and related problems.

In the discharge of this mandate, UNIDIR has not only published important research on disarmament issues but has also held conferences on disarmament-related subjects where the interchange of ideas and points of view has always been fruitful and constructive. Through these conferences UNIDIR has provided a unique forum for a mutually beneficial dialogue between the policymakers and the diplomatic practitioners on the one hand, and the scholars and members of the disarmament research community on the other. This dialogue is also enriched by the fact that the participants come from diverse regions and represent different political ideologies. The hallmark of our conferences is that we do not embark on a self-conscious task of achieving a final document or declaration crafting a consensus at whatever level an agreement has been possible. We are content with the exploration of ideas, the discussion of proposals and counterproposals, and the debate on positions held in an atmosphere free from protocol and the rigidity of recorded statements. This in itself advances the cause of disarmament being an indispensable process in creating a deeper understanding of the complex issues involved, facilitating the process of consensus building that must precede any agreement.

This UNIDIR conference is in many ways a special event. In the first instance we are, after a lapse of some years, holding a conference in Geneva where the institute has its seat. We are doing so in the distinguished presence of our keynote speaker, His Excellency René Felber, the federal counsellor of our host country Switzerland, a country that has been one of UNIDIR's consistent contributors and supporters for many years. We also have the pleasure of having the cooperation of IFRI—an institute with which UNIDIR has been privileged to have had traditional ties. I would like to thank IFRI's director Thierry de Montbrial for the contribution his institute has made toward the arrangements for this conference.

The choice of the theme of this conference and its timeliness are obvious and distinctive features that have led to widespread interest in our proceedings. What we refer to today as conventional disarmament has always been on the agenda of multilateral disarmament deliberations and negotiations from earliest times. In this century the International Peace Conference convened in The Hague in 1907 had as one of its objectives the reduction of excessive armaments and a limitation of military expenditure. More recently in the nuclear era, despite the priority attached to nuclear disarmament, the Final Document of the First Special Session of the General Assembly devoted to disarmament—surely the most comprehensive consensus statement on disarmament formulated by the international community—stated that "Together with negotiations on nuclear disarmament measures, the limitation and gradual reduction of armed forces and conventional weapons should be resolutely pursued within the framework of progress towards general and complete disarmament."

In the immediate aftermath of the Washington Treaty of December 7, 1987 eliminating the intermediate and shorter range nuclear missiles of the United States and the USSR and with a halving of the strategic nuclear missiles of these countries at the top of the agenda of their bilateral negotiations, the focus has been on conventional disarmament in Europe. Last week in Vienna the mandate of the new Conventional Armed Forces in Europe Talks was finalized and we are today at the threshold of a new phase of disarmament negotiations. Already a number of proposals have been made and a re-examination of existing strategic doctrines and assumptions is underway. General Secretary Gorbachev, in his address to the General Assembly on December 7, 1988, announced unilateral reductions in his country's conventional arms and armed forces. The rapid succession of these developments imposes upon the international community the urgent task of evaluating their impact and seizing the opportunity to achieve significant cuts in conventional weapons in Europe.

This UNIDIR conference provides a forum for such a task. Conventional disarmament in Europe has already been a subject of research in UNIDIR. Last year the third issue of our quarterly newsletter published in September focused on "Conventional Armaments Limitation and Confidence-Building Measures in Europe." It contained articles on the subject from different points of view as well as an extensive survey of the ongoing research projects in this field in various institutes. Research reports were also under preparation on the subject illustrating some of the perspectives available. One of these reports has already been published and two more will appear early this year.

This conference is therefore an important element in UNIDIR's program of work on the theme of conventional disarmament in Europe. We are grateful to all the participants for their presence. We have divided the conference into five sessions dealing with different aspects of the subject, each involving the formal presentation of two papers with interventions and a discussion to follow. Among the aspects discussed is the impact of conventional disarmament in Europe on the rest of the world highlighting the linkages that exist in disarmament and security issues globally. I am confident of a lively, instructive, and stimulating exchange of ideas. With so many policymakers present and meeting on the eve of the negotiations on Conventional Armed Forces in Europe, I believe our discussion will not be without some policy impact.

Jayantha Dhanapala

Opening Address II

Although long reduced to an essentially marginal process in the context of European security, the control of conventional forces today appears to be about to play a pre-eminent role on our continent. This development, a product of the renewal that we have witnessed in East-West dialogue over the past few years, seems to me particularly important as it affects one of the basic features of the post-war period: the political and military division of Europe with an uneven concentration of conventional forces on the two sides. In fact, the possibility of achieving effective conventional disarmament by reducing the size of the arsenals in both East and West could open up the prospect of reshaping the politico-military order inherited from the cold war—an order characterized by the presence of American and Soviet forces at the heart of a divided Europe.

Beyond the technical issues, whose importance is self-evident, the nature of the stakes involved calls for an examination of the aims of conventional disarmament on the continent. From the military standpoint, the objective is, in principle, clear: it is to improve the stability in terms of the ratio of forces at lower levels of armaments. However, we lack one essential factor for the attainment of this objective, since the very concept of stability remains very imprecisely defined. With regard to political aims, it seems to me essential to reflect not only on the modalities of disarmament itself, but above all on the type of security order that will result from the disarmament process. These uncertainties as a whole require in-depth consideration and tend to favor a primarily political approach that is gradual rather than radical and conducive to parallel and balanced results in political and military terms.

It is precisely the importance of what is at stake that led to UNIDIR, in collaboration with IFRI, to hold this international conference on the problems and perspectives of conventional disarmament in Europe. With the opening next month of further negotiations in Vienna on conventional forces in Europe from the Atlantic to the Urals, the time seems to us particularly opportune to review this highly complex subject, which is undoubtedly crucial to the future of security, not only in Europe but also worldwide. On this point, I believe it is important to stress that we wished to bring together at this conference experts belonging to many countries interested in this question, not only from Europe but more generally from East and West, from North and South. UNIDIR, which is successfully engaged not only in research but also in the promotion of international discussion on disarmament matters, is one of the institutions best able to organize a forum of this magnitude.

In the course of three working days, the very high level of the participants and written contributions should enable us to cover the main issues raised by the present renewal of conventional disarmament: analysis of the situation as regards existing forces and military doctrines; comparison of arsenals, objectives, and methods of disarmament; and, lastly, confidence-building measures, verification procedures, and the impact of conventional disarmament in Europe on international security as a whole. These discussions may thus contribute to a better understanding of the stakes and of the prospects afforded by the Vienna negotiations which are about to open, and we have made arrangements to collect the texts of the statements made on this occasion with a view to their publication.

Before the substantive work begins, I should like in particular to thank Mr. Jayantha Dhanapala, Director of UNIDIR, for organizing this conference to which we have been pleased to contribute within the framework of the excellent cooperation that has already been proceeding for several years between IFRI and UNIDIR. I should also like to express my gratitude to all those at UNIDIR and IFRI who took part in the important preparatory work for this meeting, which I hope will be able to clarify some of the sometimes crucial issues raised by disarmament for the future of our continent.

Thierry de Montbrial

Keynote Address

My observations are not those of an expert on this question; I therefore do not touch on the technical aspects of conventional disarmament, but rather I speak as one responsible for the foreign affairs of this country, Switzerland, which has the honor to welcome the conference to its territory.

We are living in a period when, for the first time since the end of World War II, we can genuinely hope for a profound transformation of relations between the East and West. These relations had hitherto been marked mainly by distrust, fear, and mutual misunderstanding, which encouraged states to strengthen their military potential and to overarm themselves. This was accompanied by the erection of social, cultural, economic, political, and ideological barriers that served only to strengthen these feelings of suspicion.

It would, of course, be simplistic and naive to think that those times are now past and that we are on the threshold of a period of perfect harmony and understanding between East and West. Nevertheless, we believe we can discern, here and there, signs that lead us to believe that, progressively, East-West relations will no longer be based solely on a policy of pure confrontation, but rather on a policy of consultation and negotiation. Who, only five years ago, could have foretold the undeniable progress that has been made in controlling nuclear armaments, the realization of the danger that proliferation of chemical weapons presents, and the profound changes now taking place in the foreign and domestic policies of the Soviet Union? This maturing of East-West relations – although not irreversible – is nevertheless cause for hope.

It is appropriate to recall here the vital contributions made by the United States and the Soviet Union, and particularly by their respective leaders, to these developments. With undeniable political determination, they have revitalized their bilateral dialogue, giving it a dimension extending beyond the control of armaments and now covering also the questions of human rights and regional conflicts. Many concrete results provide evidence of this more than fruitful dialogue. Worth mentioning in the area of armaments control is the agreement between the United States and the Soviet Union on intermediate-range nuclear forces (INF), whereas in the area of human rights there has been some opening up in the USSR and there is also the prospect of ending the crises in certain regions, such as Afghanistan and southern Africa. The thaw in East-West relations is therefore producing beneficial effects, not only on our continent, but also in many other regions. I should mention, in this connection, the efforts and initiatives of the secretary general of the United Nations to resolve regional conflicts. These have provided an opportunity for Switzerland, under its policy of availability, to associate itself with the untiring efforts of Pérez de Cuéllar. It is obvious that many difficulties remain to be overcome, but we have to recognize that we are witnessing a promising start.

Because of its geo-political and strategic position, Europe has a particular interest in these developments. There are such historical, cultural, and personal links across ideological frontiers that a qualitative improvement in relations among the European states cannot fail to be in the general interest. Whereas the *rapprochement* between East and West can be seen, for example, in the increasing interest being shown by certain Eastern countries in the European Communities and the Council of Europe, it is particularly evident in the framework of the Helsinki process. The participation in CSCE of all but one of the European countries, the United States of America, and Canada is evidence of this determination to give a new dimension to and to establish new horizons for relations among Europeans. The Helsinki Final Act must be credited for having established a global approach to the problem of cooperation among the states of Europe and North America. Switzerland has always maintained that there can be no real progress in the military field, for example, without the parallel establishment of sound cooperation in the economic field and, especially, the development of greater transparency and better observance of universally recognized standards in the area of human rights. All these things are ultimately linked: if there is to be agreement in the areas of security and disarmament, distrust must be replaced by confidence, and for there to be confidence, better contacts must be established, not only between governments, but also between the peoples of all the nations of Europe.

Europe at present faces a great challenge. That challenge is the need to reorganize East-West relations, both in the political and economic fields and in the field of military security. In this connection, the dynamic role now being played by CSCE is vital. Since the start of that conference, Switzerland has committed itself with determination to the Helsinki process and has contributed to it either by itself or within the framework of the neutral and nonaligned group. Evidence of this is provided by the active role Switzerland played in the preparation of the Vienna meeting's draft final document on the follow-up of CSCE. This meeting just concluded has shown the real determination of the participating states to continue, and particularly to enrich, the process. As a result of this, the machinery for cooperation has been substantially strengthened. What we regard as the most significant step forward is that made in the area of human rights and humanitarian cooperation, in other words what is now called the "human dimension" of East-West relations. We also welcome the agreement reached on the holding of a meeting on protection of the environment—a hitherto neglected dimension of East-West relations—and on the peaceful settlement of disputes. We also hail the encouraging progress made in the military field, involving, in addition to the decision to pursue the work started in Stockholm on confidence-building measures and security, the decision to include negotiations on conventional disarmament in the CSCE framework.

If only because of its geographical position in the center of Europe and its policy of armed neutrality, Switzerland is vitally interested in greater strategic stability on the European continent, a stability implying a balance of military forces between East and West at a lower level allowing neither surprise attacks nor major offensives. There can, however, be no question of a small neutral state such as Switzerland—which constitutes a threat to no one and whose militia army has a purely defensive role—participating, at least initially, in negotiations on conventional disarmament. Yet the formula adopted at Vienna concerning negotiations among the 23 countries members of military alliances does not in any way prejudge the further action to be taken once tangible results have been achieved and the forces in presence are more balanced. A review of the structure of the negotiations will then become necessary. It is obvious that in the meantime the recognized autonomy of the 23 must have as corollary their recognition of the national interests of which each nonparticipating country will remind them at the joint 35-nation and 23-nation meetings. In this connection, Switzerland welcomes the principle, agreed upon in Vienna, of exchanges of views and information, a principle it has always supported.

Although Switzerland, like the other neutral and nonaligned countries, will not, at least initially, be participating in the negotiations on conventional disarmament, it will nevertheless be ready, as in the past, to perform tasks of verification of international treaties, should any request for this be made to it. Such a role would be consistent with its traditional good offices policy. The performance of this role obviously also implies a requirement to have the necessary trained personnel. For this reason, in agreement with the Graduate Institute of International Studies of Geneva, the Swiss authorities established, some years ago, a program of training in security policy. This program is intended in the first place for our own civil servants, but it will also be open, from next autumn, to participants from the administrations of Switzerland's neighboring countries and other neutral states of Europe.

The aim of achieving a reduction of armed forces, troop numbers, and military equipment in Europe is an ambitious one. This will probably prove no easy task and will require of the participating states an unshakeable political will. It will involve both asymmetrical reductions and a probably complex system of verification. The INF Treaty, although concluded in an entirely different field—that of nuclear weapons—has established a precedent of which we must take advantage.

It is, of course, too early to foresee the outcome of the negotiations on conventional disarmament that are shortly to begin in Vienna. We can at most assume that they will commence under much more favorable auspices than the fruitless negotiations on mutual and balanced force reductions. The present climate of East-West relations is very different from that which prevailed in the 1970s. Furthermore, all the countries that are members of the two military alliances will be taking part and, above all, having regard to the extraordinary size of the conventional forces involved, there seems to have developed—for both political and economic reasons—a genuine determination to reduce them. In this connection, Switzerland welcomes the decision, announced in the General Assembly of the United Nations last December by Gorbachev, to reduce the size of the Soviet armed forces by 500,000 men. Whereas many of the details of this reduction are still not known and the reduction will not eliminate the existing imbalance, it nevertheless constitutes a step in the right direction, further underlined by the Soviet statement in Vienna that certain tactical nuclear weapons are to be withdrawn from the East European theater.

The lessons that the states participating in CSCE have already drawn from the system of confidence- and security-building measures now functioning in Europe and that they will be drawing from the future negotiations in this field and in the field of conventional disarmament might well be useful to the states of other regions. We therefore wonder whether the scope of the disarmament conference being held here in Geneva—which is essentially confined to chemical disarmament and nuclear issues—might not be expanded to include the two matters just mentioned, for the problems that are confronting the Europeans with particular intensity exist also elsewhere.

Neutral Switzerland, a member of no military alliance and of no supranational organization, has always favored any measures aimed at ensuring greater security, greater stability, and greater predictability of military behavior in Europe. It has not contributed only words, however, to the achievement of this objective. The considerable effort Switzerland has made to ensure a credible defense of its territory is, in fact, an act of solidarity vis-à-vis its neighbors and vis-à-vis Europe as a whole, for, by this defense effort, it is able to guarantee that its territory will not form a strategic vacuum. The existence of such a security zone is a factor of which the other European states have to take account. However, that is not Switzerland's only contribution. At a time when there is frequent reference to new defense concepts, to "nonoffensive military structures," and to "defensive defenses," Switzerland can claim to have already put such concepts into effect. It does not have a permanent army on standby but rather a militia force; its counteroffensive capability is limited, its logistics are decentralized and defensive, and its doctrine is a doctrine of combat within its own frontiers.

I make no claim that the Swiss defense structure is one that can be applied elsewhere or that it is a model to be copied, because what we have done is the result of our own history and our centuries-old traditions. Nevertheless, our experience in this field may be of some value for other states.

As mentioned at the outset, we are living in very exciting times. They are exciting because there are grounds for optimism. They are also exciting because we are all confronted with a challenge, that of building, upon new bases that will no longer be those of confrontation but rather those of cooperation, a Europe stretching from the Atlantic to the Urals. For more than 40 years Europe has been living in peace under the umbrella of nuclear deterrence while at the same time building up an arsenal of conventional and other weapons unequalled in our history. To continue thus overarming without reason is no longer a viable course. We are all convinced of this. The states participating in CSCE have the opportunity to contribute decisively to the reversal of this trend, which will be successful only if relations are established between them that reflect a higher degree of trust. I can assure you that Switzerland, for its part, will spare no effort for the achievement of this goal.

Rene Felber
Department of Foreign Affairs
Switzerland

Introduction

Negotiations on arms limitation and conventional disarmament in Europe appear to have a promising future, and this book is intended to illustrate not only their prospects but also their complexity. They have a long and turbulent history and constitute the most worthwhile regional approach, particularly as they concern the area which has the greatest concentration of weapons in the world.

It is impossible to say how they will turn out, for even though the trail has in part been marked, unexpected obstacles and unforeseen delays are always possible. Nor can a study of the past suggest what is likely to happen in the future. Yet these negotiations are taking place in a time-frame and a context whose basic outline was determined over 40 years ago and which has not known any major breakdown having been experienced. This historical framework, with the past ever present, is of decisive importance and may be contrasted with the declaratory, abstract and prophetic vision expressed more willingly in global multilateral fora.

The European context is, moreover, particularly complex and permits only a methodological, or so to say administrative, distinction to be made between the question of disarmament (or arms limitation or reduction, or yet stability, security or balance of forces—depending on the terminology used) and the various factors that shape the development of political relations in Europe. What should be borne in mind in this connection is that the process has survived crises and overcome obstacles owing to the existence of the diversity, flexibility and even ambiguity of the fora concerned.

The very idea of negotiations immediately suggests a patient search for agreement, a narrowing of viewpoints and the gradual achievement of consensus. Yet what are also important in this respect are unilateral measures, and these are frequently overlooked. It is tempting to regard them only as manoeuvres or traps if they simply take the form of announcements or unilateral declarations of intent, or as preparatory and therefore transitional measures if they take the form of genuine proposals and negotiating elements leading to agreement. Conversely, it can be said that they may be meaningful in themselves, bringing about progress while at the same time retaining their unilateral nature, and it is this aspect which is at present obvious in the European context.

**

Glancing back over some 20 years of negotiations—beginning with the M(B)FR without going back to the various proposals and agreements which prepared the way for them, and indeed without overlooking what was in fact a womb which gradually gave birth to the Helsinki Conference—what is striking is not only the slowness and complexity of the process but also its durability and, taking an optimistic view, its continuing impetus. Its development was facilitated by a sort of empiricism as if, the negotiating instrument—or rather instruments—which could give rise to positive, even if modest, results were gradually developed as a result of groping first this way and then that. The trial and error method was applied. Errors, once recognized, were corrected by adopting more suitable forms and topics of discussion. A superficial reading of events would suggest that such discussions were pointless and repetitive since they succeeded in producing only more and more documents. Yet this would be to ignore the results achieved, namely, the Final Document of the Stockholm Conference, and the progress in the negotiating methodology itself.

And yet this process constitutes almost an insolent challenge to United Nations multilateralism. It predates the first special session of the General Assembly devoted to disarmament (SSOD-I) in 1978 which gave a fresh start to the global disarmament exercise; it is part of a cumbersome historical process which is far removed from the general perspective of the SSOD-I Final Document of 1978; it concentrates on conventional weapons and deliberately ignores nuclear weapons which were the foremost concern at the first SSD; it depends to a greater extent on progress made in American-Soviet negotiations rather than on discussions in the Conference on Disarmament; and it aims at security through strategic stability rather than collective security or general and complete disarmament, which is the basic leitmotif of the Final Document. And yet, despite all that, the process is continuing.

But there is something artificial about this divergence. Taken as a whole, the various disarmament or arms reduction efforts converge and complement one another. The result of this diversity of approaches, bodies, areas and weapons does not result in incoherence and futility of the disarmament exercise as a whole. Far from frustrating such efforts, these divergences act as a stimulus and result in breakthroughs. For example, the Stockholm experience with on-site verification proved to be of advantage in connection with the INF Treaty which, in turn, may offer valuable lessons both for the CDE as well as for the negotiations on chemical weapons, even if the problems involved are of a different scope and nature and even if the technical solutions arrived at in the past cannot be transposed in their entirety.

Reverting to the narrower framework of the reduction of conventional weapons in Europe, the main question—the key to success—remains. Empiricism is always equivocal. Two tendencies are invariably apparent in negotiations. One aims at victory through the consecration of *de facto* domination which has been accepted, willy-nilly, by the partners. The other aims at agreement through a search for common interests or at least the optimum protection of the interests of each party.

In the case of the first tendency, which implies the existence of an acknowledged power scenario, agreements are easily arrived at, precisely because they merely consecrate the supremacy of the dominant party or the perception of such supremacy—which at least at the outset comes to the same thing. Yet such agreements continue to depend closely on the situation on which they were based, so that in all likelihood their existence will very soon be affected by the evolution of power relationships which are, by definition, variable. Either the parties concerned regard them as a stage on the way to further progress or, on the contrary, the weaker parties reject them as soon as they are in a position to do so; history abounds with examples of both cases. Such instruments which are rapidly and in some cases triumphantly drawn up, subsequently become subject to the vicissitudes of the changing power configuration.

On the other hand, negotiations constituting a genuine search for agreement, based on a desire for a balanced outcome and, if the formula adopted enjoys long-term validity, mutual advantage and which aim neither at effective domination by one or more participants or a desire to bring about such domination through maneuvres or trickery are much more difficult and need more time to be obtained but ensure much more lasting results. To a large extent these results are achieved by the maintenance of initial contradictions. Such negotiations must therefore perpetuate the ambiguity of individual positions, without spelling them out or rejecting them—as for example in connection with security concepts and the role of nuclear deterrence. They constitute an indefinite process whose partial results are nevertheless more firmly rooted in facts and therefore respected more easily. In this connection the system of universal collective security, with its all-powerful Security Council which is often paralysed, can be compared with the negotiations on European security which, for the time being, have resulted only in confidence-building measures that nevertheless meet with general satisfaction. Efforts aimed at the peaceful and agreed reorganization of a security system in the absence of any irresistible internal or external constraints are without parallel in the history of the world. Moreover, the stated purpose of this reorganization is not to set the stamp of approval on the domination of one State or a group of States over the others. What is highly symbolical from this standpoint is the fact that negotiations which initially began between alliances were gradually transformed into negotiations between the States of the Continent, enabling small Powers as well as neutral and non-aligned States to play a not insignificant role.

But, as a matter of fact is the situation that favorable? Does not this ambiguity also extend to cover the very nature of the negotiations, negotiations aimed at consolidating supremacy or, on the contrary, reaching an agreement that generally takes account of the legitimate diversity of the interests of all States concerned? It must be borne in mind that this entire process, this long gestation, is rooted in the absence of a peace treaty with Germany following the Second World War. To a certain extent might not its purpose be to consecrate the victor or victors of this conflict which still remains or remain to be identified once and for all. Or, putting it another way, if the intention is to put an end to the Cold War, would this be done by institutionalizing the Soviet advances that gave rise to it—which would be tantamount to recognizing their lasting nature—or, on the contrary, by discreetly bringing about the dislocation of the Soviet bloc—which would thereby signal their historical failure. The negotiations could certainly not be successful if they were presented or even conceived in this spirit. Yet this is probably one of the things at stake and one of the possible explanations for their slowness as well as their sloping development, since they cannot in themselves meet this challenge. However, they cannot be separated from this context, namely, the general political context which, in the final analysis, concerns the evolution of the power scenario on the Continent.

* *

This context can be analyzed from two standpoints: that of the scope of application of power and that of the factors constituting power.

In this sense, Europe is both more and less than the Continent in its geographical sense, just like one of Calder's mobiles which is unable to find its center of gravity. It is more than Europe in the geographical sense because the "big brothers" cannot be ignored and because much depends on their bilateral agreement or disagreement. The INF Treaty is not limited to Europe which is, however, the area of its main impact, and it was negotiated without the participation of the European countries. More also because to an increasing extent the outside world does not let itself be forgotten anymore. For example, what implications do multilateral negotiations such as the one on chemical weapons have on the region? Other examples are the implications for reductions in conventional weapons in Europe of the continuing instability and conflicts in the Third World, of armament policies or even of the rampant arms race which is tending to develop in certain parts of the Third World. The general political limits of the splitting up of negotiations and of the analytical method rapidly become apparent. It is always tempting and sometimes effective to divide a difficulty into as many elements as possible, but the interdependence of such elements should not be ignored.

Europe is also less than Europe in the geographical sense in so far as it does not regard itself as a single unit and because the growing desire for European construction and organization are likely over the short term to overcome outstanding differences of various kinds. It is obvious that the most dynamic progress is being achieved in only one part of the Continent, and this will inevitably give rise to reactions that are difficult to control on the part of countries which deliberately or otherwise remain on the sidelines. Is this long negotiating process likely to revive a European conscience, or more precisely create it, since it has never really existed before? Certainly not in terms of unity in any circumstances, but rather through new forms of competition and rivalry between States, regions and groups, for such competition and rivalry have always been the hallmark of its genius and should be attenuated and regularized rather than eliminated.

As regards the factors constituting power, it would seem that they are at present dominated by two closely associated elements, namely a relative decline in importance of military force as a yardstick of power and the increasing importance of economic strength and technological capacity—all this logically coinciding with a long period of peace.

As a result, security can no longer simply be identified with defence. It implies something much more, but by the same token something more vague, more composite and less definable. The stability of domestic society is, for example, one of its elements, not in the conventional sense but rather as correspondence between the aspirations of the governed and the conduct of those who govern. This can be achieved only if the governed exercise better control over power. The same is true of freedom of communications and trade, the predictability of behavior patterns and the State governed by the rule of law—"l'Etat de Droit." These interrelationships make it more difficult to isolate negotiations confined to weapons systems alone, and at the very least complicate any efforts to do so owing to the constant emergence of extraneous factors. This explains the emergence and subsequently the general acknowledgement of the topic of human rights as an integral part of negotiations on security in Europe in the framework of the Helsinki process.

At the same time, the relatively declining importance of the role played by military power will possibly militate in favor of specific measures aimed at the limitation or reduction of armaments, not as a result of the espousal of a pacifist ideal but because such measures are in the interest of each of the States concerned. Nevertheless, the importance of technological capability should not be overlooked. Weapons are being modernized, fewer but more skilled men are required to operate them and they are becoming more efficient but more costly. In this case, negotiations could well lead to concerted and programmed reductions which facilitate such modernization rather than genuine disarmament. In that context, arms reductions turn out to be an unexpected form of a controlled arms race, both from the qualitative as well as quantitative standpoint. Yet security remains the key word. However, regardless of the degree of cooperativeness of such arms reductions—and confidence-building measures are symbolic and offer an interesting foretaste in this respect—security remains basically an individual matter, so that what counts most in the final analysis are unilateral measures.

**

From the disarmament standpoint, unilateral measures are not well thought of, at least by the experts. First because, from a historical standpoint, the arms race was initiated, accelerated and relaunched by such unilateral measures on both sides. Secondly because it is doubtful whether they are capable of starting a disarmament race. The possibility or announcement of such measures may touch the right chord among militant organizations owing to their ostentatious manifestation of virtue and goodwill, but they cannot in themselves resolve the basic problems of disarmament. By definition they do not imply reciprocity and therefore do not guarantee the initiation of a "virtuous circle." They are likely to weaken peaceful States in relation to those which are less peaceful, thereby complicating the question of individual and collective security. Owing to their nature, moreover, they cannot be the subject of an organized verification process and they depend completely on the State that announces them and then applies them as it sees fit.

Yet this virtuous unilateralism—or rather hypocritical if it is merely intended as a stage effect designed to catch the eye of the pacifist organizations of the opposite sides and thereby to increase a multiple pressure against them—does not exhaust the wealth of practical possibilities offered by such measures. Unilateral measures in essence have three aspects, inherent in each measure to varying degrees depending on its content, on motivation and on the reactions that it generates in the counterpart or counterparts. The first, most elementary, aspect is of a propagandistic nature; the two others concern the impact that such measures may have on negotiations and the fact that they may act as substitutes for agreements by reason of their exemplary nature or even as a form of prior application of an agreement that they may represent.

It is, of course, too early to say whether such measures can play an effective role in the framework of negotiations on conventional forces in Europe. All that can be said is that unilateral measures are not at variance with agreements but rather complement one another. A quite general although modest trend towards the reduction of military expenditure—or rather efforts to prevent it from increasing—is underway, and it is clearly the result of mutual emulation. The withdrawal of troops, the phasing over a longer period of the production or modernization of armaments, thinking about the modification of strategic doctrine, all represent first and foremost an effort made by each party in respect of and for itself, in the hope of deriving benefits without jeopardizing the essential elements of its security. But at the same time these efforts create a new climate and, by offering a concrete demonstration of the reality of the objectives being sought, they may even anticipate the agreement, suggest its general outline and even constitute a prior stage of implementation. A series of convergent unilateral measures in line with the personal interest of their author and at the same time corresponding to collective aspirations are thus capable to a considerable extent of performing the functions of an agreement. In this case, negotiations serve as a womb for the production of unilateral reductions or adjustments which, in the final analysis, approximate an implicit agreement and an agreement in which no one is the winner since it expresses the decision freely arrived at by each of the partners concerned.

Yet a formal agreement is nevertheless necessary. The positive role of unilateral measures must be stressed. They can be an incentive, they can anticipate events, and they can constitute a *de facto* provisional agreement. In essence they constitute a rag-bag category of confidence-building measures. Yet agreements offer irreplaceable advantages. On the one hand, only an agreement implies a genuine commitment, since it creates a situation that can be reversed only with difficulty. On the other, the reliability of the obligations assumed obviously depends on their verifiable nature, and verification can be organized only in an international legal framework that unilateral measures are unable to provide by themselves.

Serge Sur*

---

* Deputy Director of UNIDIR. The views expressed in this paper are not necessarily those of UNIDIR.

Part 1

Conventional Forces in Europe: Present State and Strategic Doctrines

Two main topics are tackled here: (1) the impact on multilateral negotiations of the unilateral reduction measures announced by the Soviet side, and (2) to what extent it is relevant to use and discuss, as an initial element in the negotiations, basic data on the existing deployment of military forces. A third topic is mentioned briefly: the nature of military theories, as an introduction to the qualitative aspects to be considered when comparing the positions of the two alliances. Views on all these points are widely divergent, making it difficult at this stage even to draw up a systematic list of areas of disagreement.

The Western participants focus chiefly on the effects of the unilateral reductions announced by the Soviet Union, and their possible consequences for the Vienna negotiations. They do not dispute the significance and value of these measures, while emphasizing that they are not open to verification under the same conditions as joint measures. The fear is expressed, however, that they might complicate the first phase of the negotiations. Might not the Warsaw Pact countries adopt the stance of looking for some quid pro quo from the Western countries, an ill-defined expectation of no fixed duration, liable to cloud the prospects of this first session? Is the aim not to call into question the list of armaments to be considered immediately? Are the current steps not leading — as Nikolai Chervov's report (see Chapter 7) might lead one to think — to an attempt to include naval armaments, which are specifically excluded by the mandate for the negotiations? What is the significance of reductions by zones, what is meant by the concentric zones mentioned by Victor Karpov (Chapter 1), and what is the situation regarding special-status corridors? Last, what expectations would such unilateral measures stimulate in terms of NATO's planned modernization of short-range nuclear weapons? It is pointed out in this regard that the unilateral reductions announced by the Soviet Union had an impact on tactical nuclear weapons, which are and will remain outside the scope of the negotiations. It is also pointed out that the reductions in question are not sufficient in themselves to redress the existing imbalances, particularly in tanks and artillery, and that the Warsaw Pact member countries will still enjoy considerable superiority.

On the Soviet side, emphasis is placed on the scale of the unilateral reductions that were announced, and their role in eliminating asymmetries. The need is also argued, from a methodological point of view, not to concentrate unduly on drawing up initial statistics of the armed forces and weaponry at the disposal of each alliance. It is important to avoid the kind of debate that, in the MBFR talks, had proved complex and only too liable to lead to an impasse. It seems more useful to attempt to define objectives, agree on the various stages of reductions to be made, and monitor how the reductions were put into effect at each stage. It is, of course, useful to have basic data supplied for comparison by both alliances in order to show where they are starting from; but it is more important to know where they are going.

Chapter 1

REDUCTION OF CONVENTIONAL FORCES IN EUROPE—PROBLEMS AND PROSPECTS

Victor Karpov

The reduction of NATO and Warsaw Treaty armed forces and conventional arms in Europe constitutes a key problem of disarmament.

We are happy to note that the West also now views agreement on conventional forces as a political priority. Such agreement is regarded as an indication of the willingness of states to change the numerical strength, structure, and location of their armed forces in line with the principle of nonoffensive defense and, in broader terms, to place East-West relations on a new footing.

The joint efforts of all the CSCE participating states have produced an agreed mandate for the negotiations on conventional forces in Europe, which is to begin very soon [March 1989].

Our position is stage-by-stage reductions in the armed forces in Europe down to levels that would be sufficient exclusively for defense. Recently NATO set forth its proposal on stability at lower levels of armaments.

Can we build a bridge between these two proposals? I think we can.

Despite serious differences, there is a certain similarity in the positions of the two sides. Both NATO and the Warsaw Treaty stand for removing the existing asymmetries and imbalances through cuts in armed forces and armaments, above all those that have the capability of surprise attack, or large-scale offensive operations. We feel that prospects now look good for the elaboration of such an accord. To this end, we should proceed to elaborate a first set of agreements right away, while regarding the Vienna negotiations as a continuous process and without wasting time on general discussion, which, as experience shows, may only fossilize our positions.

In particular, both sides place top priority on reducing those armaments that may have the capability of surprise attack, or large-scale offensive operations. It is obvious that our attention should be focused above all on those armaments while eliminating imbalances and reducing arms. If we follow this path, i.e., single out the most dangerous types of offensive weapons (for example, attack aircraft, combat helicopters, tanks, artillery, armored personnel carriers, landing-crossing means, etc.), set ceilings on them that would be lower than the currently existing and lowest levels of NATO and the Warsaw Treaty, an agreement could be promptly reached.

The main difficulty that will confront the negotiations from the very outset concerns the numerical discussion that killed the Vienna negotiations on disarmament in Central Europe. Certainly, it would not be possible to avoid it altogether. The issue is how to minimize its dangerous consequences for the negotiations. One could also consider the possibilities of discussing in parallel the necessary data base and ways to achieve intermediate and final objectives of the negotiations.

It is also obvious that reaching agreement on a specific list of armaments and their concrete counting is an extremely complex task for the negotiations. This will give rise to disputes that are likely to last till the end of the century in the proper sense of the word, particularly if verification of all declared levels of arms is set as an objective. Therefore one could also consider the following option: to conduct negotiations on ultimate ceilings of the types of weapons to be reduced, not on the initial database. Thus verification will be applied to the achievement of these ceilings, i.e., to what is left after the reductions. Verification would be introduced gradually as these weapons are reduced. When agreed lowest ceilings will have been reached, full verification of the remaining weapons would be envisaged.

This approach would probably help avoid numerical discussions. At the same time some data exchange could be carried out in the committee of 35 if the sides agree on the exchange of information related to the strength, structure, and location of their armed forces.

Another option could be selective inspections to verify the data base. But in any case we must keep in mind that the objective of the negotiations is not the data base but ultimate levels of existing weapons that should be reduced to the lowest possible levels.

Today it is important to make the first step. The Soviet side will be actively working to this end in order to pave the way for the implementation of the three-stage reduction of forces and armaments in Europe, proposed by Mikhail Gorbachev, which would be naturally further developed, specified, and translated into the language of appropriate treaty formulas.

It is important to agree from the outset on the principles of disarmament. In this connection I would call attention to the fact that our unilateral steps, announced by Gorbachev on December 7, 1988 at the United Nations, contain as if in an embryo possible principles of future reductions: asymmetry, elimination of imbalances, reduction first and foremost of the most destabilizing weapons, forces pullback from the line of direct contact between NATO and the Warsaw Treaty, disbandment of the formations to be withdrawn, changing the structure of the divisions remaining in the zone of Central Europe for the purpose of giving them clearly defensive functions, etc.

In this context we must mention another important factor—the dialectical relationship between unilateral and multilateral steps. Thus unilateral steps, particularly in areas of great asymmetries in offensive weapons, can stimulate the entire negotiating process and make possible even further reaching multilateral agreements. At the same time we must clearly realize that there exists an objective limit to unilateral actions beyond which disarmament must take on a multilateral character.

An important point in conventional reduction is the organic relationship of that process to the elaboration and introduction of new confidence- and security-building measures in the military area. Agreements to be reached at the negotiations of the 23 and 35 states must be harmoniously interrelated, complement, and enhance each other.

The negotiations on confidence- and security-building measures and disarmament in Europe should promote the elaboration and adoption of measures that would ultimately cover activities of all kinds of the armed forces (land forces and naval forces) of the CSCE participating states.

In this context, we may also consider the idea of achieving earlier positive results at the talks of the 35 states on confidence-building measures.

One more thing: the Soviet Union reaffirms its willingness also to negotiate priority reduction of tactical nuclear weapons the moment the implementation of cuts in conventional armed forces and armaments gets underway. Obviously, it would not be possible to lend to the military formations of the two military alliances an exclusively defensive posture as long as these weapons of huge destructive capability remain on the continent.

On the other hand, given an extremely close operational, technical, and organizational relationship between armed forces, conventional armaments, and tactical nuclear systems, it is obvious that major cuts in general purpose forces would make it essential to reduce those nuclear weapons. Incidentally, that relationship is present in our unilateral steps, announced by Mikhail Gorbachev at the United Nations: the Soviet Union will withdraw from Central Europe formations and units together with all their assigned weaponry, including tactical nuclear systems. This would effectively constitute a major unilateral nuclear disarmament measure.

Clearly, those Soviet steps would create on the continent new conditions that would also favor the start of a dialogue on tactical nuclear weapons, including shorter range missiles. In the context of these Soviet steps, the West would be well-advised to consider once again its approach to the problem. Clearly, large-scale cuts in armed forces and conventional armaments, particularly in more destabilizing types, would significantly reduce the mutual threat of surprise attack or offensive operations employing conventional means of destruction and effectively remove all justification for keeping tactical nuclear weapons in the military arsenals of NATO and Warsaw Treaty countries.

Given the determination of all the states to achieve success, their first priority task should be the overcoming of the "powerplay" stereotypes and the willingness not to look at each other through gunsights.

It is well known that for many years diplomats of the East and the West have been bogged down in the discussion on what is to come first—confidence-building or arms reduction. However heated, that discussion only led to one result—inaction. In the meantime the flow of new weapons was steadily growing and international problems piled up. It has probably become clear by now to everyone that military preparations constitute not only the most obvious and condensed expression of mutual distrust but also stimulate it because they are perceived by the opposing sides as material proof of aggressive intentions.

That is why we believe that today public assurance of peace intentions and of the defensive character of one's military doctrine no longer sound convincing unless they are backed by concrete, tangible moves by a state in the sphere of its military policies, i.e., in the field of development of armed forces and armaments, their structure and location, operational planning as well as willingness to reduce the level of military confrontation through disarmament negotiations. In this connection it is particularly urgent to bring—in deeds rather than in words—the military policies of states strictly in line with the declared defensive objectives of their military doctrines, and to fill these doctrines with concrete content.

The idea is that following the restructuring of armed forces, neither their defensive might in quantitative or qualitative terms nor the military policies of states in general should push the other side toward building up its own military power or create the impression of an impending threat.

As for the Soviet Union and the other Warsaw Treaty member states, they have already begun restructuring their armed forces on the basis of the principle of reasonable defense sufficiency. As a result of the Soviet unilateral disarmament measures now underway, the numerical strength of the Soviet armed forces will be pared by 12 percent, the military budget reduced by 14.2 percent, and the production of arms and military equipment will go down by 19.5 percent. Of the troop cuts totaling 500,000 army and navy personnel to be carried out within the next two years, 240,000 will be reduced in the European part of the USSR, 200,000 in the east and 60,000 in the south. We intend to withdraw from our army groups 5,300 most advanced tanks, and of the 10,000 tanks slated for reduction in Europe, 5,000 will be physically eliminated with the rest to be converted into towing vehicles intended for civilian use or into simulators. Shortly, we plan to begin the second reduction of our troops stationed in Mongolia, amounting to 75 percent of their size, in addition to removing our air force grouping. We also intend to pull out of Eastern Europe several formations and units that lend an offensive posture of our military deployments in that region.

In short, already now it may be said that a theoretical reassessment of the defensive military doctrine of the Warsaw Treaty member states has moved to the stage of practical military deployment. What I would like to emphasize in this connection is that the unilateral reduction of the Soviet armed forces and conventional armaments has become possible as a result of a radical improvement in the international situation over the past two to three years and the introduction of the principles of new political thinking in the foreign policy of states, both in the East and in the West.

All this goes to show that we have already begun reassessing our previous perception of the military threat emanating from the West and made relevant political adjustments, including in our military policy. But it is essential that a similarly changed perception of the Soviet Union and Socialist countries assert itself in the West. Only this can make it possible to overcome mutual distrust and achieve radical progress at the Vienna talks in the near future.

The Soviet Union and the other Warsaw Treaty member countries stand ready to consider any possible proposals and measures that are likely to lead to greater stability on the continent at a progressively lower level of military confrontation and in conditions of respect for the principle of equality and undiminished security of all sides, provided negotiated agreements are made effectively verifiable.

Chapter 2

FACTUAL GROUNDWORK

Arne Olav Brundtland

I take my mission to help establish a factual groundwork for a discussion on conventional forces in Europe. The utility of such facts can be found in highly different directions. My introduction could help serve as a platform for an approach to arms control and disarmament. In other words I could try to help establish the facts that should be a starting point for an academic evaluation of military problems for the negotiations to come on Conventional Armed Forces Europe, the CAFE negotiations for March 1989, and for the Conference on Security and Cooperation in Europe (CSCE) follow-up on further Confidence and Security-Building Measures (CSBM) as well. But the military facts are also of great importance, one could say even greater importance, for an evaluation of security and strategy. They form a basis for unilateral acts of build-ups, build-downs, restructuring, and modernization. Security is the first concern, the level of armaments comes second, although the trend now fortunately is to seek security at the lowest possible level of armaments.

The problem of disagreements about military facts in Europe has a long history connected to the Mutual and Balanced Force Reductions, the MBFR talks, in which the contention of the North Atlantic Treaty Organization (NATO) has been that the Warsaw Treaty Organization (WTO) has had about 180,000 troops in excess of what has been admitted by the WTO states. This is now presumably history, partly because of new approaches to the problem as seen in the negotiations for a mandate regarding Conventional Stability Talks (CST) recently concluded with a successful outcome. The CST has, however, attacked the problems differently from the MBFR since the former has been influenced by three concepts of what really matters for stability, namely

1. Forces particularly useful for strategic surprise attack.
2. Forces with abilities to launch large-scale offensive actions.
3. Forces particularly capable to seize and hold territory.

Existing forces should be seen in conjunction with their utilities. Agreement on concepts might therefore help not only an agreement on negotiations but also an agreement on what facts should be examined.

Other speakers will penetrate problems of comparison of conventional armament systems, objectives of reduction, limitation, and stabilization, CSBMs and verification, and the impact of European disarmament on the rest of the world. By stressing the facts, however, I shall also be keeping an eye on these perspectives.

Being an academic expert without access to classified information, I am naturally forced to take as a point of departure the information brought forward by institutions that have such access in full or in parts. In view of the long tradition of treating military facts as valuable secrets, the disclosure of which has been looked upon as tantamount to high treason, the recent openness and moves toward greater transparency would be a great help in establishing the facts and their meaningfulness. This process is in full swing, but not yet completed.

The subtitle of my introduction is "present state and strategic doctrines." That indicates observations beyond a simple enumeration of military hardware.

Conventional forces amount to much more than an enumeration of military hardware and personnel. It is in the modern jargon more than a mere "bean count" as it includes a lot of imponderables of military and even political nature, e.g., readiness, mobilization, and sustainability, political decision-making. It also includes strategies, of which the forward defense and flexible response of NATO over the years has been matched by the traditional offensive defense of the WTO. Both strategies are under discussion, the WTO strategy seemingly to a greater extent that the NATO strategy.

Strategic doctrines matter; the conventional military picture cannot fully be understood without reference both to weapons of mass destruction (chemical and nuclear) and to naval forces. The complexity of the problem should, however, not be used as an excuse for not examining important parts of it. But it should help remind us of the necessity for exercising some modesty.

Furthermore, there is the problem of geography since geographical limitations are not necessarily congruent with military possibilities. For now the focus is on Europe, mostly with the designation from the Atlantic to the Urals (ATTU). That excludes important territory of both alliance systems. Furthermore, ATTU has been felt to be a somewhat inadequate description in view of the interests of the states at the flanks. Flank states would rather view Europe also stretching from the Barents Sea to the Mediterranean or from Svalbard to Sicily (ATTUSS). This gives an important underlining of the complexity of the problem. It seems, however, taken care of with regard to the CAFE talks since the one has agreed to consider the whole of Europe and to take care of measures against circumvention.

THE FACTS OF NATO

A most comprehensive collection of military facts is contained in the NATO document issued in November 1988: *Conventional Forces in Europe: The Facts*. It gives an awesome impression of WTO superiority in all major weapons systems. And it should, therefore, give a strong backing of the need for asymmetrical reductions. The NATO *Facts* lists 11 categories of weapons and military formations. All show a substantial Soviet and WTO superiority ranging from about 80 percent of the totals in category no. 2, Armored Infantry Fighting Vehicles, to about 60 percent of the totals in category no. 9, Ground Forces Personnel while oscillating around 70 percent of totals marked by most other categories. NATO figures are given in exact numbers, WTO figures in round numbers (Table 2.1).

A further characteristic of the figures in Table 2.1 is that the Soviet Union alone in most categories possesses quantities not only in excess of NATO, but in excess of the combined quantities of all other member states in the two alliance systems. Weapons in storage have

Table 2.1 NATO and WTO Weapon Categories

Categories	NATO	WTO
1. Main battle tanks in units	16,424	51,500
2. Armored infantry fighting vehicles	4,053	22,400
3. Other armored vehicles in units	35,351	71,000
4. Artillery in units	14,448	43,400
5. Antitank weapons in units	18,240	44,200
6. Air defense systems	10,309	24,400
7. Helicopters	2,419	3,700
8. Armored vehicle launched bridges in units	454	2,550
9. Personnel, ground forces	2,213,593	3,090,000
10. Divisions stationed outside national territory[1]	7⅓	31
11. Combat aircraft in units	3,977	8,450
12. Independent brigades[2]	9	8

[1] Of these divisions the United States has 4, the UK 3, and the Netherlands ⅓; all WTO divisions are Soviet. NATO *Facts* lists 20 Russian divisions in the GDR, 2 in Poland, 5 in Czechoslovakia, and 4 in Hungary, disregarding the Soviets' claim of not having reintroduced the one division they withdrew from the GDR some eight years ago.

[2] NATO figures include 5 United States, 2 British, 1 Canadian, and 1 Belgian brigade; all WTO brigades are Soviet.

not been included in the count, but it is further stressed in *The Facts* that WTO all over has more than NATO also on that score.

The single most important factor in the count might be considered the overwhelming Soviet forward deployments on the territories of its allies in Eastern Central Europe.

The report must be seen as a compilation of facts and is lacking in interpretation both as to the overall military value of the figures and the explicit value of the facts when it comes to the CAFE talks slated for March.

The Facts must be seen in conjunction with the presentation of the report entitled *Conventional Arms Control: The Way Ahead*, issued in March 1988 by NATO heads of states and governments in Brussels, in which it is emphasized that the imbalance in conventional forces remains at the core of Europe's security concerns.

In the spirit of openness, the *Facts* has been transmitted to all CSCE participating states. But it is stressed that "this information is no substitute for the data which all participants will need to provide in the course of forthcoming negotiations and that it should not prejudge the categories of forces to be covered or the degree of detail necessary."

Accessibility of reliable data naturally is a necessity, although one might argue that no meaningful agreement is achieved by agreement on data only. One is looking forward to the promise of publication of the necessary data from the WTO and one takes great interest in the statement of Foreign Minister Eduard Shevardnadze at the closing ceremony of the CSCE in Vienna to come forward with data in the near future.

While waiting for the Soviet statements of military facts, one might take courage from some other Soviet statements, first of President Gorbachev's speech in the UN and some of the official or semiofficial statements. With regard to a possible Soviet final analysis of the NATO documentation, I refer to an article distributed through the Novosti Press Service by Major General G. Batenin, in which he takes positive note of changes in NATO in order to build a common European bridge also from the Western side through disarmament of conventional military means of war. The document *Declaration on Conventional Arms Control*, as well as the communique from the meeting of NATO foreign ministers in Brussels in December 1988 are characterized as documents issued in the spirit of the policy of the new thoughts (APN December 21, 1988 no. 244 p. 5).

In general, whereas I can take note of a positive critique of the NATO document *The Way Ahead*, of March 1, also note that negative critique of the *Facts* document of November is either lacking or indeed very weak, although there have been some statements to the contrary in some conversations (e.g., at the time of or during the visit of Norwegian defense minister J.J. Holst to Poland in December 1988).

With regard to the aims of the CAFE talks to remove imbalances suitable for surprise attacks, large-scale offensive actions and the ability to seize and hold foreign territory, the four first categories on the NATO *Facts* list, seem to be the most worrisome, namely (1) tanks, (2) armored infantry fighting vehicles and (3) other armored vehicles, plus (4) artillery. In all four categories the WTO enjoys a clear superiority by having about 75 (category 1), 80 (2), 65 (3), and 75 (4) percent of the totals (see Table 2.1).

"Bean counts" are naturally not enough for giving any meaningful military picture. Many other considerations must be taken into account. But "bean counting" has the advantage of simplicity. Weapons systems can be identified, counted, moved forward, withdrawn, destroyed, verified, and inspected. And without weapons, soldiers have no significant missions. "Beans" can be negotiated.

This chapter is intended to give a picture of the situation with regard to conventional arms in Europe, not to offer an analysis on the CAFE talks. However, it seems appropriate to offer some judgements along lines of what, inspired by U.S. Senator Carl Levin, could be called beyond the "bean count."

VIEWS BEYOND THE "BEAN COUNT"

This naturally means stressing a lot of important military indicators along lines of quality, readiness, sustainability, and other values of scenario-dependent utility. Here the compilations and evaluations of Senator Carl Levin (D, Michigan) of the Armed Services Committee might be of considerable help, but not necessarily of too much comfort since the impressions of the overwhelming WTO superiority is only somewhat reduced.

Senator Levin's report; *Beyond the "Bean Count": Realistically Assessing the Conventional Balance in Europe*, 2nd ed. (July 1988), issued in his capacity as chairman of the Senate Armed Services Subcommittee on Conventional Forces and Alliance Defense, uses 13 criteria that, in the words of the subcommittee, "must be analyzed in a realistic assessment of the balance of conventional forces" (see Table 2.2). In the judgment of Levin, WTO scores on top of NATO in categories 1, 2, 8, and 13; WTO is given the benefit of the doubt in categories 5 and 12. The two alliances are considered to be equal in category 6 and doubtfully equal in 9. NATO scores best in categories 3, 4, 7, 10, and 11. (See Appendix B of the report.)

Also note the accompanying different evaluation of Mr. Karber, based on different preconditions of impact on preparation time in which he distinguishes between short warning, rapid reinforcement, and extended mobilization. With reference to short warning as a precondition for the evaluation, Karber puts WTO ahead or the two alliances on an equal footing, but does not put NATO ahead in any single category. On the basis of rapid rein-

Table 2.2 Assessing the Conventional Balance

Categories	Levin's judgment
1. Deployment of forces—capability for surprise attack and effective defense in Europe	WTO
2. Quantity of major weapons systems	WTO
3. Quality of major weapons systems	NATO
4. Force readiness	NATO
5. Force sustainability	WTO ?
6. Number of active and reserve personnel	EQUAL
7. Quality of personnel	NATO
8. Interoperability of forces	WTO
9. Command, control, communications, and intelligence (C3I)	EQUAL ?
10. Reliability of allies	NATO
11. Economic and industrial strength	NATO
12. Geographic factors	WTO ?
13. Ability to decide to mobilize prior to outbreak of hostilities	WTO

forcement as another precondition, however, Karber, with the exception of category no. 2 quantity, puts NATO either ahead or at an equal footing with the WTO. When it comes to extended mobilization as a similar precondition, WTO gains in category 5, sustainability, from equal to ahead; NATO gains from equal to ahead in categories 6, number of personnel, category 9, C3I, category 11, economic strength, and loses to equal in category 12, geographic factors.

EVALUATION OF "BEAN COUNT" versus "REALISTIC ASSESSMENT"

Any attempts to evaluate the "beans," thus, is dependant on the preconditions for the assessment and the purpose of it. A much-cited evaluation of the military balance in Europe is made by the International Institute of Strategic Studies (IISS) in London through the yearly *Military Balance*. For a number of years the IISS has arrived at about the same conclusion:

> The conventional military balance is still such as to make general military aggression a highly risky undertaking for either side . . . there would still appear to be insufficient overall strength to guarantee victory. The consequences for an attacker would be quite unpredictable.

(Here taken from the *Military Balance* 1985–86 as cited in Levin's report.) One might notice that the IISS does speak of general military aggression and not about surprise attack, large-scale aggression, ability to seize and hold territory.

Senator Levin also cites (obviously approvingly) Dr. Richard Kugler, the director of the Strategic Concepts Development Center of the National Defense University: ". . . the balance, in my view, is sufficient close, closer than is commonly believed, such that the pursuit of a viable conventional posture . . . is itself a viable programming goal with the resources that are likely to be available." Here one might note that Dr. Kugler makes his evaluation not in terms of arms control agreements but in terms of a NATO ability to improve the balance through a stronger conventional effort of which NATO is surely economically capable but politically unwilling.

One might finally note that qualities and scenario dependant preconditions might be very difficult indeed to negotiate as compared to quantitative limits.

FLEXIBLE RESPONSE

Let us turn to the question of military doctrines starting with NATO's doctrine of flexible response and forward defense based on a determination not to give up territory.

In my view the doctrine is somewhat vague and therefore robust for changes. Although it is and has been under considerable public criticism and debate, it still seems to command sufficient support to be considered official NATO doctrine. The idea of responding to aggression with force tailored to the task of stopping it should not be considered offensive in any way. The idea of not being willing to give up territory is likewise natural and it is of particular importance to the small strip of land called the Federal Republic of Germany. The necessity of preserving an ability to escalate is illustrated by the disparities in conventional weaponry, and it furthermore underlines the close connection between conventional forces and forces of mass destruction, nuclear forces in particular. The stronger the conventional defense, the higher the nuclear threshold, or the better the conventional balance, the smaller the role of nuclear weapons, which nonetheless hardly can be removed.

True, there has been much debate in NATO countries about the problems of nuclear weapons, but NATO has not felt conventionally strong enough to drop the wish to reserve for itself the possibility of even a first use, and it seems difficult to go any further than to a possible no-early-first-use, which naturally would be preferred under all circumstances. "A nuclear war cannot be won and must never be fought" — sure. But the idea of security in doctrinal uncertainty still seems to hold the day. Questions raised about the role of nuclear weapons under flexible response in relation to a no-first-use agreement or a no-early-first-use policy is closely related to matters of the conventional balance and possible missions of forces.

One might take account of the different attitudes of military commanders as well. General Rogers, in his capacity of supreme allied commander Europe, SACEUR, voiced difficulties in upholding flexible response in view of the elimination of the INF weapons, whereas his successor, the present SACEUR, General Galvin, seems reasonably confident that he stands a good chance of fulfilling his missions without the INF weapons that have been negotiated away. He even has indicated preparedness to trim NATO nuclear battlefield forces and, like many others, has been stressing the advisability to achieve a more equal military balance on lower levels of armaments in Europe through negotiations.

In these matters the policies of the Federal Republic of Germany is of particular importance, but an intelligent guess about the relative weight of forces for a change is not easy to make. The so-called crisis of acceptability is likewise difficult to evaluate. (Hans Rühl gives an interesting update in "Die Welt," January 12 1989.) At present the interaction of nuclear arms control, Soviet unilateral reductions, and the *problematique* of demonstrating conditional willingness to risk destruction of what should be defended has stimulated the discussion on the roles of nuclear weapons, and much could look different in years to come. Strategies might be changed, but nuclear weapons cannot be disinvented.

The discussion on the Western side ranges from the need to maintain and even stress nuclear deterrence à la Glücksman to far-reaching changes toward "nichtangriffsfähichkeit" à la von Bülow.

In official circles modernization in most fields of weapons is constantly on the minds of policymakers and military leaders. And so is the matter of revisions of concepts like FOFA and other considerations for making the military instrument of security viable. In particular in view of the doctrine of forward defense, however, strategic defense seems impossible without some degree of tactical offense.

On the other hand, doctrines could also be evaluated as instruments of policies. Whereas NATO has not felt prepared to issue any no-first-use of nuclear weapons declaration, it has certainly issued a long list of no-first-use of weapons statements. NATO rules of engagements for military commanders fully underline this basic nonoffensive defensive doctrine.

OFFENSIVE DEFENSE

The Soviet doctrine of strategic offensive defense has been interpreted as a doctrine of administering early crushing blows and moves forward by large forces to the territory of the enemy. The idea seems to be to bring the war to the enemy at the earliest possible time by overwhelming forces to secure the earliest possible victory should war break out. Both in doctrinal statements and by forward deployments to the territory of the GDR, the Soviets have enjoyed a solid credibility for the doctrine of offensive defense. For the militarily stronger, the doctrine is an excellent one, although it naturally is expensive to uphold.

Even to Western observers, however, this doctrine (which also might have been given other designations) is undoubtedly under revision on the official plane through declarations by WTO political leaders and by responsible organs of the pact as well. The ideas of new political thinking, i.e., elimination of threats, and the doctrine of "reasonable sufficiency" bear witness to this, and so do statements of military reorganization, i.e., the dissolution of the so-called Operation Maneuver Groups, the OMGs.

Unilateral Soviet reductions along the line of Gorbachev's UN speech of December 1988 serve as another, and perhaps even more convincing, substantiation of the doctrinal change. Acts traditionally speak louder than words. The reductions to come, according to Gorbachev, would significantly reduce Soviet offensive power in East Europe, and should be welcomed. The withdrawal of 5,000 Soviet tanks from the GDR, Czechoslovakia, and Hungary represents a 50 percent reduction of this, a most offensive weapons system. The military significance of the withdrawal of six divisions from their forward deployment in the three countries, which likewise speaks in favor of the credibility of the new doctrine, although its significance could finally be judged when the selection of actual units is made. Other declarations of withdrawals and disbanding of military formations and military hardware and destruction of the latter speak to the same effect. The recent (Shevardnadze, Vienna, January 1989) announcement that the Soviet units also will bring back their battlefield nuclear weapons is an important but nevertheless limited addition to make the doctrinal changes credible.

A point for examination should nevertheless be whether the slimming of Soviet forces, although naturally representing a real reduction, might not have so dramatic effects as seen at a first glance, since there would be a lot of possibilities by means of reorganization to lessen the loss in military effectiveness in withdrawal and dissolution. The factual implementation of the unilateral Soviet policy will be followed by very eager eyes, indeed.

SIGNIFICANCE OF DOCTRINAL CHANGES

The new transparency of the East is of considerable importance. Doctrinal changes to a more defensive platform are likewise important. The whole discarding of Cold War rhetoric and the positive use of possibilities for East-West cooperation across the board have positive security implications.

The varieties of significance of military doctrines, and in particular the display of the order of battle, might, however, be hard to judge. But any move toward "defensive defense" makes for better stability and opens for mutual respect for defensive needs and for understanding. The CSCE process bears witness to the idea that transparency and openness are of importance to stability. Further moves in the direction of insights into military thinking of the two alliances should enhance stability and give credence to the concept of common security. Approaches in the spirit of a common European home (Gorbachev at numerous occasions) or a common European village (Holst, Warsaw, December 1988) certainly will help bring the defensive thinking in either part of Europe into a common line and help stabilize detente and stimulate far-reaching arms control. The burying of enemy images and excessive negative criticism of the other side contribute to the same end. But, again, acts speak louder than words.

FROM ATTU TO ATTUSS

Most "bean counting" and other evaluation of the military situation have traditionally been centered on Central Europe. That is the region in which the WTO superiority is most strongly felt.

When it comes to other parts of Europe, south and north, however, the pictures look different. The "bean counting" approach, as one knows, regarding the south of Europe puts NATO in a superior numerical position. But southern members of NATO are countries spread along the latitude of the northern Mediterranean and they have not been too clever at modernizing their forces. A qualitative evaluation tends to downgrade NATO's numerical superiority. Countries are far apart and most have forces with local missions only. The southern flank of NATO is further characterized by tensions between Turkey and Greece, much to the embarrassment of NATO.

In the north the picture is yet another. And the evaluations depend upon how Northern Europe is designated. But speaking of the Scandinavian members of NATO—Denmark, Norway, and Iceland—and making comparisons with, e.g., forces in the Leningrad military district, the Soviets again are overwhelmingly superior in numbers. But comparison is difficult since distances are short. Forces in Eastern Europe, outside of the Leningrad military district, might have or could be given different missions. Denmark can also be said to be threatened in an emergency by forces primarily dedicated toward Germany. Denmark is strategically closer to Central Europe than is Norway and, naturally, Iceland.

A comprehensive calculation of forces in the central region or regions cannot be fully meaningful without consideration of naval assets. That follows from the nature of NATO as a "sea alliance." The same is even more the fact when one considers the Mediterranean and the northern waters, respectively. In the south, allied forces outnumber Soviet naval forces, which, nevertheless, are substantial. In the north, Soviet naval forces are regularly dominant, although allied missions and exercises represent actual counterweights while present in the region and potential counterweights because of the flexible nature of naval power. Overall NATO disposes of greater seapower than the Warsaw pact. NATO is, by its geographical configuration, also much more dependent on the sea as compared to WTO, which is a land alliance. Naval considerations shall, upon agreement, not be included in the CAFE talks and considered only in a limited way in the CSBM negotiations.

Discoursing into a Norwegian perspective for arms control in Europe, I would underline the great importance to the northernmost flank country of the present development in Europe. A balance at lower levels of armaments in Central Europe is of great security interest to Norway. Questions of war and peace in Europe have a particular bearing in the center. There have been the post-WW II political problems with potentials for outbreak of war. The problems of the flanks and in particular the problems of the northern flank are of a different military nature because of the naval factor, but the overall security is a function of the balance in Central Europe.

Nevertheless, whereas arms control in Central Europe in general is of significance and in the Norwegian interest, one is keenly aware of the potentiality of transporting imbalances from the center to the flanks. The so-called sausage theory of heydays of MBFR, of old weapons being withdrawn to new places, is in principle still of concern and so is the new possibility of a nuclear arms race, in particular in sea-launched cruise missiles (SLCMs), and air-launched cruise missiles (ALCMs), either being stimulated by the INF agreement or conducted as an alternative to it.

This testifies to the proposition that under the local northern perspective, the elements in the balance are different from the elements of the balance in the center. The significance of armor, personnel carriers, and artillery is great in the center, whereas other weapons systems in the north seem to hold a greater potentiality for surprise attack. The 76th Guard Air Landing division in the Leningrad military district and other air transportable units (mobile brigade), plus the naval infantry at the Kola Peninsula, represent in the view of many Norwegian military experts greater threats for surprise attack than do the armor, artillery, and the personnel vehicles in the north.

Security within the alliance is one and indivisible. Norway does not take exception from flexible response. Common security can be developed from the Atlantic to the Urals and from Svalbard to Sicily. Norway takes an active part in this matter. But the tactical implementation of security might differ greatly in different areas.

Chapter 3
RESPONSES

FIRST RESPONSE
William Hopkinson

The comments of Victor Karpov (Chapter 1) are welcomed, as are the many positive developments in the USSR's position in recent times. If I deal here with points of differences it is not to be negative, but to make clear the areas of difficulty.

Let us consider a number of issues raised by Karpov.
1. Verification after reductions. We must avoid a position where the West is asked to make reductions only to discover after the event that there are significant differences in the remaining levels of armaments—e.g., because of different counting rules. We certainly need to avoid the sort of exchanges that were so frustrating in MBFR—and to press on with the substantive negotiations—though work on definitions, and on verification of data, will have to go forward at an early stage, perhaps in parallel with negotiations on numbers.
2. Withdrawal from contact. It is not realistic to ask NATO to abandon forward defense. There are very real political issues at stake, as well as a lack of depth for a different defense strategy. If the Warsaw Pact puts forward proposals that may be the basis for serious negotiation, they will have to take cognizance of those facts.
3. Changes in doctrine. This causes concern to the other side, much more for the Warsaw Treaty Organization than for NATO. The latter is a purely defensive alliance of free nations; a candid examination of its policies, its decision-taking process, and its actions over 40 years demonstrates that no one could feel threatened by the idea of a NATO-launched attack. In any case, as is well known, doctrine has a very different significance for the Soviet Union and the Warsaw Pact than it has in the West. Changes in the USSR's doctrine, to make it unambiguously and demonstrably defensive, are, of course, very much to be welcomed; what the West now awaits are demonstrations that the changes that have been mentioned have moved down from the academic or diplomatic level and have started to impact on teaching in military academies, and in the carrying out of exercises.
4. Zones. We must certainly address the particular problems of particular areas—e.g., concentration of armaments on the central front. However, security of *all* must be preserved. There must be no marginalization, nor leaving certain areas out of comprehensive arrangements. As already indicated, withdrawal from contact in the center

of Europe is not a realistic option if it means NATO's forces going back well behind the inner German border. Let us rather devise limits on armaments that, applied in a uniform manner and simultaneously, meet the needs of thinning out such concentrations as are threatening. That does not require corridors or special zones, but sensible limits for the whole ATTU area, not, of course, ruling out sublimits within it.
5. Without in any way impugning the integrity or intentions of Gorbachev, we must consider the certainty that the most welcome new thinking will last. NATO does wish to move forward, but at each stage it will need to consider the East's capability as well as its stated intentions. I repeat, I am not questioning Gorbachev's desire, but history shows that changes can frustrate intentions. The USSR has enormous economic difficulties; there are problems of nationalities; even within the party itself there appear to be divisions of opinion. It is not inconceivable that some of these problems, despite Gorbachev's reforming desire, could give rise to instability. In those circumstances we need to be certain at each step that our security can be assured, given the capability and military assets of the East.

More generally, if we are to avoid frustration and to make early progress in the forthcoming negotiations, we must not attempt comparisons of numbers of one kind of weapon with numbers of another, or assessments of relative quality. It is difficult to compare one tank with another—how does one offset, say, firepower against mobility, or protection against survivability? Early agreement on such matters is just not possible. All the more would this be the case if one attempted to assess, say, aircraft against tanks.

Further, to make early progress in the areas where there can be the least dispute about what needs to be done, we need to focus on the pressing issue of asymmetries in those major assets that can seize and hold ground in Europe. There is no doubt about the relative order of holdings—whatever the precise numbers; and there is no doubt that territory can be invaded and held only by such weapons. Maritime and air assets, on the other hand, are highly mobile, often relenting to worldwide rather than European issues, and not easily dealt with on a regional basis. Moreover, though aircraft in particular can contribute significantly to the land battle, neither they nor ships can sustain a territory-seizing action on their own. I would therefore urge early concentration on the major pressing issues—tanks, artillery, and armored vehicles—and for the avoidance of highly complex and technical debates, almost certainly incapable of agreed outcomes.

However, it must be recognized that we do not pursue arms control for its own sake, but to add to security. No state can be asked to agree to proposals unless it can be assured that its security will be secured. Hence the importance at an early state of establishing the facts—i.e., verifiable data.

In estimating security, the Warsaw Pact will recognize the importance of seaborne communications to the West. One might say almost that our ships are the equivalent of their trains. We need to protect them against a formidable force of submarines. Everyone will be conscious of the grave threat posed to Great Britain in both world wars by submarines far less sophisticated and capable than those deployed today. Defense of those shipping lanes poses no threat to anyone. The USSR and its allies are land powers; frigates cannot significantly damage them, yet our lack of such assets would enable the West's very lifeline to be severed. And, of course, in considering the West's needs for maritime defense, one must measure the task not by counting the number of antisubmarine frigates held by other states, but by considering the ocean areas, the amount of merchant shipping, and the threats to that shipping.

To get into a detailed combination of such matters would not make for speedy progress on the central threat to stability in Europe—the concentration of massive ground forces, capable of surprise attack, of seizing and holding ground. The CAFE negotiations should seek early progress on those. The changes announced so far by Gorbachev are welcome, but they still leave great imbalances. The change in stated Warsaw Pact doctrine is welcome, but not in itself sufficient as a basis for Western reductions. What we must do now is order the priorities; tackle the whole of the ATTU area; avoid exclusive zones, but look to the security of all. We must address first the present great imbalances in ground forces, and press on with measures to remove those.

SECOND RESPONSE

Manfred Müller

The agreement on the mandate for the negotiations in Vienna underlines the favorable situation that now exists in Europe for conventional disarmament. This conference should not be seen as an interference or as setting preconditions for those negotiations, but it could help us to understand better the conditions under which such talks will take place.

To start a discussion of the state of conventional forces in Europe, especially the state of the forces of the two alliances, we should look at the European situation first. This situation is characterized by a profound contradiction. On the one hand, Europe, especially Central Europe, has the highest concentration of forces, both nuclear and conventional. On the other hand, it becomes clear that any use of these forces, any war or military conflict in Europe cannot be rational since it would end in the destruction only of the continent.

European, especially Central European, societies have become war-incompatible. Even if one believes that European peace can be saved, under the existing circumstances only by means of nuclear and conventional deterrence, this can already be achieved by only part of the existing forces. If we take into account the existence of hundreds of nuclear facilities, chemical plants, and modern cities in high density, then a military action would destroy what it is intended to conquer or defend. The unavoidable breakdown of the electric power systems alone would interrupt heat production, water supply, traffic, ecological protection, and so on, with far-reaching devastating consequences for societies and people, especially in urban areas. It is useless to base war—or even defense—scenarios for Europe on the experiences of World War II.

If we take this situation into account, the question arises as to what kind of military action can be regarded as possible and even useful under such conditions. To conquer another country is impossible. A surprise attack to take over limited territory may be thinkable, but nobody can be sure that the action can stay limited. In a situation where one side has certain weapons, hoping to strike successfully against sensible points of the other side under specific conditions, and the other side may have not the weapons or the power to answer in kind can lead to a new and dangerous threat. It is therefore necessary not only to look at the existing and most debated forces but to pay attention to the emergence of new weapons and new threats specifically tailored for the European situation.

Both NATO and WTO declare that they do not intend to attack the other side. Nor does either side impute to the other the intention of direct attack. But there are different assessments of the opponent's capability for attack. Whereas WTO points to the existence of offensive-capable elements on both sides that have to be abolished, NATO perceives such capacities exclusively on the side of its counterpart and denies its own. For this reason NATO demands that measures be taken by WTO to eliminate asymmetries in tanks, armored vehicles, and artillery without taking into account existing qualitative differences in these systems.

Some politicians, until now, hesitate to include in a process of reductions the modern elements of offensive strike systems. These include modern fighter bombers, tactical missiles, combat helicopters, airborne and seaborne troops, and so on. But, as noted before, it is those military forces that may be able to act in Europe. They can attack the other side's lifelines and destroy or even occupy them. Under these circumstances, one could even hope to gain territory worth conquering. In contrast, an occupation by advancing large numbers of tanks and engaging thousands of artillery systems, together with measures of response by the other side, would only result in a total destruction of both sides engaged in the conflict. Thus besides eliminating asymmetries and generally lowering the level of armed forces as laid down in the Vienna mandate, both old and modern offensive strike systems must be subject to limitations.

At the same time, we stop the process of steady modernization of nuclear and conventional weapons becomes one of the urgent problems in stabilizing the security situation in Europe. The members of WTO, as a consequence of in-depth research of the European situation, have changed their military doctrine. The new document was signed in Berlin in May 1987. The announcement, made by Gorbachev in December 1988 on unilateral reductions of forces of the Soviet Union shows that the change of doctrine was not only a declaration, like some heard in the West. Consequently, it was followed by new strategic and training documents and by new thinking on necessary defensive military structures. The fact that the 10,000 tanks to be withdrawn from the territory of other WTO members are more than the equipment of the six tank divisions that withdrew as announced shows that the reduction process is combined with steps of restructuring the remaining units to defensive missions only.

With the unilateral reductions, the GDR has announced that it will contribute to such a development. These measures not only include a remarkable reduction of its forces, but by taking out of the remaining forces the weapon systems that may be seen as specifically offensive, the GDR intends to demonstrate readiness for a general change of the role of the military in its security policy on the basis of similar actions by other states. This, naturally, is a process. It depends not only on the abilities and threat perceptions, but on the reaction of the other side, too.

Often it is said that NATO would not have any position similar to the military doctrine of WTO. Even if such a document does not exist, NATO bases the role of its armed forces on basic doctrinal thinking that ruled military strategy, concepts of training and equipment of the forces, and so on. It is high time that the two alliances start discussions of this doctrinal thinking and try to find common positions.

As long as the thinking with respect to the role of armed forces, their structures, strategy, and tactics differs basically, it is very difficult to find common ground for deep reductions. The European situation needs a common understanding between the two alliances of European security. It should be possible in such talks to formulate conditions and to find structures for the forces of both sides that may guarantee high confidence in the defensive intentions of both.

Central Europe has to play a special role in such a process of change. If a military conflict in Europe would break out, it would be started here. But if we speak of the war-incompatibility of European societies, this is true for Central European countries first. For the people of Central Europe a stable peace has become the *conditio sine qua non* of existence. They have, therefore, a special common interest, and the special initiatives undertaken by some of the governments and political forces and parties of this region have to be seen in this light. Realized as special and separate measures between the states of Central Europe or within the context of all-European agreements, a development toward military disengagement in Central Europe is necessary. It can be started with rather simple steps, not even tricking the existing forces, but with special measures of confidence-building and monitoring. Cooperative steps of crises prevention and common evaluation of events can follow. Finally, a special military regime has to be agreed upon within all-European solutions. All this must be based on the existing realities and built on similar military structures. To change the situation in Central Europe for the better, the only region in which the two alliances have a common border of more than 1,000 kilometers, seems a central element within a process of change of the armed forces on both sides to a reasonable, and with the European situation corresponding, role.

THIRD RESPONSE

Théodore Winkler

The reflections here should not be taken as those of the Swiss Confederation or the Federal Military Department, though they may reflect perhaps the concerns of many small countries. When I look at the international situation, I cannot but be impressed by the positive turn that international relations and the crucial task of arms control have taken. The sad period a few years ago, when negotiations had been interrupted and there appeared to be hardly any prospect for an improvement in East-West relations, belongs to the past. We do not only see progress, but are presented, in rapid pace, with new initiatives and ideas.

These initiatives are certainly well timed since the conventional arms control dialogue is due to resume again in Vienna. They almost seem, however, to outrun the slower step at the negotiating table to which we have, perhaps unfortunately, become accustomed. This may in many respects be positive. It contains, however, the risk that we do not know precisely where we stand. As Goethe after he met Aegel had to say, "I still feel puzzled, but at a higher level."

Let us address some simple questions, however, in which all of us are interested.

Foreign Minister Shevardnadze has said that negotiations on conventional forces in Europe should—to avoid the bitter experience of MBFR—focus on how many weapons each side should be allowed to retain under an agreement rather than to quarrel about how many it has right now. And so has Minister Karpov [Chapter 1]. There is some merit in that approach. It also raises questions, however.

Does it mean that the Soviet data on the existing balance, which have been promised to us, will be strongly different from those NATO presented a while ago? If so, in what way?

Does this, furthermore, mean that the USSR has dropped, or changed, the first stage of the three-part proposal presented to the United Nations last year? The essence of that stage was—to cite Colonel General Gareyev:

> during the first stage it is proposed to identify and eliminate all imbalances and asymmetries between NATO and the Warsaw Pact both in numbers of troops and main armaments. In order to identify the imbalances and asymmetries, it is envisaged that there be an exchange of initial data on existing armaments, and that these data can be carefully verified, including by on-site inspections.

What will happen to this verification possibility? Does the Soviet Union still believe in its utility should the data sets be far apart from each other? Is the Soviet Union perhaps even prepared to have its announced unilateral reductions to be verified—and thus to enhance their importance even further? With respect to NATO, if the Soviet data are rather different from those presented to NATO, will it be prepared to focus on ultimate objectives for the various weapons categories, or will it insist on a common data base as a precondition for agreement?

Foreign Minister Shevardnadze has declared that the six tank divisions to be withdrawn from Eastern Europe and to be disbanded would take their nuclear delivery means with them. It is important to know what these means precisely consist of. It has been argued by some that this might not include SS-21 missiles because those would have been transferred from divisional to army level. To detail Shevardnadze's important announcement may thus be highly important indeed—and so is the question of what will happen to this equipment and its associated warheads.

General secretary Gorbachev has announced in New York that six tank divisions, 50,000 men, and 5,000 tanks are to be withdrawn from the GDR, the CSSR, and Hungary. How many divisions from each of these countries will be withdrawn is important, but as yet unknown. Moreover, consulting the military balance of the IISS leads to the conclusion that six tank divisions—particularly if additional assault units are added—exceed 50,000 men. Six tank divisions have, on the other hand, clearly less than 5,000 tanks. Has one to read the discrepancy as implying that each of the remaining 24 Soviet divisions in Eastern Europe will lose in a linear fashion 120 of the tanks incorporated to it? Some concrete details about what the restructuring of these divisions will precisely entail would be very important. Gorbachev has, finally, declared that out of the 10,000 tanks to be reduced, 5,000 would be destroyed, the rest either put to civilian uses or used for training purposes. The latter two categories seem not entirely clear. Similarly, is it correct to assume that the 8,500 artillery pieces and 800 aircraft also involved in the important Soviet announcement will be destroyed? These questions need a clear answer—or at least we might need to know by when an answer can be expected.

NATO has been rather reluctant, it appears, to consider to negotiate a reduction of its tactical air forces deployed in Western Europe. Where do we stand in this matter? Is there, let's say, a tank-to-aircraft exchange rate at which that reluctance might be overcome? If not, what will this mean for the negotiations ahead in Vienna? Can there be an agreement at all without a reduction of air forces?

In Switzerland, we make excellent watches. We have learned that the tiny little pieces that compose a watch are difficult to assemble in the first place and that it is utterly impossible to make a watch if you miss some pieces or do not know what they look like. Reaching arms control agreements and assembling watches seem — in that respect — quite comparable undertakings, which after all might be one of the reasons why so many important arms control negotiations and this important conference take place in Switzerland.

Part II

Problems of Comparison between Different Conventional Armament Systems

Concentrating on the question of whether to include qualitative factors in the comparison of conventional armaments, the participants from Western countries maintain that including such factors is very difficult if not impossible and would therefore significantly complicate the negotiations. They say, however, that the present negotiating position of the NATO alliance aiming at stability at a lower level of armaments is not based on a purely quantitative approach. There are several aspects that transform the basically quantitative approach into a qualitative one. The aim of reducing weapon systems particularly suited for surprise attack and invasion, the stationing rules, and other proposed measures contain such qualitative elements. These stability measures complement the quantitative approach. Notwithstanding, this so-called bean counting was said to be a necessary element despite its pejorative connotation. A participant of a Western country points out that, although parity could not be the only feature of an arms control agreement, a treaty that would leave one country numerically inferior because the comparison of armaments was based on qualitative factors as well, would not be acceptable to the British government or parliament, for example. It is acknowledged, however, that the approach supported by NATO is not perfect. As to the manageability of the negotiations, the participant of a Western country feels that the Warsaw Pact countries should stick to the agreed mandate for the talks and not try and introduce, for example, naval forces through the back door.

The negotiating position of the Warsaw Pact countries is that European stability should be strengthened by reductions of conventional armaments to levels sufficient exclusively for defense. A Warsaw Pact participant maintains that he could not imagine negotiations that did not take into account qualitative factors in the comparison of existing conventional armaments. He underlines this necessity with the example of the combat value of tanks or aircraft. He concedes, however, that the introduction of qualitative elements could make negotiations difficult, but says that the consideration of such aspects is necessary. Negotiations on categories for qualitative aspects should be held at the beginning of the Vienna negotiations. Detailed data from both sides should be put forward in order to undertake a deep and substantive analysis and to conclude which reductions would be required.

Some attention is also devoted to the unilateral steps taken by some Warsaw Pact countries. These measures are welcomed. Nevertheless, the interdependence between unilateral and multilateral steps is stressed. A participant of a Western country, for example, points out that NATO did not ask for more unilateral reductions. A participant of a Warsaw Pact country, on the other hand, states that the unilateral steps of Warsaw Pact states will be developed and that NATO should examine similar, if only symbolic, measures.

The remark by Gyula Horn (Chapter 5) saying that COCOM has complicated the development of defense technologies in Warsaw Pact countries is briefly referred to by two Western participants. To one it is a strange idea to use COCOM as a reason for applying qualitative criteria to the comparison of conventional armaments. To the other, to complicate the development of new military technologies is precisely the purpose of COCOM.

The link between conventional disarmament and nuclear weapons is noted by a participant of a Western country, who says that conventional stability, the aim of the Vienna negotiations, can only be relative. Even if a most favorable outcome of the talks is reached, the nuclear factor would still be needed to backstop the results achieved.

Chapter 4
PROBLEMS AND PERSPECTIVES OF CONVENTIONAL DISARMAMENT
Jon Gundersen

Problems discussed here are related to the comparison between different conventional armament systems. I concentrate on the *problems* not because I believe that they are insurmountable, but because they must be understood and addressed if they are to be surmounted. I also discuss the issue of military doctrine as well as the issues of the quantity and quality of conventional weapons.

First, however, let us put the upcoming conventional arms control talks in a conceptual framework. An initial draft for the final declaration at the Paris Conference on Chemical Weapons noted the will of the international community to promote the cause of disarmament throughout the world in all fields. What could be wrong with such a declaration? During the 1970s many came to see weapons per se, particularly nuclear weapons, as evil incarnate; consequently, the goal became the elimination of various weapons systems. The most comprehensive expression of this line of reasoning is found in the Final Document of the United Nations First Special Session on Disarmament.

The position of the United States at Paris, as it has been in the last two Special Sessions on Disarmament, was to place disarmament within a conceptual framework. This has also been the approach taken by the United States in its bilateral *negotiations* with the Soviet Union.

What are the assumptions underlying this conceptual framework? First, arms are not the cause but a symptom of international tensions. Second, disarmament is a means, and not an end. The end—or goal—is international peace and stability. Third, parallel progress on other aspects of the international situation, such as peaceful resolution of regional conflicts and respect for human rights is also necessary. In other words, international stability cannot be enhanced through disarmament measures alone.

Thus in Paris the wording of the final declaration was changed to place the pursuance of effective disarmament measures in the context of the Charter of the United Nations and its objective of maintaining and promoting international peace and security.

The NATO approach to the negotiations on Conventional Armed Forces in Europe has been characterized by a similar understanding. The objective of these negotiations is not

---

This chapter does not necessarily reflect the views or positions of the United States government or any agency thereof.

the reduction or elimination of armaments themselves, but rather the achievement of peace and greater stability in Europe. Western participants in the Vienna Mandate Talks therefore dubbed the future talks as Conventional Stability Talks, or CST, long before there was agreement on an official title—Negotiations on Conventional Armed Forces in Europe, or CAFE Talks. (Editorial writers will surely put the title "Vienna CAFE Talks" to good use over the next few years.)

The whole idea of "stability" is, however, not particularly amenable to common understanding. For some, it means a panoply of zones, areas, and restrictions. Others would argue that a certain stability already exists in Europe; still others would define stability more esoterically, perhaps on the basis of computer modeling and simulation descriptions.

In any case, it seems fair to say that in the context of conventional arms, stability requires that balanced and predictable military force capabilities be established and maintained over time.

But how does one measure the military balance? How precise must this balance be? What tolerance, for example, can be accepted as older equipment is replaced by newer, more capable gear? How does one monitor the dynamics of military forces to protect the stable balance sought in an agreement? In assessing these questions, let us address the issue of military doctrine as well as the quantity and quality of conventional weapons.

The importance of a state's military doctrine is being increasingly recognized as a major element in the problem of assessing force balances. The value of a tank or an artillery piece or any other item of military equipment is directly relevant to its intended use. In other words, what does a tank do? What does an artillery piece do? Is a specific tank design intended to maximize its ability to fight other tanks, to be capable of high rates of speed and mobility, to provide direct fire capability, to provide a breakthrough capability, to be merely survivable in battle, or to reflect a combination of such requirements? These questions bring us to the importance of what the West generally refers to as military doctrine and the Warsaw Treaty states call military art: strategy, operational art, tactics, plus command and control.

It may be assumed that each state participating in the CAFE talks uses different analytical processes and techniques for assessing the force balance. Some stress that the global totals of all armaments in any state involved in the negotiations must be taken into consideration in assessing the balance. Some resist this approach in recognition that the modest size of their military capability does not threaten any other state and therefore must be considered of secondary importance. Others stress the geostrategic importance of a particular area or region. Nearly everyone understands the need to deal with those regions where armaments are the most numerous, such as in Central Europe.

The quantity and quality of conventional equipment also informs the doctrinal debate. The amount of a particular type of equipment possessed by a state usually changes the value of that equipment. One absolutely superior tank may be able to engage and defeat several other less capable tanks, but this principal has its limits. Where are such limits: 3:1, 5:1, 10:1. 20:1? This concept also changes when other items of equipment either add to the tank's survivability or detract from it. Any given ratio would change substantially if the superior tank were to be accompanied by a large number of antitank guided missiles mounted on other weapons systems or vehicles. However, this new enhancement of the superior tank's capability can also be degraded by other factors such as antitank aircraft (such as the American A-10 and the Soviet Su-25) and combat helicopters armed with various antitank systems. Greatly superior numbers also weigh very heavily on the balance scale. The bottom line goes something like this: if all the superior armaments are eliminated but only 95 percent of the comparable less-capable ones, then the side with the greater number of less-capable armaments has won.

There is no accepted formula for evaluating quality versus quantity. Perceptions abound to the effect that quality compensates for quantity, yet no one has been able to explain definitively just where the two attributes cancel each other out. Some would argue, with some justification, when there is a three or four to one asymmetry in a given weapons systems such as exists between Warsaw Pact and NATO in tanks, artillery, and infantry fighting vehicles, that quantity has a quality of its own. Generally, one may also assume that there are certain penalties for quality; such as cost, size, weight, mobility, maneuverability. Moreover, compensating measures can be developed that, at least for a time, denigrate quality. Such measures may involve physical modifications (an example might be the addition of reactive armor to Soviet tanks) or modifications to tactics (extensive use of smoke, dust, electronic countermeasures, smaller, more mobile, units and formations, etc.).

Apart from the difficulties touched upon above as they relate to quality, there is another aspect that merits mentioning. For example, let us say that an American Abrams (or MIAI) tank has qualities superior to a Soviet T-62. This comparison should not be acceptable. But, should it be suggested that the German Leopard-II or the Soviet T-80 is better than the Abrams, we would have a very long discussion indeed. We then begin to speak of prestige and technological prowess and even of impact on the business of foreign military sales.

More crucial, however, than questions of commerce and prestige are those related to assigning weighted values to particular weapons systems. Such values are frequently used to conduct computer simulations. Again, for example, what are the relative weighted values of an American M-1A1 as compared to any given tank in the inventory of WTO states. I question whether the weighted value, even once calculated, could remain constant.

As tough as it is to compare like systems, i.e., tanks and tanks, it is tougher still to compare unlike armaments. In terms of capability, one might look at assigning relevant values to the Soviet-built BMP, an armored fighting vehicle, with an American-produced M-48 tank. In extremis, one could say that both are armored, both are intended for battle, both have guns, both move on tracks. The dissimilarities, however, are of far more consequence than the similarities. The M-48 is larger and has a larger gun with greater range. Its crew is meant to operate from inside the tank. The BMP is smaller, but carries more people; these personnel can fight from the vehicle by firing out of its small portals, but generally they dismount and fight as infantrymen. But there are more than 26,000 BMP and its airborne relative, the BMD, in the inventories of Warsaw Treaty states. Remembering that we are discussing the comparison of unlike systems, how many BMP/BMD equal one M-48?

Now consider the inherent difficulties in comparing tank with helicopter, artillery with antitank weapons, air defense systems with aircraft, aircraft with tanks, etc. If these systems were not intended for different roles and purposes, they probably would not exist. It seems, therefore, a bit futile to force their particular shapes and forms into the round, fruitless hole of this kind of analysis.

The option that is easiest to manipulate in statistical situations and is also easiest to explain is to treat all weapons within a given category as being of equal value. Simply stated: a tank is a tank is a tank.

The advantages of such an approach are evident. No lengthy negotiations are required to assign relative values; the negotiating issue is clear and the ultimate outcome would most likely establish a numerical cap on future quantities.

This approach is not without its drawbacks. Since the objective of the CAFE negotiations must be greater stability through the elimination of certain offensive capabilities, balance is a key criterion. Too many qualitative disparities could complicate the process of maintaining a secure balance after an agreement comes into force.

Problems of modernization, for example, have bedeviled the history of strategic arms negotiations, i.e., when is a modernization modification actually a new system? One approach to resolve the issue of modernization would be to follow the concept of the draft Chemical Weapons Convention; that is, to list the items to be covered and to monitor newly developed systems with exchange of information, notification, and verification measures. To those who would argue that not defining all treaty limited items would lead to too much ambiguity, I would refer them to a statement by a U.S. Supreme Court Justice on the subject of defining pornography, "Don't ask me to define it, but I'll know it when I see it."

Theoretically, it should be possible to establish classes of weapons within categories. Although it is not possible to be definitive in providing illustrations, one could, for example, think of the German Leopard-II and American M-1A1 tanks as being in the same class with the Soviet-produced late models T-72 and T-80.

Managed properly, modernization could be built around such a concept preserving parity within a class while accounting for an acceptable balance of capability in like armaments. However, an enforceable commitment would have to be undertaken not to exceed mutually agreed modernization limits relative to the basic items within that class.

The advantages of such an approach relate to maintaining military balance over time, reducing motivation for a qualitative arms race, and making it difficult to circumvent definitions by developing new equipment.

Every coin has another side. Whereas major producers begin to constrain their own efforts, other states not involved in the negotiations could undertake further developments of existing armaments and develop still other systems that would remain legally unrestrained. And such a complicated approach also would require an extremely intrusive monitoring system.

If negotiators in the new CAFE talks are able to reach an agreement, it will be because the states involved, East and West, will have recognized it is in their interests to have such an agreement. In the mandate talks, both NATO and Warsaw Pact nations have already agreed that the key objective of the conference is to enhance stability in Europe, which, in turn, presumably would lead to enduring peace and security. Conventional arms control, when properly formulated, and faithfully implemented, can contribute significantly to that objective.

Security, however, cannot be divorced from economic, ecological, and humanitarian concerns. The participating states in the CSCE acknowledged this interrelationship when the Stockholm conference noted that "respect for and the effective exercise of human rights and fundamental freedoms are essential factors for international peace, justice and security." This interrelationship was most recently reaffirmed in Vienna last week.

Behind these questions is the concept of assessing the balance in Europe. Without being exhaustive, this Chapter attempts to demonstrate the complexity of comparing weapons systems. It focuses on tanks, artillery, and armored fighting vehicles not only because their reduction characterizes the Western reductions proposals, but because the difficulties that lie in comparing them are child's play as compared to attempting to draw any conclusions whatsoever between wholly unlike systems.

Some of the problems raised here may give the impression that I am a pessimist regarding the upcoming CAFE talks. I suggest that the definitional problems involved are immense.

Furthermore, the necessary verification and information exchange regimes will require an unprecedented degree of intrusiveness and comprehensiveness. A CAFE agreement, in effect, will require a new type of thinking regarding openness and predictability, as well as a new approach to the concept of cooperative security. It will require an evolution in how some nations, particularly closed societies, approach the concepts of secrecy and sovereignty.

If you had asked me 10 years ago, even three years ago, if such an ambitious accord were possible, I would have had to answer in the negative. The problems that bedeviled MBFR for over 14 years—where one side refused even to address such basic issues as an acceptable exchange of data—made it impossible to reach agreement on even that modest endeavor.

Today there has been a welcome evolution toward accepting such fundamental concepts of security—long espoused by the West—as openness, predictability, and verification. Recent experience in the CDE and INF negotiations and implementations also allows room for cautious optimism.

Thus I chose to view the CAFE talks as a chance to address—perhaps for the first time— some of the fundamental questions of conventional force structure, deployments and doctrine, which have been a source of much of the distrust and concern in Europe since World War II. Sadly, heretofore these issues have too often been shrouded in secrecy.

Today we stand at the threshold of a dynamic new negotiation on conventional armed forces in Europe. For its part, NATO enters these negotiations with a sense of realism. We realize that genuine peace and stability cannot be achieved without steady progress on all aspects of the confrontations that have divided Europe for more than four decades. At the same time, we approach these negotiations with a sense of vision. We welcome the fact that much has changed for the better both within and among the states of Europe during the past few years. Our vision, as noted in the most recent NATO communique, is of a continent where military forces exist only to prevent war and to ensure self-defense, not for the purpose of initiating aggression or for political or military intimidation. If I can paraphrase the new U.S. president, what we seek is a kinder and gentler continent.

Chapter 5
PROBLEMS OF COMPARISON
Gyula Horn

We citizens of small and medium-size states in Europe welcome most readily the fact that the questions of conventional disarmament in our continent have come into the focus of attention. We hope that the forthcoming talks in Europe will eliminate security resting on centuries-old military confrontation and a balance of fear in this continent. It must be replaced by real security built on political cooperation and the removal of the material basis of military threat. It is necessary to abandon thinking in the terms of "friend and enemy," in the category of black or white, and to start easing, step by step, by concrete deeds in the very near future and thereafter, the political, economic, and psychological burdens placed on our peoples by the existence and maintenance of large regular armies.

Favorable conditions for setting out on efforts in this direction have been created by changes in the international situation. We are aware, however, that there are on both sides forces that are not interested, though for quite different reasons, in radically changing the current state of affairs, because they have vested political, economic, and existential interest in the maintenance of large regular armies. We are nevertheless determined to achieve, both during the talks and through other possible forms of cooperation, a breakthrough in real disarmament, inclusive not only of armies disbanded and armaments dismantled, but also of militant ideologies and their exponents disarmed.

As a country directly concerned, the Hungarian People's Republic wishes to play an active role, in a spirit of initiative, in conventional disarmament. We take a complex approach to this question, placing it in the context of the entire process. We are aware that the possibilities of progress in nuclear disarmament, particularly the reduction and destruction of tactical nuclear weapons in Europe, are closely interrelated with the results achieved in the field of conventional disarmament.

We find it most important to reach accords that will be conducive to the attainment of our goals in a balanced way and on the basis of the principle of balanced security. With this end in view, we shall do our utmost, within our system of alliance, to adopt a realistic and constructive negotiating posture taking into account the security interests of both sides, making for substantive progress, and enabling the negotiating parties to make further steps. Moreover, we are working actively together with our partners outside our alliance to ensure that the talks will produce early results and the measures to be adopted will affect Hungary, too, at the very beginning of the process.

In the current situation, unilateral steps may also be needed to promote conventional disarmament in Europe. Therefore we were especially pleased with the decision of the Soviet Union, announced by General Secretary Gorbachev on 7 December, to undertake a unilateral move. We are convinced that by that move the Soviet Union and the Warsaw Treaty Organization have not only taken a significant step toward laying the military basis for a defensive doctrine, but have also created a considerably better situation for the talks due to begin soon on conventional disarmament in Europe.

A most important element of the Soviet decision is a complex of measures that point far beyond quantitative cuts. The very nature of the Soviet measures indicates that what is involved here is not a mere disarmament move, but the first real step toward changing the military doctrine into a defensive one.

In this context let us discuss the way we look at the possibility of achieving structural offensive incapability.

We start from the premise that structural incapability to launch an offensive must be achieved by other than unilateral additional force modernization, defensive though it may be. It is through cooperation between the countries of the two military-political alliances that the components of military potentials should be determined in such a way as to meet the security interests of individual countries and different groups of states and not to threaten the other side with particular emphasis on the need for military parity to be maintained at a much lower level of armed forces and armaments. Accordingly, in our view, structural incapability to launch an offensive should be achieved not by separation of offensive and defensive weapons alone. At the same time, radical cuts in specifically offensive armaments constitute an important element of this concept. It makes no sense to distinguish between possible forms of attack, between weapons suitable for acquisition of territory or for depth destruction because both categories are capable of launching large-scale surprise attacks. Therefore we lay principal emphasis on radical cuts in armored forces, long range conventional and rocket artillery, and strike air forces, not forgetting about tactical nuclear weapons, combat support units, and automated reconnaissance and strike systems.

To achieve offensive incapability, attention should be devoted primarily to forces stationed close to the line of possible engagement. This makes it necessary to effect, within the framework of global measures, essentially larger cuts in first-echelon troops, or to pay greater attention to reducing their offensive capability through appropriate reorganization and replacement of armaments.

Changes in the principles governing the use of armed forces are another important element of structural offensive incapability. They mean, in the first place, abandonment of explicitly offensive concepts posing the greatest threat to the other side. So I have in mind, above all, the need to abandon concepts about the large-scale use of operative maneuvering units, for they are clearly capable of carrying out offensive operations. Also to be abandoned are, in our view, that concepts that envisage depth strikes, such as those conceived within the framework of FOFA, against forces of the adversary. The new operational principles should also be implemented in the training of armed forces as soon as possible.

Last but not least, we find it important to increase openness in the armed forces as well. Since the talks require publication of information in sufficient detail, we see no obstacle to having such data, not a secret anymore, released to the public at large.

Under the complex approach to conventional disarmament, we maintain that this process should embrace the armies in Europe as a whole, including land and air forces. The ultimate goal should be to establish a balance of forces in which both systems of alliance will have much less weapons than those they have now. This also means gradual reductions in military capabilities threatening the other side.

We resolutely reject, however, attempts to include air forces in the scope of measures in some distant future, under the pretext of artificial arguments that, for instance, air forces are incapable of launching a surprise attack or the problems of verification are yet to be solved. Since, obviously enough, air forces are particularly capable of dealing rapid, unexpected strikes, we believe that air forces should be the first to be reduced. As regards the problems of verification, they cannot be declared at the beginning of talks to be insoluble. We should leave it to the negotiators to solve them!

I find it a contradictory idea to view military parity exclusively in numerical terms. If during the talks both alliances are to seek an equal number of tanks, armored vehicles, and artillery pieces as well as aircraft, I am not sure that they will do a good service to the cause of security, peace, and parity. Any comparison of figures alone is likely to give false results in view of the great and growing differences in aspects of quality.

There is a need for fresh ideas, for a new approach in this field. Determination of the balance of forces has always embraced a much wider area than the scope of mere numerical comparisons. When we say that in Europe that there is rough parity between the conventional forces of WTO and NATO, we do not claim that both sides have the same forces. The balance of forces cannot be considered except in view of purpose and circumstances. In our case, the balance of forces in Europe can be taken to mean that neither side has enough strength to impose its will on the other by military force.

Of course, this type of comparison cannot be used at the disarmament talks to take stock of armed forces and to determine the final result of reductions, or of the reduction process. Nevertheless it is very important to know that the talks will be conducted against this background and that the final result should not, in this one respect, be any different from the point of departure.

We should go beyond mere quantitative comparisons also for reliably measuring military strength during the disarmament talks. Without considering and comparing qualitative parameters it is impossible to establish a stable balance likely to guarantee—with reliability as well as with less risks and at less cost than at present—the security of all countries in Europe. It is indispensable to take qualitative factors into account because, as a result of historical development, the armed forces of the two military alliances have evolved into rather different structures. A mere quantitative approach is therefore objectively favorable to those who have developed their armed forces at a higher technological level, by laying emphasis on quality. To take realistic account of the prevailing situation requires acceptance of this fact as well! During the disarmament talks it would therefore be practicable for military experts to devise appropriate methods by which to make real comparisons between the opposing military potentials, while not impeding progress in, but working parallel to, efforts at exchanging quantitative data and reaching the first accords. This would also provide a basis for establishing levels of defensive sufficiency and for lowering the military forces of the participants to such levels.

The consequent implementation of COCOM restrictions by the NATO countries, which made the development of defense technologies in the WTO countries definitely more difficult, also contributed to the fact that different trends in military technology occurred in the two alliances. The WTO was forced to replace missing technological possibilities by quantity. So, as a result of NATO measures, aimed at the restriction of technology transfer, the fear of threat has been strengthened in the NATO countries. It is more than logical—also in this context—that restrictions on technology exports be mutually removed parallel to the increasing confidence in Europe.

During the talks attention should also be paid to the existence of asymmetries that are objectively impossible to eliminate. I refer, among others, to the imbalance that is perhaps of the greatest concern to the West and that is due to the fact that the Soviet Union is a European state, too, whereas the United States is not. It is by emphasizing this geo-strategic difference that the West deems it indispensable to station American units in Europe and to stage large-scale military maneuvers.

We accept the facts. We do not deny that reinforcement is much easier on land than by sea or air. It is also a fact, however, that the infrastructure of Eastern Europe, particularly as regards transport, lies behind that of Western Europe and that in times of war the land routes of reinforcement become highly vulnerable as well. In this context I only would like to remind you of the substantial naval superiority of NATO. This notwithstanding, we stand ready to give due consideration to such concerns of NATO during the talks.

We would expect our NATO partners to show a similar readiness to consider consequences of asymmetries that allow favorable conclusions to be drawn by WTO. What I have in mind is that in the European territory of the Soviet Union there are conventional forces that meet all the criteria of forces convened by the talks, but, given their purpose, would be used against NATO forces not included in the talks on conventional armed forces in Europe. This can be best illustrated by Soviet national air defense, a part of which is undoubtedly destined to avert strikes by NATO's European forces that are land-based and covered by the mandate, but another part of it is deployed for defense against American strategic air forces, sea-based cruise missiles, and naval air forces. It is not less important for this specific feature than it is for the other consequence of geographical asymmetry as aforesaid to be taken into account during the talks.

Hungary wishes to adopt an autonomous disarmament policy in keeping with its national conditions and interests and is ready to act accordingly during the conventional disarmament talks. We know that planners of military operations in neither system of alliance consider Hungary as a part of the central theater of war. Frankly speaking, we are very glad of that! At the same time we are convinced that a division of countries for theaters of war, dictated by purposes of planning military operations is unsuitable for the elaboration of disarmament measures. In our view, disarmament measures can be effective only if they extend to the whole of Central Europe at the very first stage. Any idea to omit any part of this geographical unit, Hungary or any other region, to exclude it from this process artificially, by military criteria alone is doomed to failure.

In addition to promoting the success of the disarmament talks, Hungary is directly interested in seeing progress made in conventional disarmament in Europe and in contributing thereto. In our present economic situation we are seeking, and are able, to spend less and less on the development of our armed forces. Moreover, we believe that the reform of our political system, too, calls for a different concept of security and, accordingly, a different, smaller, and cheaper army relying on qualitative factors and better integrated into the society. This presupposes a new system of relations in the field of security policy in Europe, one that every state of Europe has not only the sovereign right, but also the duty to help bring about by joint efforts.

Hungary is not content with hopes in the successful outcome of the disarmament talks. The desire to march in the vanguard of conventional disarmament is not a mere phrase on the part of Hungary. We believe that our country has special possibilities to do so within

WTO: though cuts in armed forces in Hungary do not have a direct influence to bear on the central balance of forces, they are of sufficient significance and have a symbolic value. The increasingly pressing need for reducing our forces and those stationed in Hungary and achieving their structural offensive incapability becomes easy to understand if we recall the changes with the states in our immediate and wider environment over the past decades and that have placed our feeling of security and that of our alliance on new foundations.

In light of all these developments, real possibilities are at hand, insofar as the forces in Hungary are concerned, for taking steps that will not only adjust the military component to a situation that has radically changed in respect of its other components, but will also be significant enough to demonstrate that the military forces of a country belonging to an alliance can acquire nonoffensive character based on a new concept of security. We are aware that to do so depends in no small measure on other factors than our own resolve, because it is only within the framework of conventional disarmament talks that such a decision can be translated into practice and can produce lasting results.

We are confident that the success of these talks will convince skeptics in all countries of Europe that attainment of this goal is possible and that building a new structure of security is consistent with the criteria of national security and can be set as a real objective of talks in respect to the alliance as well.

Chapter 6
RESPONSES

FIRST RESPONSE
Joachim Krause

The issue before us sounds like a rather technical one, and to a certain degree it surely is. However, more than merely technical problems are involved. The critical question is how much emphasis is put on force comparisons during the CFE talks. Given the experience with MBFR, it can be assumed that attributing too much importance to force comparisons will result in an increased likelihood for the talks to become bogged down. Through various official and semiofficial Eastern statements, a certain philosophy seems to transpire according to which comparisons between different conventional armaments systems should run very prominent during the CFE talks. This would imply that, in the initial phase of these talks, East and West shall arrive at a common assessment of the actual conventional balance in Europe.

During such a common stock-taking approach, everything that pertains to the military balance would have to be taken into account, including differences in qualities. Part of this overall effort would be a comparison between different weapons systems and technologies in order to find common ground for tradeoffs between different weapons systems or weapons technologies. Eventually, these tradeoffs should form the basis for agreements on upper limits for weapon systems. What is implicit in such reasoning is that weapons systems not belonging to the same categories are able to balance each other and that quality can outbalance quantity.

From an intellectual standpoint, this is a fascinating question. From a political standpoint, it is a rather questionable undertaking. It is hard to imagine that West and East will get together and arrive at a common assessment of the actual balance of conventional forces in Europe, including qualitative factors. This has not proved to be feasible even in the West, and it seems hardly imaginable that something of that kind will succeed in an East-West context, and it is also questionable if we think in terms of result orientation.

If, for instance, we take the most prominent example, the equation aircraft versus tanks, the shortcomings of such an approach might become visible. It is correct, at least in very general terms, to state that NATO is offsetting the Warsaw Pact tank superiority by putting more emphasis on air power. But does this warrant to trade tanks against aircraft in arms control talks? At least from a Western perspective, the answer would be negative, since the issue is not only how to compare different weapons systems or trading large tank cuts on the Eastern side against large aircraft cuts on the Western side. If one looks at what is at the heart of the Western interest in the CFE negotiations, it is rather the overall offensive character of the Warsaw Pact military preparations than only the tank superiority. The West conceives the Warsaw Pact as disposing of a nonnuclear invasion capability that is made up of a lot of components, from which the large tank and armored fighting vehicle component is one of the most crucial ones.

Thus the West is not looking for cuts in tanks as a goal in itself, but as part of an endeavor to reduce the Eastern invasion capability in Europe. Since such an invasion capability is not existent on the Western side, it is hard to see why a tradeoff between cuts in the number of tanks and cuts in the area of aircraft will have to be established.

One might argue that air forces are a vital component of any offensive capability, and that especially those refinements of air power that are currently introduced in the West under the heading of "Follow-on Forces Attack" (FOFA) will boost Western offensive capabilities. Thus one could ask whether it might not be sensible to trade an Eastern offensive capability (i.e., the tank superiority) against a Western offensive capability (FOFA).

If we agree that the reduction, if not elimination, of invasion capabilities should be the purpose of conventional arms control, this equation cannot be made. FOFA systems alone, usually like all air forces, do not allow large-scale offensive operations by which territory is taken. They are intended for destroying targets in the depth of an enemy's territory but not for conquering that territory, as long as no ground force component capable of exploiting these effects is available. In other words, any attempt to reduce existent invasion capabilities must begin with reductions of those ground force components that are crucial for the taking of territory on a large scale. Air forces surely will have to become subject to arms control measures, too. Yet, there seems to be no reason to link them to reductions of ground forces and their equipment.

On the contrary, one should rather be prudent in establishing linkages of that kind, since air forces would be extremely difficult to cover under a regional arms control regime. Due to their high mobility and versatility it will be hard to devise sensible and verifiable parameters for such regimes. It would thus be more expedient to put aircraft or air forces rather at the end of the arms control agenda.

To sum it up, problems of military stability or instability in Europe are of a rather complex nature and, hence, have to be treated in a complex fashion. However, there is no point in trying to start conventional arms control in Europe by seeking complicated procedures for comparing actual or purported advantages in ground forces and air forces with each other in order to base some kind of tradeoffs on it. A conventional arms control regime for Europe should rather encompass a set of upper ceilings for those weapons systems and armed units that are most suitable for conquering territory in a short time combined with a set of associated measures, like regulations concerning stationed forces of foreign countries, restrictions on capabilities for force generation, and reinforcement and redeployment provisions for weapons systems or other important items. Also, confidence-building measures to increase military and political openness, constraint measures to impede clandestine preparation of offensive operations, and an effective verification system should become further building blocks of such a regime.

SECOND RESPONSE
Kari Möttölä

The question of the weapons systems to be reduced, limited, or constrained does not only affect the assessments between the direct negotiating partners, it affects, in a tangible way, *the security interests of nonparticipants* as well.

When analyzing the impact on nonparticipating countries, at least the following considerations should be taken into account:

- *The strategic context* of the subregion or the country. The Nordic neutrals (Finland, Sweden), the Alpine neutrals (Switzerland, Austria), and Yugoslavia are all situated in a strategically significant location, in terms of deployment patterns or military doctrines of the major powers and alliances, but in different ways. The strategic significance, again, affects their *threat perceptions* and, consequently, their national security interests to be pursued in conventional disarmament.
- *The pattern of collateral or sequential effects* of conventional disarmament effects. Because of the interdependencies within the European security system, reductions or other measures do not take place in a vacuum. Pressures and opportunities will be created in other parts by *(sub)regional differentiation*, for example, of weapons systems and/or zones in conventional disarmament.
- *The totality of integrated security policy* means, for example, that conventional weapons cannot be separated from nuclear weapons, or certain types of conventional weapons from others, in evaluations of the security-political situations. An uneven development in scaling down the armaments levels, and perceived threats, may have destabilizing effects for various nonparticipating countries.

Some well-known historical cases illustrate the *problematique* raised here. In the connection of the MFR talks, there were worries of competitive increases in the northern and southern "flanks" left outside the guidelines area. In the aftermath of the INF Treaty, a similar risk of "compensatory" armaments and deployments measures in the adjacent sea areas has been widely discussed. The possibility of a zonal sequence in *the mandate of the CAFE negotiations*, again, has put onto the agenda the issue of political and military symmetry in subregional configurations to be tackled later. So, the question of a hierarchy of priorities is not only a problem for nonparticipants but also for those participants outside the central zone.

The *management* of this problem area will be a test of the 23/35 linkage set up by the Vienna document; how effectively the nonparticipants will have their views expressed and considered, and their national security interests respected, as far as the agenda and decisions of the 23 forum is considered. On the other hand, there are possibilities within the competence of the 35 forum to contribute to solving the issues of the 23 agenda.

As for the *substance* of solutions to the *problematique*, there are some guidelines that should be adopted. The general principle of *equal security* presupposes that destabilization or increases of military tension anywhere in the European system should be precluded as reductions, limitations, and stabilization measures are taken in the center.

Constraining and reducing *offensive capabilities, ground and air*, benefit neutral countries located in-between by strengthening the credibility, and stabilizing effect, of their indigenous denial capabilities. This is the case, typically, in Central Europe, where a surprise attack, and a potential use of neutral territory in reaching strategic targets outside, is part of the threat scenario.

In the north, however, the situation is more complicated because of the central role of military components outside the present agenda, namely *naval forces*, and *strategic nuclear forces*. For example, a driving force in military tension is the competition between the U.S. naval forces targeted on land, and Soviet land-based naval air force targeted on sea. Furthermore, the increasing but uncertain role of dual-capable, sea-launched cruise missiles in the north and the Arctic is a significant factor in Finnish and Swedish security assessments, and also in the strategic calculations affecting their positions.

Similarly, in the Baltic region, which connects the Nordic area with the Central European zone, the tactical air forces and its counterweapons, as well as amphibious and airborne forces, constitute a special threat typical of the subregion. On the other hand, ground forces do not play such a central role as in Central Europe.

In conclusion, the issue of comparison between different conventional systems is raised as a recognition that symmetrical disarmament measures do not necessarily have symmetrical benefits for the parties to the arrangement. That is why asymmetrical measures are needed. This complexity of the existing situation is a wider phenomenon; parallel and asymmetrical measures may be needed *outside the CAFE negotiation terrain* to make an equal impact for the whole of Europe.

This means that subregional processes, bilateral U.S.-Soviet strategic processes, and a process concerning the remaining European nuclear issues all have direct relevance. Results are needed here to guarantee stability and strengthened security.

Within the CAFE process itself, some kind of *de facto freezing* of the situation outside the immediate zone of measures is one way to approach the problem. Politically, this may not be difficult, since no need to aggravate the situation is foreseen. But there is automaticity in armaments technologies that may lead to negative repercussions in subregions outside the controlling effect of the negotiation under way.

And finally, measures within the *CSBM* negotiations can help in averting any negative consequences from the *CAFE* negotiation, and can also help facilitating results therein. Constraining measures, and eventually, supplementing the Madrid mandate to include independent naval and air measures are routes to be taken to address the requirements of equal security impact.

THIRD RESPONSE

Hans-Peter Neuhold

At the risk of repeating points already made in previous chapters, the following aspects seem worth mentioning—even once again—in the present context.

It is generally agreed that the measurement and above all the comparison of the military value and combat power of conventional forces are very difficult tasks indeed. Most experts are also of the opinion that "bean counting" is an inadequate method for assessing military balances. This is rightly said to be particularly true of the conventional forces facing each other on the European continent, where the two alliance systems have deployed unprecedented—at least in peacetime—military potentials.

History proves that mere numbers do not decide the outcome of battles or wars.[1] In particular, the frequently quoted rule according to which an attacker needs a 3:1 quantitative superiority in order to be assured of victory is not fully confirmed by historic evidence. On the one hand, even numerically inferior forces attacked successfully, for instance, the German invaders of France in 1940.[2] On the other hand, attackers who enjoyed a quantitative advantage exceeding the "magic" 3:1 margin failed to defeat the defenders.

It might be added that, in any event, military history leaves today's analyst with a nagging question: To what extent is experience even from the recent (prenuclear) past relevant to the present-day military realities in Europe? Doubts may even be raised as to the applicability of insights gained from armed conflicts on other continents to the European theater.

As regards the quantitative approach to conventional military balances, one important qualification is already in order on this level. What counts is not so much the overall numerical relationship between opposing forces but rather a local, albeit temporary, superiority at crucial breakthrough points.

It is also stating the obvious to emphasize the need for taking important qualitative factors into account, thus for going beyond simple and simplistic "bean-counting." All these additional variables are, unfortunately, hard to evaluate and quantify individually, let alone to measure with any single indicator. They include the quality of various weapons, above all, their fire power, range, and accuracy; mobilization and reinforcement capabilities; logistics; command, control, communication, and information (C^3I); geography, as the terrain may favor the attacker or defender, depending, first and foremost, on the existence or the lack of natural or man-made obstacles. Other, even more elusive, but equally important factors range from the strategies adopted by the adversaries involved (on which depends in turn, *inter alia*, the achievement by the attacker of the potentially decisive surprise element), leadership as well as the training and morale of the troops, to such political determinants as the readiness to proceed quickly to mobilization on the basis of correctly interpreted intelligence, or alliance cohesion, if more than one country fights on one or the other side.

Given this complexity, experts have been trying to develop more sophisticated measuring techniques that take account of at least some of these qualitative aspects. Most assessments based on such methods lead to the conclusion that the alleged superiority of the WTO is less dramatic than if mere troop and weapon figures are compared. The following examples may be mentioned here: the ADE (Armored Division Equivalent) yardstick used by the Pentagon, which focuses on a U.S. armored division as the basic reference unit for comparisons and includes mobility, survivability, and firepower; the Attrition—FEBA (Forward Edge of the Battle Area) Expansion model developed by Barry Posen, who also takes into account mobilization and C^3I^3; or (another extension of the Lanchester equations[4]) the Adaptive Dynamic Model used by Joshua M. Epstein, with its emphasis on movement and the trading of space for time.[5] These two scholars, as well as John Mearsheimer[6] doubt whether the quantitative advantages of the WTO in some sectors could really result in a meaningful qualitative superiority that might tempt rational Warsaw Pact leaders to launch an attack against NATO.[7]

However, three comments ought to be made here. First, unfortunately, there exists no consensus even within the academic community in the West on the most appropriate and accurate method for measuring the qualitative variables that are most relevant to a conventional military balance. Second, there is no consensus on the degree of superiority that is militarily significant and poses a genuine threat to the weaker side. Finally and most importantly, even if the assessment that the conventional forces of the two military blocs in Europe are already equivalent is correct, there is no reason for complacency. The crucial factors that shape this relationship are in continuous flux. The problems of surprise attack and decisive local superiority still remain to be solved.

In the light of the widespread criticism of "bean-counting" among experts, it seems legitimate to ask why claims founded on simplistic numerical comparisons, according to which one side holds a menacing advantage, die so hard. One explanation may be the need to convince parliaments and taxpayers that high defense expenditures must be maintained or even increased, even if political relations with the adversaries are improving. This also means that a possible shift to a new approach will have to be explained to those parts of public opinion that have come to firmly believe in the relevance of the numbers of soldiers and weapons.

Another reason for the continued emphasis on these figures that comes to mind are worstcase assumptions from which strategic planners proceed in order to be on the safe side.

It is also worth mentioning that the "man and woman in the street" is confused by contradictory data from various Western sources, as official statistics frequently differ from those compiled by independent research institutions. NATO figures in particular have also been contested by WTO spokespeople. The main problem with the Eastern alliance, however, used to be the reluctance to provide data of its own. Therefore, the announcement by Soviet Foreign Minister Edvard Shevardnadze at the concluding session of the third CSCE followup meeting in Vienna that the WTO would—for the first time—publish detailed statistics on its conventional forces and armaments by the end of January 1989 was generally appreciated.

Even more welcome was the actual implementation of this promise, although it did not fully settle differences of opinion between the blocs, and considerable data discrepancies still remain. Using different counting methods, each side is still trying to demonstrate the assets of the opponent and minimize its own strength. Whereas the WTO is thus attempting to prove an already existing rough military equality between the two alliances, NATO keeps asserting the pact's superiority.[8] It may be suspected that political propaganda considerations may prevail, every now and then, over scientific rigor on one side or the other. That is why agreement on some data appears as an inevitable prerequisite before conventional arms control and disarmament in Europe can get underway. Asymmetrical reductions could then result in equal ceilings for troops and certain categories of weapons—as spelled out in the CFE mandate hammered out in Vienna.

However, another caveat should not be lost sight of in this connection. Reductions of military forces and even the elimination of disparities need not produce conventional equivalence and stability in all cases. For instance, deep cuts that establish numerical equality on a lower level might at the same time change force-to-space ratios in the attacker's favor so that breakthrough operations could even become easier than before.

Furthermore, another obvious conclusion must be drawn from the above considerations. Due to partly inalterable asymmetries such as geography and hardly measurable qualitative variables, strict conventional military parity between the two blocs is out of reach; a future agreement on conventional force reductions will therefore require a "political investment" in terms of confidence in the trustworthiness of the other party and a certain amount of risk.

The final question to be addressed here at least briefly concerns ways and means for facilitating such an agreement in these circumstances. At least four approaches can be recommended to pave the way for a more stable European security system.

1. Reductions should include those forces and weapons that each side perceives as most threatening. This approach may in turn raise the issue of possible tradeoffs, perhaps also over time, for example, between WTO tanks and NATO aircraft.[9]
2. If the possibility of surprise attacks is regarded as *a* — if not *the* — principal problem (as it is in the CFE mandate), increased military transparency and operational constraints could contribute to a solution. To begin with, this would need the strict implementation of the already accepted CSBMs laid down in the Stockholm Document.[10] Future agreements could increase transparency by tightening and improving the CDE parameters already in force and by adding new measures to the existing *répertoire*. Moreover, the breakthrough toward "objective" CSBMs at the Stockholm conference, important in principle but of little military significance, should be followed by more meaningful measures, for instance, the withdrawal of troops and equipment particularly suited for offensive operations from border areas. Consequently, the new round of CSBMs negotiations among the 35 CSCE participating states provided for in the Vienna Document has an important task. Along the same lines, a thorough verification system will have to be part and parcel of an eventual CFE treaty.[11]
3. The shift to defensive strategies should also be given high priority. Mere proclamations are not sufficient; they must be reflected in actual force postures, the training of troops, etc.
4. In a broader perspective, stability ought also to be promoted by political efforts aimed at causes of tension other than military factors and at increasing mutual interests in preserving peaceful relations and avoiding resort to armed force in order to change it. Progress in the field of human rights and economic cooperation — although the latter is seen by some as a double-edge sword that could lead to dangerous dependence and strengthen the adversary's military potential — seem to lend themselves particularly well to achieve this objective.

To sum up, the road to conventional disarmament and stability is long and strewn with obstacles. For the first time in many years, however, there is real hope and not just wishful thinking that those roadblocks may be removed or surmounted.

Notes

1. Examples are given by Joshua M. Epstein, Dynamic Analysis and the Conventional Balance in Europe, *International Security*, 12 (4), Spring 1988, 154–165.

2. Kim Holmes, Measuring the Conventional Balance in Europe, *International Security*, 12 (4), Spring 1988, 166–173.

3. Barry Posen, Is NATO Decisively Outnumbered? *International Security*, 12 (4), Spring 1988, 186–202.

4. F. W. Lanchester, *Aircraft in Warfare: The Dawn of the Fourth Arm* (London: Constable, 1916).

5. Epstein, Dynamic Analysis.

6. John J. Mearsheimer, Numbers, Strategy and the European Balance, *International Security*, 12 (4), Spring 1988, 174–185.

7. For a critique of these optimistic estimates, see Eliot A. Cohen, Toward Better Net Assessment: Rethinking the European Conventional Balance, *International Security*, 13 (1), Summer 1988, 50–89; for an attempt at assessing the conventional balance in Central Europe, see Heinz Magenheimer, Zum Kräftestand in Europa-Mitte, *Österreichische Militärische Zeitschrift*, 25 (2), March/April 1987, 128–138.

8. Heinz Kozak (ed.), *Konventionelle Rüstungskontrolle in Europa: Dokumente und Kräftevergleich* (Vienna: Institut für strategische Grundlagenforschung an der Landesverteidigungsakademie, 1989).

9. Robert D. Blackwill, Specific Approaches to Conventional Arms Control in Europe, *Survival*, 30 (5), September/October 1988, 429–447.

10. John Borawski, Stan Weeks, and Charlotte E. Thompson, The Stockholm Agreement of September 1986, *Orbis*, 30 (4), Winter 1987, 643–662; Richard E. Darilek, The Future of Conventional Arms Control in Europe: A Tale of Two Cities: Stockholm, Vienna, *Survival*, 29 (1), January/February 1987, 5–20.

11. Michael Krepon, Verification of Conventional Arms Reductions, *Survival*, 30 (6), November/December 1988, 544–555.

Part III

Objectives and Methods of Reduction, Limitation, and Stabilization

Two contrasting reports are presented in Chapter 7 by Nikolai Chervov and in Chapter 8 by Jerôme Paolini. The two positions with respect to the objectives of the Vienna negotiations can be distinguished. On the one hand there is the tendency to see those negotiations in the global and wider perspective of a European security system; on the other, their more limited nature is stressed. It is, for example, pointed out that although the larger political aim of establishing a new international security system in Europe should certainly not be brushed aside and does merit analysis, it is not the object of the negotiations in Vienna. Arms control and disarmament alone cannot carry the whole burden of the necessary improvements of East-West relations. The more limited aim of the Vienna negotiations was that of the reduction of conventional forces and of establishing a better and more stable balance in Europe. Similarly, nuclear forces, as well as any discussion on nuclear deterrence, should remain outside these negotiations.

At a certain stage of significant conventional force reductions, i.e., at a stage where conventional weapons would have reached a level that would not give an advantage to either side, would there still be justification for nuclear weapons in the military arsenals of NATO and of Warsaw Pact Treaty countries? The Western side stresses that nuclear as well as conventional weapons will for the foreseeable future continue to form the basis of the NATO defense strategy of war prevention. In other words, even with a successful outcome of the negotiations, a credible defense and deterrent posture, in both conventional and nuclear terms, would still be needed.

Looming large behind this question is the idea of a third zero option and its implications as to the matter of the denuclearization of Europe. Particular reference is made to the modernization of tactical nuclear weapons both in the East and West. The quantitative superiority of Soviet tactical nuclear weapons is noted and the question raised if the announced unilateral force withdrawals from the GDR, Czechoslovakia, and Hungary would have any incidence on the level of the tactical nuclear forces SS21 and FROGS stationed in those countries.

It is also noted that whereas the recently announced Soviet unilateral measures were welcomed by all, their unilateral nature was also stressed. By definition unilateral measures need no reciprocal answers. As one participant notes, unilateral force reductions were often also the result of a process of modernization and of a more rational, i.e., economic use of resources. The French force reductions of 1975-78 and 1982-84 are an example.

As in previous chapters, Western participants voice fierce opposition to any suggestion that naval forces should be included in the CAFE negotiations. The geostrategic and geopolitical differences between the NATO alliance and the Soviet bloc, and NATO's high dependency on long seaborne lines of communication are emphasized, stressing that the Soviet submarine threat to those lines of communication is insufficiently recognized.

There is note of the distinction made by Chervov in Chapter 7 between interceptor and strike aircraft. Many aircraft are capable of performing both roles and interceptors add substantially to the force of attack aircraft. By escorting the latter they inter alia increase the survival rate and ensure better penetration.

The concept of reasonable sufficiency, stability, and the question of what is defense as opposed to offense are briefly covered. With respect to reasonable sufficiency, the concept should apply to the armed forces of the United States and the USSR, of the Warsaw pact and of NATO, resulting in force structures sufficient only for defense and not for attack. This entails a rejection of being the first to start a war and a sharp reduction in conventional forces down to a level where each side can ensure reliable defense but cannot carry out an attack. Reasonable sufficiency cannot be achieved by unilateral measures alone. The importance of maintaining a balance in the field of strategic weapons between the United States and the USSR at the lowest possible level is also underlined in this respect.

Chapter 7

LIMITATION AND REDUCTION OF CONVENTIONAL ARMS: OBJECTIVES AND METHODS

Nikolai Chervov

We are living at a time when war between East and West—not only nuclear but also conventional war—is totally senseless. It cannot solve any problem—political, economic, or other.

From the military point of view, war between East and West is madness. Calculations show that after 20 days of conventional warfare Europe could become another Hiroshima. Therefore we must work out forms of long-term cooperation. Before it is too late, we must radically reduce our military potentials and rethink our military doctrines.

The reduction by 500,000 men is for the USSR no simple solution. But that step may become a model for further actions by East and West.

The West's proposal that armed forces should be reduced to the level of 95 percent of NATO's armed forces is not a solution. Both sides—the Warsaw Treaty Organization and NATO—must be deprived of the capacity to launch a sudden attack; they must be deprived of their attack potential. The USSR initiative shows the true way toward that goal.

What is happening in connection with our decision is not always correctly interpreted in the West, and so I should like to draw attention to some distinctive features of the Soviet armed forces reductions and, first of all, their scale (equivalent to the Bundeswehr of the Federal Republic of Germany). With respect to Europe, Soviet troops are to be reduced in the German Democratic Republic, Czechoslovakia, Hungary, Poland, and the European part of the Soviet Union—a total of 240,000 men, 10,000 tanks, 8,500 artillery systems, and 800 combat aircraft.

Along with the large scale of the reductions, fundamental qualitative changes are taking place in our armed forces, which are being given a nonoffensive structure. The Soviet Union's military strategy is changing. The reductions will involve modern types of weapons (5,300 of the most modern tanks are to be withdrawn from army groups). The tank divisions to be withdrawn from the GDR, 4, Czechoslovakia, 1, and Hungary, 1—i.e., a total of 6 (about 2,000 tanks)—are to be disbanded; disbanded, not redeployed elsewhere. The divisions remaining for the time being in allies' territories are to be restructured. A large number of new tanks (about 40 percent, or a total 3,300 tanks) are being withdrawn from those divisions, and the divisions are being given a defensive structure.

Bearing in mind that, simultaneously, tactical nuclear systems, assault-landing and water-crossing formations and units together with their weapons and equipment are to be withdrawn from the army groups, the sudden attack potential of the Soviet troops is being drastically reduced. This removes grounds for concern in certain Western circles about the grouping of Soviet forces. Ask the NATO generals; many will unequivocally say that practical implementation by the Soviet Union of the measures announced will genuinely lead to a reduction of the offense capabilities of the Soviet armed forces.

We have sometimes been told that our defensive military doctrine is only words. Where are the deeds? These are concrete deeds. Soviet allies, too, will no doubt take steps in the same direction. All this confirms the consistency of the course steered by the USSR and by the Warsaw Treaty Organization as a whole toward reorganization of their armed forces on the principles of defensive sufficiency.

It would be desirable if NATO's military doctrine and armed forces were also restructured on defensive principles. The doctrine of "nuclear deterrence" does not meet the present situation; it became outdated long ago and is marked by internal contradiction. One cannot speak about the defensive character of a military doctrine that is based on the first use of nuclear weapons. The two are incompatible. Various circumstances will nevertheless oblige NATO to undertake not to use nuclear weapons first (like the People's Republic of China and the Soviet Union).

Someone said that a 500,000-man reduction still does not do away with Soviet superiority and that further unilateral reductions are therefore necessary. Such statements testify to the other side's lack of readiness for real action, for serious steps toward disarmament. Such statements are not even in NATO's own interests, since they do not correspond to the situation, are out of tune with public opinion, and are far from the truth.

What is needed is a broader look at the military potentials of the two alliances. I do not deny the Warsaw Treaty Organization's superiority in tanks. But tanks do not constitute the whole of military potential, nor are they its main element by any means. NATO has substantial advantages, as follows:

- The strategic offensive weapons of the United States include almost 4,000 more nuclear charges than the Soviet Union.
- NATO's total number of nuclear weapons exceeds the Soviet Union's by many thousands of units.
- NATO has a total of approximately 570 fighting ships of the main classes as against the Warsaw Treaty Organization's 300 or so.
- NATO has a superiority of 5:1 in terms of capacities and means of strategic transport of troops and equipment and of 10:1 in terms of marines.

Our estimate of the balance of forces in Europe and its adjacent waters is as follows: strength of armed forces of WTO, 3.5 million men; of NATO, 3.6 million men. Whereas the numbers of tactical combat aircraft of the air forces, air defense forces, and navies are approximately equal, NATO has 1.5 times more strike aircraft and twice the number of combat helicopters. In tanks, the Warsaw Treaty Organization has superiority. As to artillery, the question is debatable. Yet the figures do not instill confidence. Why choose artillery of 100 mm caliber and above? If one takes all kinds of artillery, NATO has an additional 25,000 pieces, and the ratio is equal. A better count is needed. As for assessment of the state of the infrastructure and of the qualitative characteristics of many forms of weapons, it is in NATO's favor.

Such are the facts. We should like the NATO countries to take into account our concern over the above-mentioned imbalances, especially the considerable superiority in naval forces.

We are disturbed—and will always be disturbed—by the many hundreds of U.S. military bases encircling the USSR in a vast ring.

We are disturbed by NATO's strike air power. World War II and every war since started, not with tanks, but with aircraft. In the space of an hour or an hour and a half, an air force can deliver powerful blows to a depth of 1,000 km or more. During the same time, tanks cannot even reach the frontier.

An air force is an invasion potential. To say that it is difficult to distinguish between offensive and defensive aircraft is not an argument. They are quite different. That is no problem. Besides, there is inspection to help us. If we are of one mind about reducing offensive potential, the first thing to reduce are aircraft (along with tanks).

Conventional arms reduction will proceed not only by way of arrangements reached at future talks but also through unilateral steps on both sides. There is nothing to prevent the United States and NATO from responding with some equally constructive steps. We have given an example of trust, of turning from arms build-up to arms reduction. A good example deserves to be followed. We are not demanding similar steps from the United States and NATO. However, my expectation is that our unilateral initiative will provoke a positive reaction from the NATO countries and that they will come forward with initiatives of their own. They could reduce those of their conventional weapons in Europe in which there is an imbalance in their favor. As a result of such joint efforts, the military confrontation in Europe would be substantially lowered even before arrangements were reached on the mutual reduction of armed forces and conventional armaments from the Atlantic to the Urals.

New talks are to start in March. It is hard to tell how they will go. But it seems that our initiative on a 500,000-man reduction will be a strong influence for their success.

The position of the Warsaw Treaty countries is well known. We are proposing that the armed forces of both sides be reduced in three stages.

During the first stage, we propose doing away with imbalances and asymmetries, reaching approximately equal aggregate levels in terms of the numerical strength of armed forces and the quantity of conventional weapons.

Where to start? We can start by agreeing on a list of the arms to be reduced. Then we could put all our cards on the table, in other words, exchange the initial data for the talks. We should not be afraid to "talk figures" if the sides agree to strict verification of the figures (including on-site inspections).

During the second stage, each side would make a substantial reduction (by, say, 500,000 men). At this stage we would have to begin reducing naval forces and weapons, otherwise NATO would gain a dangerous superiority.

At the third stage a situation would have been reached where the sides would be left with forces and systems needed for defense only, but insufficient for attack.

Other scenarios are also possible: (1) for instance, to begin straightaway with equal-percentage reductions from the start (scope and phasing of reductions to be agreed on), or possibly, (2) to agree on some reduced level of the armed forces of the size needed for defense but useless for attack. From the agreed "defensive minimum" we could then go on to make the necessary reductions. However, in that case it would be frivolous to speak only of ground troops and air power, leaving out naval forces. The NATO countries must eliminate their naval superiority.

On the topic of our conference, we must find answers to some particular questions:

Are the NATO countries prepared for an exchange of negotiating data and for their verification by on-site inspections?

Are the NATO countries prepared to revise the structure of their armed forces with a view to making them defense-oriented?

When will the NATO countries clearly explain their approach to the new talks in response to our proposal for a three-stage reduction of military potentials?

We look forward to talks that are frank, open, and above board, for this is not a game played to see who takes the prize. Everyone must win, or else all will lose.

Chapter 8
FUTURE NEGOTIATIONS ON CONVENTIONAL STABILITY
Jerôme Paolini

The recent acceleration in the debate on conventional disarmament is due to a set of convergent factors – the growing importance of conventional forces in security policies in the East and in the West and, above all, the spectacular impetus given to the entire issue of disarmament by the new Soviet foreign policy. However, it remains the case that the negotiations on conventional stability expected to begin very soon immediately strike the observer as being a fundamentally new exercise. All deliberation on the prospects for conventional disarmament in Europe must have as its starting point understanding of what will be at stake in the future negotiations as regards the future of the political and territorial order in Europe.

There are, therefore, three preliminary points to be made at this stage.

1. To speak of disarmament or of reduction of the conventional forces in Europe is also to speak of ineluctable alteration of the politico-territorial order inherited from World War II, an order dominated by the confrontation of the alliances and the presence of U.S. and Soviet forces in the center of Europe. In an international context characterized by great fluidity due to the renewal of East-West rapprochement, the process of reform under way in the USSR and the disarmament dynamic, and to the gradual rebalancing of transatlantic relations, what is really at stake in the negotiations on conventional forces is indisputably the future of Europe's security system. The negotiations should above all be an occasion for juxtaposing differing visions of that future as well as a tool, a vehicle for change. Clearly, then, the outlook is radically different from the experience with the MBFR, which were not only confined to the area of Central Europe but marked by the immobilism implicit in the maintenance of the status quo. In these circumstances, it is extremely important not to view the future negotiations as an isolated initiative, but, on the contrary, as an integral part of a wider whole comprising a cluster of proposals each relating to the drawing-up of a political and military blueprint for tomorrow's Europe.

From this point of view, the people of Europe will have to be especially vigilant as regards the account taken of their specific interests. It must be emphasized that each country taking part will approach the future negotiations as a country – once again an obvious difference in comparison with the MBFR, which involved two military organizations – whereas the East-West rapprochement of recent months with respect to arms control has inevitably been dominated by a strong dose of Soviet-American bilateralism. In this regard, the lessons of Reykjavik and of the negotiating of the INF Treaty—where the Europeans' vital security interests were overthrown with sometimes disconcerting haste and lack of consideration—must not be forgotten. Because of the central role of the American and Soviet military presence in the politico-military order of postwar Europe, the same bilateralism is also likely to affect the future conventional negotiations. The Soviets are certain to give the United States—where questions of the continued presence of GIs in the Old World and of "burden-sharing" within the alliance are again coming to the forefront of debate—every opportunity for a negotiated withdrawal either within the framework of bloc-to-bloc exchanges or outside the negotiations, or again by playing on the differences of approach in the West.

2. The second point is that the presence of American and Soviet forces in the heart of Europe also brings out a dilemma, which might be termed conceptual, facing the West: the very approach to arms control, by being simultaneously numerical and purely military, tends to hide what is a fundamental difference between the presence of the United States on the one hand and that of the USSR on the other in the midst of a divided Europe. The first of these presences, freely entered into and accepted, contributes to the defense of a group of democratic nations. The second, imposed by force of arms 43 years ago, underlies the very existence of régimes whose legitimacy is, quite simply, nonexistent. The very logic of the process now underway—tank for tank, division for division in the striving for the objective of equal ceilings on armaments—could lead not only to the forgetting of this fundamental aspect of the problem, but even, to some degree, to the legitimization, through its banalization, of the Red Army's role in Europe. There has been much talk lately, in the East as in the West, of the concept of asymmetric reductions in particular categories of armaments but—and here lies all the irony of the situation—this very notion of asymmetry and its logical corollary as regards arms control, *parity* in the final balance of forces, tends to bolster the misconception that there is a legitimacy that is also symmetrical between the presence of the Soviet forces in Eastern Europe and that of the U.S. forces in the West.

Whence the following difficulty for the West: how to negotiate on the forces now facing one another without accepting ipso facto the resultant political symmetry? How to ensure that withdrawal of all or part of the super powers' forces from Europe does not entail adverse developments in the political order not only in the West, but also in Eastern Europe?

The implication of this second point is that preference should be given to a primarily political approach, an approach that is gradual rather than radical and that seeks parallel results in the political and military spheres. The linking of the future negotiations on conventional stability to the CSCE process is of vital importance in this regard.

3. The third point is that the course of the conventional negotiations is likely to be very heavily influenced by the dynamism of Gorbachevian diplomacy. It is true that, even in the era of the "Brezhnevian immobilism" that is so strongly decried these days in Moscow, the Soviet Union always showed the importance it attached to its "policy of peace." Under Gorbachev, however, the theme of disarmament has acquired an altogether fundamental importance in the application outside the country of the "new thinking." It can even be said that, along with domestic cultural and political change, it is disarmament that seems to have been the subject of the new Soviet leadership's main priorities. Over the past three years, there has been a veritable flood of proposals and agreements on the whole range of disarmament issues, from the Washington INF Treaty, START, and conventional and chemical disarmament to unilateral cuts such as those recently announced by Gorbachev at the United Nations. Placed end to end, the Soviet initiatives both in the nuclear and conventional fields result in a coherent and steadfast policy serving constant geopolitical

objectives: the "common European home" above and beyond the alliances and the marginalization of the United States on the continent.

Thus the anti-deterrence rhetoric coupled with the themes of global nuclear disarmament and the dismantling of the two military alliances that form the essence of the current Soviet proposals, far from signaling equitable recognition by the USSR of the Europeans' legitimate security interests, are, on the contrary, reminiscent of the leitmotifs of postwar Soviet diplomacy. What novelty there is is certainly not in the nature of the political and military objectives, which remain fundamentally unchanged, but in the strategy adopted in pursuit of those objectives. The new Soviet diplomacy seems admirably to have learned its lesson from the failures of the Brezhnev approach in the 1970s by substituting for the traditional exclusivity of a strategy of military saturation of NATO at all levels of the system of escalation a new approach based on the deliberate psychological, moral, and material demobilization of the West. This strategy passes through two poles of prime importance: on the one hand, a change in the overall external image of the Soviet Union and attenuation of the threat resulting from its military might; on the other, the systematic use of the renewal of East-West détente, and of disarmament on terms fixed by Moscow as the instrument of choice of the Soviet designs in Europe.

The whole formed by these convergent factors—the Soviet disarmament drive, the dilemma inherent in the exclusive objective of parity, the prospect of reapportionment of the politico-military map in Europe—is an indication that, for the future, a number of basic precautions should be taken in the conduct of the negotiations on conventional stability.

Above all, it is vital that no gulf should emerge between the perception and the expression of the respective interests of the Europeans and the Americans in these negotiations. Such a hiatus would be liable to create the conditions for a Balkanization of Western security policies that would soon be reflected in an equivalent number of separate races for entente and disarmament with Moscow, with, in the long term, de facto cleavage of the Western and even the European positions. This risk also applies to the sphere of human rights (which is connected to the process of disarmament in Europe in the context of CSCE), where there is a risk that some will seek disarmament for its own sake, whereas others will base their approach on a balance between human rights and disarmament, or even on the preponderance of the political and human aspects. This problem is of particular importance for the Europeans, confronting them with a difficult dilemma that could restrict their room for maneuver in the process now beginning. On the one hand, because of the European imperative they need to avoid the risk of a Euro-American break and thus of finding themselves involved—in order to try to make their voice heard—in a process that necessarily smacks of bloc-to-bloc relations and is itself strongly impregnated with Soviet-American bilateralism. The risk is, of course, that the voice will end up by being covered by the process itself, a development that could in time place Europe's leaders in the difficult situation of having to accept either a joint position at variance with their views or gradual marginalization in the negotiations.

Conversely, resisting the process by following the autonomy track might put the Europeans in a situation of growing political isolation and cause them to lose most of their influence not only as a leading player in the Euro-American ensemble, but also on the development of the substantive negotiations.

A second matter of vital concern is that the negotiating strategy that is chosen and the conduct of East-West relations in general must avoid repeating the error of the 1970s where arms control became the keystone of détente. On the one hand, it would be to forget that the aim of the new Soviet foreign policy is not just the stabilization of the balance of forces, but the veritable restructuring of the political and military order in postwar Europe: disarmament and conventional stability in a great forum from the Atlantic to the Urals are but the preferred means to a political end, that of the "common European home." On the other hand, it would, in view of the difficulties that are inevitable in negotiations on such complex topics as the counting of forces or the very sophisticated inspection régime essential to conventional disarmament, be to make East-West relations hostage to their strictly military aspect and to risk an abrupt reversal of a favorable trend. If the Western and the Eastern countries' priority objective is, in essence, to attain the "demilitarization" of the whole range of East-West relations, it is not certain that overly rapid disarmament is the best way of going about it. Paradoxically, for armaments to weigh less heavily on future East-West relations, the scope of those relations must, on the contrary, be expanded beyond the bounds of military questions *stricto sensu* by as coherent as possible a group of initiatives in other fields. This points yet again to the importance of the parallel and properly respected progress of conventional disarmament and gradual harmonization between East and West in the political, humanitarian, and economic spheres within the context of the Helsinki process.

As regards the Soviet Union, one must always keep in mind the fundamental contradiction between *internal reform* and a *revolution in European security* that characterizes Moscow's "new political thinking." On the one hand, Mikhail Gorbachev misses no opportunity to impress upon us how much the implementation of internal reforms in the Soviet system is a difficult and slow undertaking requiring more time, more patience, and our understanding, not to say our active assistance. On the other hand, what is simultaneously proposed to us in the sphere of security is nothing less than the complete revolutionizing of the European system through the elimination of the "intolerable risk" inherent in nuclear deterrence, the denuclearization of Europe, the "restructuring" of conventional forces for defense, and drastic cuts in conventional forces leading to the withdrawal of the American troops from the Old World. The contrast is not only flagrant; it is akin for the West to the signing of a veritable blank check, whereby the mere promise of internal change in the USSR and in its stranglehold on half of Western Europe would be traded for a model in which it is very hard to see any evidence of the Europeans' legitimate interests. The Soviets must understand that, after more than 70 years of the building of the unparalleled military power that the USSR has become, Europeans cannot agree to discard an order qualified as "old thinking" without tangible proof that it is indeed outmoded. That is, in fact, an essential political test of the Soviet Union's sincerity and genuineness in its approach to disarmament in Europe: the movement toward truly common security must, without fail, include the recognition by the USSR of the legitimate security interests of the other inhabitants of the continent, beginning with the full and entire recognition of the legitimacy of nuclear deterrence as a means of preventing war and thus of reinforcing the stability of the system and that at the time when that system might be in a phase of radical transition. Similarly, the Soviets must accept that a drive for disarmament in Europe is not something to be controlled by them alone to their own advantage but, of necessity, a step-by-step process linked to the Soviet system's internal development in the military and in the economic and human spheres.

Finally, and to conclude on a more specifically military note, progress toward genuine stability in the balance of conventional forces in the European theater must of necessity be accompanied by and even depend on the in-depth revision of defense doctrines and policies on each side. Over and above the cuts, ceilings, and verification that can be envisaged, it is very much in this regard that the challenge must be taken up if a different European security system is to put an end to the postwar legacy of division.

Above all, the Soviet Union will have to give proof of its genuine desire for disarmament by reviewing the whole of its military doctrine, meaning, to employ the Soviet conceptual approach, not only its "socio-political" aspect, but also its "technico-military" aspect. It ought as a preliminary to recognize the maintenance of nuclear deterrence in Europe as an essential element of every future military equilibrium. Should these two conditions be met, under the protective guarantee of limited, truly deterrent nuclear postures, conventional disarmament could then shift the current balance of conventional forces toward general stabilization from the Atlantic to the Urals. Reducing and deconcentrating troops and matériel and limiting reserves and arms stockpiles would then be conceivable as ways of forestalling at each stage all possibility of surprise attack and prolonged war—all this around nuclear arms as the central stabilizing element in the period now opening of change in the European security system.

Finally, the countries of the Atlantic alliance, and more specifically those that are members of NATO, will, for their part, also have to undertake the re-evaluation of their military posture if the current trend toward absence of East-West confrontation is confirmed in the years ahead. How, indeed, can conventional disarmament be viewed with equanimity when disagreements persist within the West concerning the type of posture, whether nuclear or conventional, that should be maintained in the future? Here again, a global strategic concept entered on a deliberately limited and truly deterrent capacity (i.e., a capacity precluding all form of conflict, however limited, on the continent) having as its accompaniment reduced, efficient conventional forces alone seems compatible both with genuine conventional disarmament and with the gradual end of the division of the peoples of Europe.

Chapter 9
RESPONSES

FIRST RESPONSE
Benoit d'Aboville

To initiate discussion of the reports [Chapters 7 and 8], I note that all negotiations start by taking stock of divergences. This is a natural process. It is also a healthy process by means of which ambiguities are eliminated. The reports offer rather contrasting views. We should not necessarily draw the conclusion that the gap cannot be bridged, but I think it would be worthwhile to remove the ambiguities, in a sense. These two reports raise four questions.

The first question relates to the dialectic of the unilateral and the multilateral, to use Karpov's phrase [Chapter 1]. We have a twofold ambiguity concerning the concept of unilateral measures: on the one hand, these are measures that fall outside the negotiations but that, it is clearly stressed, have been taken with the negotiations in mind; on the other hand, these are unilateral measures in the sense that they will be pursued regardless of the behavior of the West—at least that is my understanding—but at the same time General Chervov says that he expects the USSR's unilateral measures to meet with a response, in a sense. So we have a new "animal," which is no longer truly unilateral and which raises certain questions. Fundamentally, does the USSR consider that it must adapt its arrangements for its own reasons, operational reasons, linked to technological development, resulting from reflection on adapting these arrangements, or for political reasons, in other words for the purpose of creating a favorable climate for the start of the negotiations? If this is the case, if these measures have a justification in themselves, on what grounds should they be accompanied by measures in response?

The second question has to do with the issue of data in the future negotiations. Karpov tells us that an MBFR-type war of figures must be avoided and that the ceiling approach would make it possible to do so. Chervov seems to have attached greater importance to the data issue. But the question of data cannot be reduced to that of the method used to draw up an inventory. The problem here is the problem of the scope of the negotiations. Concerning verification, transparency, the Western countries have no difficulty with increasing transparency, and thus going well beyond Stockholm measure number one. There is no difficulty with strengthening a verification régime, nor with agreeing to verify the implementation of unilateral measures. Thus, in fact, what is involved is the purpose of the verification: what are the categories of arms on which data are to be verified? Here we touch upon a problem that is less one of data than of the very definition of the scope of the negotiations. Whereas General Chervov, of course, considers that tanks constitute the backbone of forces in Europe—and on this point I think there is no disagreement with the Western countries—at the same time he sets out three categories of forces: the American strategic forces, naval forces, and a third category made up of logistical facilities for reinforcing the American alliance in Europe, for which it is difficult to see how they could be defined at the European level. If we are to speak of data, then it is global data that are actually involved. Thus behind this matter of data, we much acknowledge, lies the scope of the negotiations.

The third ambiguity that needs to be clarified relates to the role of nuclear weapons in relation to the imbalance in conventional forces. From Chervov, one has the impression that nuclear weapons essentially constitute a fighting weapon—in a sense pieces of conventional superartillery that would cease to be legitimate once the balance of forces was restored. This is not at all the concept that exists in this part of Europe. Because of the enormity of the damage they cause, nuclear weapons have a deterrent function *by their very nature*. They also have a linkage and escalation function, and consequently the sufficient and necessary quantity of nuclear weapons cannot be considered to be linked to the balance of conventional forces.

The fourth ambiguity should truly be at the center of our discussions. Ultimately, what is reasonable sufficiency, and what is a defensive posture? Is it—since this is the justification for the unilateral measures as it has been presented—a question of moving closer to a defensive posture? And what is a defensive posture?

Last March and last December the countries of the Atlantic alliance gave their version of what a defensive posture is. In reply to one of Chervov's questions, we have a clear concept. The concept of the objective of the negotiations is very simple: it is sufficiency, a term also used on the Soviet side. But what may this sufficiency involve? It is defined in relation to the existing state of affairs. Can we consider, for example, that it is normal, politically and militarily healthy, that the Soviet Union should have one tank in two in Europe? Is it healthy, is it reasonable, not least from the viewpoint of balance in political relations, that a single country should have more than a third of the forces in Europe? It is true that there is no magic formula for sufficiency, but at least one can grasp intuitively and politically what goes beyond sufficiency. This will certainly be one of the negotiating topics.

The second clear objective: stability. Here, too, the positions are well known and have been clearly set out—means preventing a surprise attack and its reinforcement. It is also the idea that no aggressor must be in a military position to be able to resort to aggression with a chance of success or a minimum risk that could encourage the aggressor to embark on such aggression.

The third concept is that of transparency. From this point of view, it is a concept that had a difficult start but has advanced soundly over the past 10 years. Defensive posture; what would General Chervov say it consists of in military terms? Does it mean the capacity to repulse the aggressor by means of a rapid counteroffensive? We read often in Soviet literature that the battle of Kursk can show the way regarding what a defensive posture means. But we also know that nearby, on the Ukrainian front, there were reserve units ready to intervene, a concentration ready to pitch into the battle. So how—in general and on the basis of this historical example—can defensive posture be a criterion? This is one of the topics of the negotiations. It is a topic that can be pursued at the same time in the negotiations on stability, but it is also a topic that can be tackled, for example, on the occasion of a seminar on doctrines, which I believe the Western countries have no problems with, but which in fact they would welcome.

SECOND RESPONSE

Rolf Ekéus

The agreed objective of the negotiations on CAFE is to strengthen stability and security in Europe. This objective is to be realized through reduction of forces. In other words, the task for the negotiators is to agree on such reductions that strengthen the stability and security in Europe.

The CAFE negotiations are reductions talks, and as such they replace the MBFR talks. A major concern must be to avoid stalling the CAFE negotiations as the MBFR talks were stalled. How to avoid that is a major problem that should be addressed during the preparatory stage of the negotiations. In general terms the CAFE negotiations benefit from the present favorable international political climate, not the least in the relations between the two major military powers. Furthermore, in order not to repeat the shortcomings of the MBFR talks, it would be strongly advisable to emphasize what differs CAFE from MBFR. Thus differences should be identified and given specific attention when the outline of the negotiations is made. The following fundamentally new characteristics can be identified: (1) that security and stability should be strengthened in the whole of Europe, not only Central Europe, (2) that the area of application for the reductions is the whole of Europe, from the Atlantic to the Urals and from Svalbard to Sicily, and (3) the negotiations are to take place within the framework of the CSCE.

The *first point* underlines that reductions should be carried out in the interest of all CSCE states, thus including the 12 states that do not participate in the CAFE reductions. The question is if security in Europe can be achieved without taking into account the security concerns of the neutrals. It is generally recognized that the reduction of the forces of the NN states at present would not contribute to the aim of stability and security in Europe. But it must also be generally recognized that the undermining of security or the destabilization of, e.g., any of the neutral states would not be conducive to the objective of strengthening the stability in Europe. In other words, if no security for the neutrals, no security for Europe.

From the *second point* follows that reductions should be applicable not only to Central Europe but to the whole of Europe. The Nordic neutral states of Sweden and Finland cover little less than half of the whole stretch from north to south in Europe. In addition, the territories of Austria and Yugoslavia, interposed between WTO and NATO controlled areas, cover an important part of the southern region of Europe. The structure and character of reductions will have a specific impact on the security of the states mentioned. The impact of various weapon systems differs considerably from region to region. Heavy tank and artillery units no doubt are of great relevance in the Fulda Pass area, whereas their relative importance in Northern Europe is limited in comparison with movable units, like air force and airborne or amphibious forces. A security-enhancing approach to force reductions in Europe presupposes a careful analysis of the specific character in security terms of each part of the European theater. Such analysis can most effectively be done together with the affected states in the relevant regions. It is highly questionable if a solid evaluation of the security situation in the north of Europe can be carried out without taking fully into account the concerns of Finland and Sweden.

The *third point* emphasizes the fact that the CAFE talks in a stricter sense are not talks between the two alliances but between the members of the alliances. Furthermore, it establishes a link between the reduction talks and the broader objectives of the CSCE process, with its stress on cooperation with regard to security, economy, human dimensions, and human rights, encompassing all states participating in the CSCE process. The CSBMs negotiated in Stockholm would constitute important collateral measures with regard to confidence building in the CAFE talks and to some degree to verification. The talks on CSBMs, which are to begin at the same time as the CAFE negotiations, create good opportunities for the support of the CAFE talks. New and improved measures of confidence- and security-building character could thus directly facilitate the progress of the reduction talks as well as complement the scope of the talks and assist in obtaining the goal of strengthening stability and security in Europe. Of course, early results in the negotiations on reductions would enhance the prospects for good progress in the CSBM talks. The participation of all CSCE states in the CSBM talks would guarantee that problems specific to certain regions would be fully taken into account, and that the security concerns of all, not the least of all the NN states, would be addressed.

The negotiations on CSBMs and CAFE should thus interrelate for the purpose of mutual improvement and early and tangible results.

THIRD RESPONSE

John van Oudenaren

Like other people here I was very struck by the differences between the two reports [Chapters 7 and 8]. Let me make a few remarks on General Chervov's report [Chapter 7] and then devote the bulk of my remarks to the other [Chapter 8]. I have three points to make. The first concerns the tone—the somewhat alarmist tone. Chervov talks about an exceedingly dangerous military confrontation, invokes the specter of Hiroshima, and talks about "before it is too late." This is a theme that runs through a lot of Soviet statements, but I find it unhelpful. I think everybody agrees that war in Europe would be catastrophic and that we must not be complacent and we must do all we can to try to eliminate the possibility of war in Europe. But I don't think it is all that helpful to try to generate a sense of emergency that we need to take immediate steps. The fact is, the postwar order in Europe has been remarkably stable, and Europe is one of the few regions in the world that has not had major conflicts. Therefore I think we need to be cautious about fundamentally restructuring the European order. And so this notion that we should rush into change is one that I find a little objectionable.

The second point concerns the unilateral steps that were announced by Gorbachev in the United Nations General Assembly in December. General Chervov has disparaged the motives of the people who questioned whether the cuts are enough and talked about reciprocal steps from the West being expected. I would make two points on this. First, like everyone else, I welcome the Gorbachev move and I welcome the lowering of the Soviet forces in Europe. But I think it is unrealistic of the Soviet Union to expect that everyone in the Western world is automatically going to give a reciprocal response. The fact of the matter is that every government in the world, particularly governments in the West that are responding to parliamentary pressures and public opinion, impose unilateral restraints on their forces. They don't always go in front of the United Nations General Assembly and make a big noise about it, but countries have cut their forces, do place limits on their forces because of economic reasons, because of financial reasons, demographic reasons, and so on. The notion that only the Soviet Union ever exercises restraint or cuts forces unilaterally is an incorrect one, and I think it should be clarified.

The third point has been raised already and this concerns the naval theme and also to some extent the nuclear theme that runs very prominently through the Chervov report. People have objected to the raising of the naval issue on substantive grounds. I would stress the procedural grounds for staying away from the naval issue. We have terms of reference, we have a mandate that excludes naval issues and as a practical matter the talks will become hopelessly bogged down if we continue to bring in these extraneous issues. It also should be pointed out that mandates—agreements on terms of reference—are international agreements. They are not like the ABM Treaty or the SALT Treaty where they need to be ratified by the United States Senate, but they are international agreements. Admittedly there is always some vagueness in a mandate—if you didn't have that ambiguity and vagueness you would not need a negotiation—but to flagrantly go against the terms of reference by bringing in naval issues is really ignoring an international agreement and I would hope that the instructions that go to the Soviet negotiators in Vienna take into account the mandate and what it says about the exclusion of naval forces.

Now I turn to the Paolini report [Chapter 8], which is a very rich and complex paper—a very broad paper that makes three general points. The most interesting point is that Paolini sees a new forum for arms reduction in Europe as leading to change in the political order. He hopes that such change will occur. I would like this to be so, and I wish I could share his optimism, but I am a little more skeptical about change in the political order—positive change in the political order through arms control. Paolini has made numerous contrasts between the "good" new forum and the "bad" old one of the seventies. There is some validity in doing this, but if you go further back into the fifties and sixties there is a long history of efforts, mainly by the West but to some extent by the East as well, to use arms control to foster political change. In the fifties—1952 to 1957—conventional arms control discussions were totally divorced from questions of European political order. You had a subcommittee on disarmament, and there were proposals that the United States, the Soviet Union, and China lower their forces to one to one and a half million men, and France and Britain lower theirs to 700,000 to 800,000 men. This was a proposal that the West put forward and the Soviet Union, with modifications, actually accepted in 1955. But the point is that this proposal had nothing to do with the European balance *per se*. It had to do with the fact that these were the great powers and the idea was that the great powers would take reductions first and then other powers would follow suit.

Then there were subsequent moves by the West to introduce an arms control component as a way of getting some movement on the reunification of Germany. You had the Eden Plan in 1955, you had disengagement proposals, and even a remnant of this existed in the Harmel exercise, which really gave an impetus to MBFR from the Western side, in that the Harmel report talked about solving the underlying political issues. These were all attempts to use arms control as a vehicle for introducing positive political change of the type that Paolini is talking about. None of them worked, partly because of resistance from the Eastern side. Thus I am a bit more skeptical as to whether this new forum, which in many ways is superior to the MBFR forum as an arms control forum, will produce this positive political change. In fact, I think there is a downside danger from the Western point of view that this new forum—this new all-European, only-European arms control forum—actually could lead to political change that the West would see as negative. I can see some kind of European security order in which the Soviet Union tries to become the "security manager" of the European continent. If you look at some of the things that are being pushed on the Eastern side, hotlines, institutionalized consultations, crisis centers, very strong emphasis on verification, you begin to see a little bit of a hint here of creating an institutionalized structure that the Soviet Union, still being a very large power, would use to try to exert a lot of leverage over events in the rest of the continent. So at a minimum I hope that Paolini is right and we get positive political change, but there is also a downside danger of negative political change. The outcome may be a stand-off in which we just get some modest arms control.

Let me go to the second point regarding parity, or the moral equivalency shall we say, of the United States and Soviet forces. I imagine this is a controversial point with some of the people from Eastern Europe, but let me enter into the spirit of it. I would agree with Paolini; I think that if you do get into arms control negotiations and conclude a treaty or an agreement in which United States and Soviet forces are limited, you run a great danger of legitimizing the presence of forces in Eastern Europe that you don't want to legitimize. You could even take this further and say you legitimize the division of Germany and so on. This is a great danger. But it is a little bit late now to be raising this. This involves maintaining a position of principle that the West really moved away from in the late sixties. We were pushing MBFR on the Soviets, including the discussion of Soviet forces in Czechoslovakia, within months after they had occupied the country. Twenty years later it is going to be practically very difficult to raise this issue. I think maybe all you can hope for is some clever drafting by international lawyers in the French and other foreign ministries that will skirt around this issue.

The third point that Paolini makes is about the Gorbachev style. I would agree completely with what he says here. There is a dramatic difference between the internal pace of the Soviet reform, which is slow and difficult, and the Soviet Union's call for new thinking and rapid change internationally. This really brings me back to where I began, with the criticism of the Chervov report. It is not directed so much at the report *per se* but at a general trend. There is something depressingly old about the Soviet new thinking. There are new elements, but a lot of the tones, and especially the idea that the Soviet Union has all the answers in these kinds of things, I find kind of depressing. I hope that the Soviet

Union moves away from this and, as Paolini says in his report, moves toward a genuine acceptance of the legitimacy of European security concerns. That would be real new thinking from my point of view.

FOURTH RESPONSE
Zdeněk Pagáč

In recent years much has been said about new political thinking. We can witness the erosion of old biased dogmas and prejudices. Former security concepts are becoming anachronic and urgent need for common endeavor is being felt practically in all spheres of international life. Positive tendencies enable us to formulate new initiatives with good prospects that they may come true. In this context emphasis has been put upon the role of the so-called small and medium-size states to which my country belongs. I would like to make a few comments on the Czechoslovak foreign policy initiative for creating a zone of confidence, cooperation, and good neighborly relations on the line of contact between the Warsaw Treaty Organization and the NATO countries. As an objective we can see a common European house with a wide system of firm security guarantees, Europe free of nuclear and chemical weapons where conventional forces will undergo sweeping changes, that is, they will be substantially cut and restructured exclusively for defensive purposes. In such a Europe, military confrontation and ideological animosity will yield to a fruitful competition and cooperation. From a conceptual point of view we consider all aspects of international relations as sectors influencing security, confidence, and cooperation among states. Those aspects include political and military questions in the first place, but also cooperation in economic, ecological, scientific and technological, cultural and humanitarian fields. In this respect a number of suggestions have been raised both at governmental and nongovernmental levels. In the field of conventional disarmament we are preparing our own unilateral measures in conformity with the defensive doctrine of the Warsaw Treaty Organization. A dense net of relations and contacts with our West European neighbors, namely the Federal Republic of Germany and neutral Austria, contribute to enhancing confidence and cooperation in central Europe. Our initiative is organically connected with all European processes; the proposal is not a definitive closed one. It is open to discussion not only with the NATO countries but also with the neutrals. Even though we have a comprehensive approach to problems to be solved, we do not condition progress in one area on a progress in another. If we cannot move in one direction, we will seek another way; even better, we may proceed wherever it is possible. We believe different progress is possible in different subregions.

There is no doubt that the level of our mutual security will be determined in the first place by progress reached in disarmament talks. As far as Vienna talks on conventional disarmament are concerned, they may at a certain stage facilitate the establishment of a chemical weapon-free zone and nuclear-free corridor in Central Europe, which had been proposed by the German Democratic Republic and Czechoslovakia and endorsed by three political parties including West Germany's SPD. At the same time a new political climate and arms reduction could revive a number of other subregional initiatives in Europe that have been presented in recent years by the governments, parliamentarians, political parties, and various organizations and institutions on both sides.

There is a great potential of ideas that might be transferred into practice. What we will need now at the negotiating table in Vienna is a flexible approach and the art of compromise. This may be in the broadest sense of the word the best method of conducting talks to avoid repeating the bitter experience of the protracted rounds of the MBRFR. In my view a promising and realistic way out has been explained in the report by Nicolai Chervov [Chapter 7] and I believe that he has shown in a very convincing manner that there is a strong political will on the part of the Warsaw Treaty Organization to promote conventional disarmament in Europe.

Part IV

Confidence-Building Measures and Verification

The discussions following the reports in Chapters 10 and 11 concentrate on such questions as linkages between Stockholm I and Stockholm II and between CAFE talks and Stockholm II, on the future verification régime in Europe, and political assessment of the Vienna document.

In discussing the future of the CSBMs, it is pointed out that some measures that were rejected in Stockholm I might be acceptable in Stockholm II. The more flexible approaches of the WTO on the establishment of fast communication mechanism, exchange of structural information, and improvement of on-site inspections are mentioned in this respect.

On the relationship between CAFE and Stockholm II, it is argued that the Vienna document did not have a conceptual definition of the link and that it was not clear how CSBMs agreed to in Stockholm II would be incorporated into the CAFE framework. A response to this view is that the lack of definition of the linkage between the two talks should not be considered a serious shortcoming of the Vienna document. An attempt to elaborate and agree on such a definition could have been a nonstarter. A failure of CAFE could lead to a setback in the future CSBMs. That setback could not be compensated by the Stockholm II since it would be left with comparatively unimportant CSBMs, which was detrimental to the interests of neutral and nonaligned states not participating in CAFE talks.

In discussing the scope of Stockholm II, it is pointed out by participants from the WTO states that Western countries, especially the United States, are not interested in the extension of the CSBMs to the maritime activity because they believe they have a privileged position on the sea and do not need control and verification. WTO participants feel the threat from the sea and think that the naval CSBMs are necessary. The argument of "mandates linkage" is not workable since the CAFE mandate does not determine what CSBMs would be agreed to on Stockholm II. In reply, it is maintained by a U.S. participant that the CAFE mandate explicitly excluded naval activities and that the Stockholm II mandate only included these naval activities that were functionally linked to land activities.

Verification, it is pointed out, could be a means for overcoming the debate on figures and could play an important crisis prevention and management role in Europe. With respect to conventional disarmament in Europe, it is suggested that two aspects are to be taken into consideration: the limits of the technical means, and the difference in the technical means of individual countries. To overcome the problem of unequal possession of NTM, an integration of satellite data in a joint and structured verification system is proposed.

Concerning the dichotomy between the talks of the 23 and that of the 35, it is argued that this dichotomy meant political regress for the Vienna document. In response it is pointed out that the document could not be regarded as a regress; in fact, it was a very balanced compromise achieved between different interests of the participating states.

In response to statements by Western participants, a Soviet participant confirms that the USSR did not modernize its short-range missiles.

Chapter 10
CSBMs IN EUROPE: A FUTURE-ORIENTED CONCEPT*

Adam-Daniel Rotfeld

Confidence- and security-building measures (CSBMs) occupy a special place in the various concepts of arms control and disarmament in Europe. Hopes pinned on a system of military confidence-building measures were increasing particularly at periods when talks on the reduction and limitation of armaments produced little or no concrete results. The special treatment of CSBMs has sprung from a conviction that they not only would alleviate international tensions but would also foster disarmament. Yet efforts to strengthen confidence and security of states made by the Geneva Surprise Attack Conference, 1958, or at the early stages of the Geneva Eighteen-Nation Disarmament Conference, 1962, did not yield the desired effects. During the same period the first serious theoretical studies highlighted the role and significance of direct communication lines, early warning and notification, exchange of military missions, national technical means of control and monitoring/radar systems, satellite surveillance and establishment of observation posts and inspection zones.[1] Those measures have been designed to decrease the risk of an outbreak of war through accident, miscalculation, or lack of communication; see the Working Paper on Reduction of the Risk of War Through Accident, Miscalculation or Failure of Communication, ENDC/70. The Soviet and American proposals made then spoke in one voice about the need for advance notification of major troop movement and military maneuvers, rapid and efficient communications between the respective heads of state and the UN secretary general. On June 20, 1963 the United States and the Soviet Union reached agreement on a direct line of communication between the Kremlin and the White House. Since then it has been technologically upgraded on the basis of a 1985 accord. Under subsequent Soviet-American treaties, certain national means of control have been set up such as satellite surveillance and radio-electronic early-warning systems. In 1976 the right to on-site inspection was agreed on in connection with the Soviet-American Peaceful Nuclear Explosions Treaty. These have been the first modest attempts to establish international procedures. After a period of detailed analyses and studies,[2] they have been gradually integrated into the pro-

---

* This chapter is based on the contribution prepared for *Conventional Arms Control and East-West Security*, ed. by Robert D. Blackwill and F. Stephen Larrabee. Not for quotation without the permission of the author and the Institute for East-West Security Studies.

cess of shaping a system of confidence and security between East and West. An important step in this direction has been the incorporation into the CSCE Final Act of a section on confidence-building measures.

CSBMs AND THE CSCE DECISIONS

One is struck by the contrast between the broadly conceived and somewhat anticipatory aims and the actual scope of the operative decisions of that part of CSCE decisions. The Helsinki document provided in practice five confidence-building measures in the military sphere:

1. Prior notification of major military maneuvers (involving more than 25,000 troops).
2. Prior notification of other military maneuvers.
3. Prior notification of major military movements.
4. Exchange of observers.
5. Other confidence-building measures, e.g., exchange by invitation of military personnel, visits by military delegations, etc.

These were rather modest measures. Only in the case of prior notification of major military maneuvers was there any precise definition of parameters—ceilings, operative area, and degree of obligatoriness. It is fair to say that by and large the confidence-building measures envisaged in the CSCE Final Act were neither militarily significant nor of obligatory nature. The zone of their application did not cover the whole of Europe nor was any provision made for verification and control procedures. Nonetheless this was the first multilateral document testifying to a political will to initiate a process of reduction of the danger of armed conflict in Europe and elimination of the possibility of surprise attack. The recommended measures aimed at preventing misunderstanding, miscalculation, or misinterpretation of military activities.

The provisions on confidence-building measures included in the CSCE Final Act had more of a political and psychological than military significance. The next important step was the decisions of the CSCE Madrid Meeting (September 6, 1983). The mandate eventually adopted at Madrid, which formed the basis of the Stockholm accord of 19 September 1986, was of a compromise nature. An indication of the interest shown by other states is that a total of five proposals relating to military aspects of security were submitted by, in addition to Poland, France, Romania, Sweden, and Yugoslavia.

The document finally adopted by the Stockholm conference on Confidence- and Security-building Measures in Europe[3] comprises six chapters (104 provisions) and four annexes forming an integral part of the agreement reached.

The following brief recapitulation of the decisions of the Stockholm conference shows that they incorporated a number of qualitatively new elements in the field of confidence- and security-building measures.

First, the decisions adopted at Stockholm are politically binding and so, in contrast to the Final Act, obligatory.

Second, they are militarily significant in that they not only make it possible to form a picture of military activity in Europe (notifications and annual calendars) and observe its conduct, beginning at relatively low quantitative ceilings (17,000 troops), but are also conducive to a certain limitation of its scale. This is of importance with regard to both major maneuvers and to an even greater extent troop transfers. Essentially, these are new steps hitherto unknown in the practice of relations between CSCE countries, still less between states belonging to opposed alliances.

Third, the zone of application for military CSBMs is much wider than in the Final Act, and it is also worth noting that the extension has been effected entirely eastward. The formula "from the Atlantic to the Urals" encompasses the whole European territory without including even a part of North America, whether the United States or Canada. Furthermore, the measures agreed at Stockholm are not applicable to independent naval activities unless they form an integral part of land operations on the European continent.

Fourth, there is no precedent in East-West relations for the verification measures agreed. Of particular significance are the decisions relating to on-site inspection, which will unquestionably contribute to the greater credibility of the entire system of confidence- and security-building measures. They are evidence of a fairly fundamental change in the Warsaw Treaty states' position on this issue. Bearing in mind that it has been a sticking point in arms limitations, it will be seen that the new control and verification measures should serve as a kind of proving ground that could forward agreement on conventional force and armaments reductions.

The controlling theme of the decisions contained in the Stockholm document is a wish to see all CSCE states feel more certain that surprise attack in Europe is impossible. The security of states is founded in the contemporary world on a triad of forces: land, sea, and air. National security policies, based in effect on the concept of deterrence, depend on an equilibrium embracing all elements of the triad. Given an international system so organized, confidence- and security-building measures ought to correspond to the existing threats. Analysis of the decisions of the Stockholm conference indicates that the agreed measures apply chiefly, if not exclusively, to conventional land forces. Military activity on the sea or in the air comes within the scope of CSBMs only if it is an integral part of military activity on land. In other words, independent major naval exercises or large-scale deployment of air force units are excluded from the applicability of the Stockholm conference decisions. However, a policy of effective prevention of the possibility of surprise attack must, in the case of Poland and still more the USSR, make provision to an equal, if not greater, extent against threats from the sea and air as the land. In an analysis of the military problems of Polish security, experts from the Polish Army General Staff Academy have written that "in the initial and most difficult phase of war we will not be faced with the necessity of confronting land forces or countering firepower of these forces. The chief threat will come from air strikes or airborne and amphibious operations. Nor can the possibility of operation by diversionist groups be ruled out."[4]

The Warsaw Treaty states' acceptance at Stockholm of measures offering greater insurance against land attack by conventional forces than sea or air strikes involving nuclear weapons should effectively demolish the hoary old arguments about a "threat from the East."

Looking back over the two years that have passed since the adoption of the Stockholm decisions, a general picture is beginning to emerge of how effective they have been and what impact they have made on the overall developments in Europe. It certainly has been a period of gathering experience and not infrequently also experimenting with the new measures, whose scope—it will be remembered—is without precedent in East-West relations.

Notifications received in 1987 and 1988 in accordance with the requirement to exchange annual calendars of military activities aroused no reservations. They conformed to the provisions adopted. A comparison of the 1987 calendar with the 1988 calendar shows decreasing numbers of military activities that are subject to prior notification. It is, however, hard to say just how far it has been determined by economic considerations such as high cost of maneuvers, and how far it could be attributed to a more relaxed atmosphere and political will to restrain military activity. A certain weakness of the Stockholm decisions is that they do not provide for limitation of frequency, number, and ceilings for military exercises that are conducted during the same period of time. Another thing is that concentration of troops participating in maneuvers is much greater on the NATO side than on the side of the WTO countries. (For example, in September 1987 the NATO states conducted maneuvers with 394,000 troops whereas the total number of the WTO troops in simultaneous maneuvers did not exceed 90,000.) The provisions on notification, observation, and control were in principle respected. There were some differences in the interpretation of the relevant provisions in this respect.

Strict and scrupulous implementation of the confidence- and security-building measures agreed at Stockholm will undoubtedly help to some extent to reinforce convictions that the intentions of states conducting military activities are peaceful and that the maneuvers carried out be them are not of a threatening or aggressive nature.

Nevertheless it remains a fact that both present and future confidence-building measures have to do chiefly with the sphere of perception; they do not contribute to a reduction of military capabilities, of forces and armaments in Europe. Without a simultaneous decrease in military arsenals, these measures can be an additional source of tensions, frictions, and mutual suspicion. The Stockholm conference was from the outset treated as the beginning of a process of negotiations. Moreover, both France and Poland, the authors of the principal proposals submitted on this question in Madrid, assumed that in the next stage the conference would, in accordance with its name, deal not only with confidence- and security-building measures but also with disarmament in Europe.

For this reason, on December 1986 Poland tabled at the Vienna meeting a proposal for supplementing the mandate agreed at Madrid so that it included "consideration and adoption, on a basis of equality of rights, equilibrium and reciprocity, and equal respect for the security interests of all participating states, steps aimed at reductions of conventional forces and armaments in Europe. They will be examined parallel to confidence- and security-building measures that have been or will be submitted by any of the participating states. Particular consideration will be given to essentially new confidence- and military-strategic stability-building measures directly connected with conventional force and armaments reductions and facilitating achievement of agreement in these matters."[5] The Polish proposal's aim was to ensure continuation of the Stockholm conference along lines of seeking the broadest possible common denominator:

- In the substantive sphere parallel discussion of confidence- and security-building measures on the one hand, and force and armaments reductions on the other.
- In the procedural sphere the participation in the negotiations of 35 states on an equal basis in accordance with the principle that the CSCE process cannot permit the introduction of different categories of states and different "degrees of initiation."

During the informal meeting of "Group 23" (16 NATO and 7 WTO states) in Vienna, the question of participation of neutral and nonaligned states in the future conference has turned into a major contentious issue between the East and the West. The NATO states—

except for France—demanded that arms reduction matters be excluded from CSCE process. The diminishing of military potentials in Europe was meant to be the exclusive subject of interbloc talks.[6]

A different approach was taken by the Soviet Union, Poland, and other WTO states. They proposed that:

1. A mandate agreed by the 23 NATO and WTO states form an integral part of the concluding document of the CSCE Vienna meeting.
2. A mechanism be devised to ensure a two-way institutional link between talks within Group 23 on reductions and military stability in Europe, on the one hand, and the negotiations on CSBMs conducted by the 35 CSCE states on the other.

A basis for a compromise solution was eventually provided by drafts submitted by Sweden,[7] Yugoslavia,[8] and Cyprus.[9] The solution adopted at Vienna was initially included in the comprehensive proposal by NN states tabled on 13 May 1988. The document articulated the accords reached after months of hard work in working bodies and drafting groups. On the question of future negotiations on CSBMs by 35 states, the document reads: "The participating States have agreed that negotiations on confidence- and security-building measures will take place in order to build upon and expand the results already achieved at the Stockholm conference with the aim of elaborating and adopting a new set of mutually complementary confidence- and security-building measures designed to reduce the risk of military confrontation in Europe. . . ."

As regards negotiations by Group 23 concerning stability and conventional force reductions in Europe, the document reads: "These negotiations will be conducted within the framework of the CSCE process and in accordance with the mandate agreed upon by the participants. . . ."

In this way a link has been established between the two planes of negotiations—one, within the framework of the CSCE process, and the other, without damage to the autonomous character of talks by the 23 countries.

The future system of building confidence and security in Europe depends less on procedural arrangements or relationship between the two negotiating planes than on their context and scope of future CSBMs. The Vienna document defined the aims of future negotiations as follows:

1. To build upon and expand the results already achieved at the Stockholm conference.
2. To elaborate and adopt a new set of mutually complementary CSBMs.
3. These CSBMs will be designed to reduce the risk of military confrontation in Europe.

It would be interesting to establish what kinds of measures could match those expectations and requirements.

THE STOCKHOLM DECISIONS AND THE NEW MEASURES

It stands to reason that the measures tabled and discussed at the Stockholm conference, but that had not won consensus, could as well be put again on the negotiating table during talks on new CSBMs. In view of such a possibility it could be expected, immediately after the closure of the Stockholm conference that:

- WTO states will repeat their postulates on supplementing the zone of application of CSBMs by the sea area and airspace around Europe,[10] including independent naval and air force operations in areas surrounding Europe,[11] they will also seek decisions restraining military activity.
- NATO states will seek the expansion of military information, new measures to enhance the regime of verification, inspection and communications.[12]
- NN states will again advance postulates that will be closer to WTO proposals on certain issues, for example, limitation of military activity, and on some other matters closer to the NATO position, like greater access to military information. They are also expected to present their proposals reflecting their specific position vis-a-vis East-West relations, e.g., with regard to a draft proposal to hold on demand ad hoc multilateral meetings on CSBMs to exchange views "on the routine implementation of the measures."[13]

Trying to reduce the whole problem of future measures to those postulates that had been tabled at Stockholm but were not included in the document of 19 September 1986 would be making things look more simple than they in fact are, specifically in the light of the experiences that have accumulated over the past two years since the Stockholm conference ended, regarding the implementation of its decisions and the debates held at Vienna.

Recent changes of the politico-military situation in Europe and especially the Soviet-American INF Treaty on the elimination from Europe of two types of missiles and also the opening of talks on conventional stability, have now created an atmosphere encouraging negotiations on a set of confidence-building measures much more ambitious than envisaged earlier. The question remains what these measures should actually be and whether they should lead mainly to reductions of military activity or perhaps to an expansion of military information (access to data) and greater scope of control and on-site inspection.

It now looks that the new generation CSBMs cannot be seen in isolation from the processes going on along the East-West line. CSBMs never have been, are not, and perhaps never will be the main determinant of the politico-military situation. They can, however, considerably influence its shape within the framework of broader processes including the relations among the nuclear powers, relations between states from the two military blocs (talks within Group 23) and, ultimately also relations between participants of the all-European process (talks within the 35 CSCE states). CSBMs could foster reductions of armed forces and conventional armaments in Europe. A new element that emerged after the Stockholm conference was a certain convergence of views of the three groups of countries (NATO, WTO, and NN) over the essence of the new measures. For example, Warsaw Treaty states, which in the past viewed with reserve measures designed to facilitate openness and predictability, especially verification, inspection, and exchange of information, have now included them into their recent proposals. In making their move the WTO states were falling back on their heretofore experience from the way the multilateral CSCE recommendations as well as the Stockholm decisions and also the INF Treaty on the elimination of medium and shorter range missiles have been put into practice.

NEW PROPOSALS

The Jaruzelski Plan. Poland has proposed (para. 4 of the plan) that an agreement could be concluded "on appropriate far-reaching confidence- and security-building measures and the mechanisms for the strict verification of compliance with the undertaken commitments, including such which for various reasons it would be difficult to introduce to Europe as a whole."[14] Such measures could envisage:

- An agreement on parameters to constrain the size and/or the intensity of the specified types of military activities.
- The exchange of military information.
- Procedures for the prompt clarification of situations arousing the concern of either side.

The Polish document devotes much space to national and international means of control, including a possibility to establish a control mechanism with the participation of the interested states and third parties. The control mechanism might visualize:

- An exchange of information indispensable for effective verification.
- Notification of the commencement and completion of the withdrawal or reduction of armaments and their observation.
- Establishment of control points on the borders of the zone through which the arms would be withdrawn, as well as at large railway junctions, airfields, sea ports, and other measures.

The system could include a procedure of bilateral and multilateral consultations. On its part, the Polish government expressed its readiness to accept, on a reciprocal basis, any method of control indispensable to attain the purpose of the plan.

It is true that the Polish proposal is restricted only to the territory of Central Europe. That area—under the Jaruzelski Plan—embraces a zone that is wider than that mentioned in earlier Polish initiatives for an atom-free zone (the Rapacki Plan, 1957), or a nuclear freeze (the Gomulka Plan, 1963-64), which covered only the territories of the two German states, Czechoslovakia and Poland. In the latest Polish proposal Central Europe is meant to cover the territories of the FRG, Benelux, and Denmark, on the NATO side, and the GDR, Czechoslovakia, Poland, and Hungary, on the WTO side.

The statement of the Polish government of 14 June 1988 contains a proposal to elaborate and accept new parameters constraining ground force activities by applying "correspondingly further reaching measures as the distance from the line of contact is decreased." The document explains that "such constraints could be applied to the movements of force, to the size, number, duration and frequency of military exercises including, for example, the possibility of simultaneous exercises, and also to bans on large exercises." That postulate is quite understandable in view of the fact that the Stockholm conference decisions have brought about a certain restriction of the military activity. Even more importantly, that self-imposed limitation or constraint approach in military activity by states has been forced to a greater extent by financial considerations and improved East-West climate than by an obligation to respect concrete recommendations.[15]

The catalogue of the new CSBMs proposed in the Polish statement covers the following:

- Exchange of military information.
- Procedures for the clarification of situations related to the military activity and arousing concern of either party.
- Establishment of a system of "hot lines" between the highest state authorities and military high commands (such communication lines already exist between Washington and Moscow and between Paris and Moscow.

- Extension of contacts among representatives of armed forces (study visits and regular bi- and multilateral working meetings).

The system of control envisaged in the Polish proposal would comprise observation and on-site inspection without the right of refusal. The system of mutual control could encompass:

- Exchange of indispensable information, including lists of the types and kinds of armaments being withdrawn and their dislocation.
- Notification of the commencement, progress, and completion of the various measures.
- Establishment of permanent observation posts on the borders of the zone, at large railway junctions, airfields, and sea ports through which the arms, equipment, and specified military units would be transferred.

Also subject to control would be the weapons decommissioned from the armed forces as would-be compliance with levels attained as the outcome of the reduction and/or withdrawal process.

Poland expressed readiness to establish an international consultative body with the possible inclusion of interested third parties. It would be primarily concerned with observation and inspection activities and would also investigate controversial issues. An important role in that organ could be played by representatives of NN states.

The Polish proposal refers first of all to Central Europe, but it remains in strict relationship with the situation and security requirements and solutions on an all-European scale. During work on the document its authors have listened to opinions and suggestions of Western partners expressed both at official consultations with governmental officials and during meetings with experts on a nongovernmental basis.

Center for prevention of surprise attack in Europe. On 11 July 1988 Mikhail Gorbachev announced in the Polish parliament that "there is a need for a European centre to temper the threat of war that could serve as a place for co-operation between the NATO and WTO. Such a centre, which would be a permanent organization, could be transformed into a useful structure enhancing the trust in the infallibility of peace in Europe." Speaking in support of that initiative Wojciech Jaruzelski said that it corresponds to the Polish plan. He also expressed a readiness to actively contribute to the establishment of the center for prevention of surprise attack in Europe. "Poland," said Jaruzelski, "is ready to engage immediately into consultations on the Centre, at the same time offering — should states interested consent — its territory as the center's seat."[16]

The idea to have such a center is not new. It is related to a broader concept of crisis management mechanisms. In the United States it has been discussed chiefly in the context of providing reliable handling of crisis situations. A need for a mechanism that could track the developments and remain in control was suggested by the experience of the Cuban crisis of 1962. In their report to the U.S. Arms Control and Disarmament Agency published in 1984, William Langer Ury and Richard Smoke from Harvard Law School wrote: "Four key features of a crisis make it especially dangerous: little time to decide, high stakes, high uncertainty, and few usable options."[17]

The task of the European center would be not so much resolution of crisis situations but rather preventive activity, information, and control. It would be a kind of a clearinghouse for politico-military matters in Europe.

The idea for a European center has been mooted for quite some time at scientific symposia and conferences attended by representatives from West and East. Some experiences on joint control and prevention of escalation of tensions and crisis situations has been gathered by institutions operating within the Allied Control Council for Germany. Some of those bodies as, for example, a Committee for the Security of Flights in air corridors into Berlin are still operative.

On 22 March, 1988, acting on a bilateral basis, the United States and the USSR established nuclear risk control centers in Moscow and Washington. That such solutions for the entire European continent are being looked at is best evidenced by various nongovernment documents and reports.[18]

In May 1987 a Joint Working Group of the PUWP and SPD issued a proposal for a European Council for Building Confidence designed to serve as a forum for dialogue that would promote elaboration of political measures preventing tensions and crisis situations and encouraging the construction of peaceful structures in Europe. In July 1988 a similar working group of SED and SPD submitted to the governments of the two German states a proposal to establish in Central Europe—along the line of contact of the two blocs—a zone of confidence and security. The regime of the zone was designed so as to convince both parties that for all their respective military capability neither of them intends to launch a surprise attack. A qualitatively new element in the SED-SPD document is an idea to create centers for confidence-building as permanent organs entrusted with the task of exchanging militarily important information and the results of observations. This would facilitate the governments involved in their efforts to forestall crisis situations in Central Europe and/or to resolve them through political means. The centers would use data from an agreed joint European satellite surveillance system. These data would also be supplied to every CSCE member state.

The Committee of Foreign Ministers of States-Members of the Warsaw Treaty Organization in session in Budapest on 28 October 1988 incorporated a draft for the establishment in Europe of a center for diminishing the threat of war and prevention of surprise attack into its joint statement on confidence- and security-building measures and disarmament in Europe. The center would perform such tasks as information exchange, communications, consultations on operative clarification of situations arousing concern and suspicion. Matters concerning the center will be open for talks during a conference of 35 CSCE states devoted to CSBMs. The outstanding issues include the scope and nature of information exchanged, organizational framework, mode of procedure, financing, and many others. It is nonetheless certain that such a center—even allowing for the fact that in its initial stages its functions would be limited to information exchange only—would contribute to stabilizing the military as well as political situation in Europe. The agreement to have a European center alone would be eloquent proof of serious change and progress in building confidence. It would set in motion a process of shaping lasting structures for preventing, controlling, applying, and resolving crisis situations in Europe. So far the NATO states have responded with caution.

The United States for its part remains stubbornly negative to two other concepts: a gradual transformation of military doctrines toward giving them a defensive character, and expansion of CSBMs to sea and ocean areas.

Transformation of military doctrines. The new approach of WTO states to military doctrines articulates deep political changes and reappraisal of their approach to matters of security. The idea to include the problem of doctrines into East-West discussions has been advanced for some time by experts from Western Europe working on alternative concepts of security.[19] The document "On the Military Doctrine of States-Members of the WTO," adopted on 29 May 1987 in Berlin during a session of the Consultative Political Committee of the States-Members of the Warsaw Treaty, reads that:

- The military doctrine of the Warsaw Treaty as of any state that is party to that treaty is designed to serve the task of blocking the eventuality of a war, be it nuclear or conventional.
- That doctrine is of a strictly defensive character and rests on an assumption that under present conditions the use of military means in order to resolve any contentious issues is inadmissible.
- WTO member-states will never and under no circumstances start hostilities against any state or alliance unless they themselves become an object of armed assault.
- WTO states have never sought nor are they seeking to have the armed forces greater than it is indispensable for defensive purposes.
- WTO states seek to maintain equilibrium on an ever lower level and do not advance claims to greater security than that of other states.

One of the WTO states' goals under the defensive war doctrine according to the Berlin document is the establishment of zones of thinned-down armaments and enhanced confidence and implementation of military measures of confidence-building in Europe on the principle of reciprocity and also reaching agreements on the application of those measures on the sea and ocean areas.

What lies in the core of joint activity for ensuring an evolution of military doctrines in such a way as to make them reciprocally seen as defensive? The answer can be found in documents of the Polish government clarifying the essence of the Jaruzelski Plan.[20] These documents advance a postulate to base the doctrines on the principle of adequacy, which would justify the possession by a state only of such a military potential as is indispensable for effective defense. In order to achieve this end it would be helpful to hold joint discussions and comparison of military concepts and doctrines and analyze their nature and development trends.

Following bilateral consultations with several NATO states, including representatives of the United States and FRG, it turned out that difficulties in mutual understanding begin already on the level of terminology. What the WTO countries define as "military doctrine" the NATO states call "strategy." Therefore the statement of the Polish government of June 1988 says as follows: "It would be desirable to interpret mutually the terminology connected with doctrines, and their practical reflection in the system of troops organization and training."

It remains an open question whether military doctrines could be the subject of negotiations. The NATO states and especially the United States fear that as a result of such talks the WTO states could win droit de regard, regardless of the fact that all agreements would in actual fact be based on the principle of reciprocity. These fears are not determining the positions of all NATO states in equal measure. Both France and FRG have expressed their interest in talks on doctrines. Taking into account the need for flexibility, the Polish document of June 1988 adopts a broad formula. It suggests that the issue of the doctrines could become the subject matter at meetings of political representatives and of high-ranking military commanders. It could likewise be tackled within the framework of, or in connection with, the CSCE process. The pragmatic approach adopted by Poland and the FRG to start talks on doctrines found its expression in a joint initiative by the two governments to hold, at their invitation, in 1989 a symposium attended by government experts and army representatives from the interested CSCE states. Contacts of a similar kind could help pave the way toward future decisions on this issue.

CSBMs on the seas. The matter of expanding the zone of application of CSBMs to waters around Europe and making independent naval operations part of the regime of the agreed measures has been and still remains a major contentious issue.

In the official American assessment the extension of the CSBMs zone of application to the Urals was correctly defined as "quite significant." On the other hand, the Soviet idea of extending the geographical area into the North Atlantic Ocean as compensation for its extension to the Ural Mountains cannot be rejected simply with the argument that the Soviet objective is "to negate the international principle recognizing free use of the high seas and thus possibly to interfere with movement of U.S. forces in contingencies involving areas of the world outside Europe."[21] The reasoning is not convincing for many reasons.

First, as a rule, international treaties and agreements limit sovereign rights of states, including the freedom of naval activities; by conclusion of agreements the sovereignty of states is reflected in respect of their equal rights and the principle of reciprocity.

Second, free use of the high seas is reduced in many respects not only by the law of the sea, but sometimes even unilaterally, e.g., American and Soviet announcements about closed areas on the oceans for military testing.

Third, some limitations as far as the "adjoining sea and space area" is concerned that are included into the Final Act are not considered as negation of the free use of the high seas.

Finally, the conferences in Helsinki, Madrid, and Stockholm as well as in Vienna were and are concerned with the problems of security in Europe. This can by no measure be reduced to military activities on the European continent. It would be hard therefore to accept the unilateral U.S. interpretation of the mandate as it would clearly exclude independent air and naval activities from coverage.[22] For the time being, though, the problem of surprise military attack cannot be reduced to land activity only and should also encompass in agreed scope, the surveillance and observation of naval forces, including submarines, aircraft, and other instruments of surprise attack deployed on the sea and in the air, as stipulated by the Western experts at the Geneva Surprise Attack Conference.[23]

"The inclusion of naval and air exercises in CBMs could have both beneficial and detrimental effects on security," wrote one of the Canadian researchers.[24] He argued that many states, among them Norway, find Soviet naval maneuvers worrisome. But CBMs could also—as he has said—reduce military flexibility by depriving certain states of the minimal level of secrecy needed for an effective defense. "Thus while Norway, from a regional point of view, may favor notification of naval maneuvers, the United States, from a global naval perspective, may well find notification and exchanges of observers detrimental to coping with current and new military problems. Therefore, before such measures are introduced, regional and global strategic interests will have to be reconciled.[25]

In the Soviet view the climate of confidence can be enhanced "through the limitation of naval activities in some sea and ocean areas."[26] The Soviet initiatives are directed at limitation and lowering of the level of military presence and activities, where the conflict situations are most probable. The Soviet Union is interested in withdrawing missile-submarines, especially from the regions of combat patrolling, while limiting the mutually agreed areas of navigation. It aims at limiting deployments of new ballistic missile systems on submarines and prohibiting the deployment of Long-Range Submarine-Launched Cruise-Missiles [LRSLBM] and Ground-Based Cruise-Missiles.[27] In other words, from the Soviet view point the question of extending the CSBMs to seas and oceans is of vital importance for its security policy. This approach supported by the other Socialist states did not find understanding on the Western side during the Stockholm conference.

The idea of expanding CSBMs by the naval activity of states has recently gained greater currency. It has been discussed by PUGWASH experts[28] and directly between representatives of political parties from the Baltic region. A number of new solutions have been advanced. Particularly interesting are the postulates submitted by the Norwegian defense minister, Johan J. Holst, in his paper read at a PUGWASH symposium. Its title was "Northern Europe and the High North. The Strategic Setting: Parameters for Confidence-Building and Arms Restraint." His examination of CSBMs at sea suggests the following tentative conclusions:[29]

- There is a need to develop such measures in a period of change in the operational pattern of the major naval powers in northern waters. The purpose is to prevent an unintended sharpening of tension and competition in sensitive waters.
- Particular emphasis should be attached to confidence- and security building measures that could build upon traditional rules of behavior. Consistent with the principle of freedom of navigation measures should be considered which promise to contribute to the prevention of incidents, inadvertent conflict, and escalation. A basis for multilateral instruments exists in the Soviet-American and Anglo-Soviet agreements for the prevention of incidents at sea.
- Potential confidence- and security-building measures must be considered concretely. Measures that would contain and regulate the access of flag states to particular ocean areas could cast heavy shadows constraining the political freedom of action of coastal states unless they take into account relevant geopolitical asymmetries. Norway depends on not being confined by the shadows cast by the Soviet naval forces, which are homeported on the Kola peninsula. For this purpose allied "countershadows" are needed.
- Confidence must be constructed on a reciprocal basis. Reciprocity in northern waters must comprise the naval powers of particular importance for the defense of Norway. Measures that create distance between Norway and its allies do not contribute to Norwegian confidence. Consequently, confidence- and security-building measures for northern waters should be negotiated by the two alliances. Measures involving mutual notification and observation should include the major flag states as well as the coastal states affected because of their location.

CLOSING REMARKS

The new "third" generation CSBMs ought to be seen as an integral part of the process of diminishing military threat and consolidating politico-military stability in Europe. From this point of view, of crucial importance will be the following:

- Measures leading to restraining military activity. They would mean introduction of a regime of building down the scale and number of simultaneous exercises, their fre-

quency, and also putting limits on troop transfers and their equipment. Of serious importance would be an agreement to restrain military activity near state borders of other CSCE states.
- Expansion of the zone of application of CSBMs to independent naval and air activity and creation of zones of confidence and security, especially areas that are particularly sensitive in military terms in view of the accumulation of great arsenals of weapons and concentration of troops. One of the components of the Central European zone of confidence and security is the Baltic Sea area, where an agreed regime of application of specific CSBMs should be introduced. The Baltic coast states are interested in such a solution (it would not impair the security interests of any other state).
- The matter is now ripe for initiating negotiations on the establishment of a center for prevention of surprise attack in Europe and lessening the threat of war.
- Opening of East-West debate stimulating change in rendering the military doctrines strictly defensive in character.
- Setting up a special system of communications for clarification of certain situations arousing concern; and development of contracts between political leaders and military commanders from all states and establishment of contacts between alliances.
- Refraining from steps in the sphere of arms buildup, which would be incompatible with the goals of negotiations, and in particular nonenlargement of armed forces.
- Agreements on measures for elimination of negative stereotypes and "enemy image" and initiation of moves toward a better mutual understanding and strengthening confidence.

The search for a new generation of CSBMs must not be confined to certain types of measures that are of interest for one group of states only. This requires rejection of the dichotomous perspective in favor of a concept of an international system based on partnership.

Notes

1. Thomas C. Schelling, Arms Control: Proposal for a Special Surveillance Force, in *World Politics* (October 1960), and The Role of Communication in Arms Control, in Evan Luard (ed.), *First Steps in Disarmament* London 1965, 210–225. For a review of concepts see: Charles R. Planck, Sicherheit in Europa. Die Vorschläge für Rüstungsbeschränkung und Abrüstung, 1955–1965 (München 1968), 29–96.

2. Jonathan Alford et al., (eds.,) The Future of Arms Control. Part III—Confidence-Building Measures. Adelphi Paper no. 149, London 1979; Comprehensive Study on Confidence-Building Measures. UN Disarmament Study Series no.7, New York 1982; Karl E. Birnbaum (ed), Confidence-Building East-West Relations. The Laxenbourg Papers, no.5, Wien 1985; F. Stephen Larrabee and Dietrich Stobbe (eds.): Confidence-Building Measures in Europe. New York 1983; Wolf Graf von Baudissin (ed.): From Distrust to Confidence. Concepts, Experiences and Dimensions of CBMs. Vol. II, Baden-Baden 1983; Karl Kaiser, Confidence-Building Measures. Proceedings of an International Symposium, 24–27 May 1983 at Bonn 1983; Adam D. Rotfeld (ed.): From Confidence to Disarmament. Warsaw 1986; Rolf Berg and Adam D. Rotfeld, Building Security in Europe, in Allen Lynch (ed.), CBMs and the CSCE. New York 1986; R. B. Byers, F. Stephen Larrabee, and Allen Lynch (eds.), Confidence-Building Measures and International Security. New York 1987; Karl E. Birnbaum, and Bo Huldt (eds.), From Stockholm to Vienna: Building Confidence and Security in Europe. Conference Papers 9, Stockholm 1987; Ingo Peters, Transatlantischer Konsens und Vertrauennbildung in Europa. Baden-Baden 1987.

3. The full title of the document is: Document of the Stockholm Conference on Confidence- and Security-Building Measures and Disarmament in Europe Convened in Accordance with The Relevant Provisions of the Concluding Document of the Madrid Meeting of the Conference on Security and Co-operation in Europe. Stockholm 1986. The course of the negotiations were outlined by John Borawski in: From the Atlantic to the Urals. Negotiating Arms Control at the Stockholm Conference. Washington, D.C. 1987.

4. Julian Kaczmarek, Wojciech Lepkowski, and Zbigniew Paluch, Wojskowe problemy bezpieczenstwa Polski (The Military Aspects of Poland's Security), in Adam D. Rotfeld (ed.), Miedzynarodoweczynniki bezpieczenstwa Polski (International Factors of the Security of Poland). Warsaw 1986, 66.

5. CSCE/WT.1, Vienna, 8 December 1986.

6. Cf. document CSCE/WT.129 tabled by NATO states at Vienna on 10 July 1987.

7. CSCE/WT.131, 31 July 1987.

8. CSCE/WT.133, 22 September 1987.

9. CSCE/WT.134, 22 September 1987.

10. See: Contributions to a Seminar on the Stockholm Conference and the CSCE Process organized by the Swedish Institute of International Affairs, 4–5 June 1987, Karl E. Birnbaum (ed.), *Stockholm to Vienna: Building Confidence and Security in Europe*. Stockholm 1987. Also see: Adam D. Rotfeld, New CSBMs. A Polish View, in: PISM Occasional Papers. Warsaw 1987, 24.

11. Concrete proposals were tabled at Stockholm on 20 May 1985 by the delegations of Bulgaria, Poland, and the USSR–SC/WGB.3 (naval exercises), and by the GDR, Hungary, and USSR–SC/WGB.2 (air force operations).

12. CSCE-WT.129, Vienna, 10 July 1987. For more on the NATO position, see J. Borawski: From the Atlantic to the Urals.

13. CSCE/SC.7, Stockholm, 15 November 1985.

14. Memorandum of the government of the Polish People's Republic on Decreasing Armaments and Increasing Confidence in Central Europe, Warsaw, July 1987. Text in: *Polish Plan to Decrease Armaments and Increase Confidence in Europe*. Warsaw 1987, 57–58.

15. In 1987 CSCE states exchanged a total of 47 notifications: 17 NATO, 25 WTO, 5 NN states. By comparison with 1987 the 1988 annual calendar shows a decrease in both the number of exercises and the number of troops involved. It is, however, premature to assess to what extent it is the effect of budgetary constraints and how much responsibility could be laid at the door of improved international situation.

16. For texts of the two speeches, see *Trybuna Ludu* daily, 12 July 1988.

17. W. L. Ury and R. Smoke, Beyond the Hotline: Controlling a Nuclear Crisis. A Report to the U.S. Arms Control and Disarmament Agency. Harvard University, 1984, III.

18. The Declaration on Security and Co-operation in Europe, adopted by the 10th Congress of PUWP (Warsaw, 3 July 1986) reads as follows: "... we come out for the establishment of a European mechanism which would serve the purpose of reaching agreement on the means and methods of preventing and easing tensions and crises on our continent. This would help to reinforce the mutual CSBMs now being elaborated within the CSCE process," In Adam D. Rotfeld. (ed.), *Poland and the Implementation of the CSCE Decisions*. Warsaw 1986, 147.

19. See recent publications reviewing the literature of the subject: E. Bahr and D. Lutz, eds: Gemeinsame Sicherheit. Konventionelle Stabilität. Bd. 3: Zu den militärischen Aspekten struktureller Nichtangriffsfähigkeit im Rahmen gemeinsamer Sicherheit. Baden-Baden 1988. H. Harvey (ed.), Special Issue on Non-provocative Defence, in: Bulletin of the Atomic Scientists. September 1988. NOD–Non-Offensive Defence published by Centre of Peace and Conflict Research at the University of Copenhagen, UNIDIR Newsletter – Conventional Armaments Limitation and CSBMS in Europe, no. 3, 1988.

20. Memorandum of the Polish government on Decreasing Armaments and Increasing Confidence in Central Europe, Warsaw, 17 July 1987, point 3, op.cit., p.57. Statement of the Polish government, June 14, 1988, points 21-24.

21. M. M. Kampelmann, An Assessment of the Madrid CSCE Follow-up Meeting, Department of State Bulletin, September 1983, 64.

22. Ibid.

23. Documents on Disarmament 1945-59, vol. II, doc. 319, 324, et al.

24. Aurel Braun, CBMs, Security and Disarmament, in Robert Spencer (ed.), *Canada and CSCE*. Centre for International Studies, Toronto 1984, 223.

25. Ibid, 223-234.

26. I. Khropunov, Mery doveriya: problemy i perspektivy. (Confidence Measures: Problems and Perspectives), in Diplomaticheskiy Vestnik 1984, 61.

27. Ibid.

28. Anders Bøserup, Maritime Defense Without Naval Threat. The Case of the Baltic. 5th Workshop of the Pugwash Study Group on Conventional Forces in Europe. Castiglioncello (Italy) 9-12 October 1986. Bjørn Møller, A Non-Offensive Maritime Strategy for the Nordic Area. Working Paper of Center of Peace and Conflict Research, Copenhagen 1987, no.3.

29. Naval Forces: Arms Restraint and Confidence-Building. 52nd Pugwash Symposium, Oslo, 23-26 June 1988.

Chapter 11

VERIFICATION OF CONFIDENCE- AND SECURITY-BUILDING MEASURES

Joseph Schärli

As a participant to those negotiations that ultimately led us to the Stockholm document, I refer here only to those verification provisions and confidence- and security-building measures mentioned in the Stockholm document. Verification of compliance is carried out by means of NTMs and on-site inspections, which means not through observation of notifiable military activities equally contained in the Stockholm document.

I am a citizen of a state that has gained neither active nor passive verification experience, i.e., that has neither received nor conducted an inspection. Thus I am somewhat handicapped insofar as I do not dispose — as an insider would and could — of the respective findings of an inspection — all the less since the inspection reports that make their way to the public rarely spread remarkable detail information but usually confine themselves to information of a rather general scope.

I therefore have to bow to the constraint and analyze as an outsider, who knows his want of knowledge, the practice of verification as it has evolved since 1987.

My exposé is structured as follows:

1. Verification of confidence- and security-building measures: the status quo in the light of the principal provisions.
2. Analysis of the current practice.
3. Possible developments and improvements.

As a representative of a CSCE state member of the Neutral and Nonaligned (NN) Club, I occasionally indicate briefly positions that these states have advocated with regard to the respective verification provisions in the course of the Stockholm negotiations.

FUNDAMENTAL PROVISIONS OF THE VERIFICATION CHAPTER OF THE STOCKHOLM DOCUMENT

Fundamentally, the chapter on compliance and verification of the Stockholm document provides for:

- The recognition of the role of National Technical Means, which clearly include, although do not specify satellite monitoring (ELINT, SIGINT), in monitoring compliance.

Switzerland—supported by other NN states—had advocated deletion of this paragraph which unilaterally favored the big powers because, on the one hand, it merely repeated already existing bilateral agreements—thereby stating the obvious—whereas, on the other hand, it introduced an element of inequality into the CDE agreement, which in paragraph 22 reconfirms the commitment of all CSCE participating states (pS) "to the basic principle of the sovereign equality of States" and stresses "that all States have equal rights and duties within the framework of international law." The element of inequality is due to the fact that two of the CDE signatories (USA, USSR) possess a satellite-monitoring capability and thus dispose of a verification advantage that other states have to miss. The attempt to gain access to satellite-generated monitoring data covering CDE-relevant information of military activities had failed.

- Any pS will be allowed to address a request for inspection to another pS on whose territory, within the zone of application for CSBMs, compliance with the agreed CSBMs is in doubt (para 66) (zone of application: the whole of Europe as well as the adjoining sea area, refers also to ocean areas adjoining Europe, and air space, usually determined as "from the Atlantic to the Ural").
- Despite the fact that "doubts" need not be specified, para 70 establishes the obligation that "the pS which requests an inspection will state the reasons for such a request." Para 78.1 underlines the importance of reasons: "in its request, the inspecting State will notify the receiving State of the reasons for the request." However, "any possible dispute as to the validity of the reasons for a request will not prevent or delay the conduct of an inspection" (para 72).
- No pS will be obliged to accept on its territory within the zone of application for CSBMs, more than three inspections per calendar year (para 67), and no pS will be obliged to accept more than one inspection per calendar year from the same pS (para 68).

In spite of requests—raised particularly by NN states—to specify the kind of doubts, the participating states decided that "to have doubts" was sufficient justification requiring no further specification. NN states argued that the inclusion of the general formula "on whose territory compliance is in doubt" would introduce an element of suspicion into an agreement mainly aiming at the building of confidence. Furthermore, there was an apprehension that inspections might be called wantonly or without a proper factual justification (e.g., reciprocity in number and locations of inspections, matters of prestige). Finally, however, they came to accept that such arbitrariness would be contained by the obligation to present the reasons for demanding an inspection.

The interpretation of the agreement allows only very vague conclusions on the contents of doubts:

- The conformity of the notified activity to be inspected with the contents of the notification (overlapping with observation).
- The monitoring: whether an actual military activity would have been notifiable or not; whether or not a connection exists between several activities conducted simultaneously and a notified activity, when no such connection was notified, etc. Obviously the agreement allows for the possibility to debate and even contest the justifications provided with an inspection request: however, as stated above, such a discussion must not obstruct the timely materialization of an inspection.
- The pS that has received a request will reply in the affirmative in the shortest possible

period of time, but within not more than 24 hours; within 36 hours after the issuance of the request, the inspection team will be permitted to enter the territory of the receiving state (para 71, 79). Rejection of an inspection request is not possible.
- The pS that requests àn inspection will be permitted to designate for inspection on the territory of another state within the zone of application for CSBMs, a specified area. The specified area will comprise terrain where notifiable military activities are conducted or where another pS believes a notifiable military activity is taking place. The specified area will be defined and limited by the scope and scale of notifiable military activities but will not exceed that required for an army level military activity (para 73). In the specified area, the representatives of the inspecting state accompanied by the representatives of the receiving state will be permitted access, entry, and unobstructed survey, except for areas or sensitive points to which access is normally denied or restricted, military and other defense installations, as well as naval vessels, military vehicles and aircraft. The number and extent of the restricted areas should be as limited as possible. Areas where notifiable military activities can take place will not be declared restricted areas, except for certain permanent or temporary military installations, and consequently those areas will not be used to prevent inspection of military activities. Permanent or temporary military installations as exceptions should, in territorial terms, be as small as possible (para 74). The dimension provided in para 73 as terms of reference for the size of a specified area equals the zone of operations of a Soviet-type army and translates, in the case of Switzerland for example, to the zone of operation of an army corps that would train as an operative unit within a coherent geographical area. Switzerland and Sweden in particular were interested in the inclusion of provisions to protect the secrecy of permanent, classified military installations. Exceeding the initial Western starting position of "sensitive points," the neutrals succeeded in firmly implanting the concept of military and other (total) defense installations.
- There will be no more than four inspectors in an inspection team. While conducting the inspection, the team may divide into two parts (para 84). Inspection will be permitted on the ground, from the air, or both (para 76). Representatives of the receiving State will accompany the inspection team, including when it is in land vehicles and in aircraft from the time of their first employment until the time they are no longer in use for the purposes of inspection (para 77). Within 48 hours after the arrival of the inspection team at the specified area, the inspection will be terminated (para 83).
- The inspecting state will prepare a report of its inspection and will provide a copy of that report to all participating states without delay (para 95). Switzerland insisted up to the last moment of the negotiation on a fixed period of time within which inspection reports have to be submitted (7 days). The proposal stood no chance; it had been substituted by "without delay."
- Each pS will be entitled to obtain timely clarification from any other pS concerning the application of agreed CSBMs (para 98). This paragraph is almost the only "leftover" of the "observation upon request" concept submitted to the Stockholm conference by the NN states. Originally belonging to a framework of consultations that were intended to precede on site-inspection requests, the idea had been turned into an authorization of pS to ask for clarification in case of unwillingness of a pS to proceed to an inspection. Clarification could namely be sought by a pS that had doubts, whose doubts, however, might not have justified an inspection request or who perceived inspection less as a routine than as an extraordinary measure.

Numerous detailed provisions set the standard for carrying out an inspection; they refer to the content of a request, to board and lodging, to the equipment of inspectors, to rights and duties of the inspecting and of the receiving state.

Some unpleasant experience gave rise to certain concerns as to the subject and purpose of on-site inspection according to the Stockholm document. Interestingly enough, the Stockholm document is not unambiguously clear as to the subject or purpose of inspection. According to para 73 and 74, inspections seems to aim *at the territory* on which military activities are (supposed to be) conducted. Para 75, however, points out: "the forces . . . will also be subject to the inspection . . ."

Indeed, depending on its prime interest, an inspecting state can thus focus emphasis either on the inspection of a *territory* or on the inspection of a *military activity*. In a teleological interpretation of the Stockholm document, Switzerland, together with a majority of CSCE participating states shares the view that an inspection should relate to an *activity* (presumed or notified) within a specified area. Considered as military activities are, according to para 31 of the CDE document, activities in the zone of application for CSBMs of formations of land forces, of military forces either in an amphibious landing or in a parachute assault by airborne forces, or of formations of land forces of the pS in a transfer from outside the zone of application for CSBMs to arrival points in the zone, or from inside the zone of application for CSBMs to points of concentration in the zone, to participate in a notifiable exercise activity or to be concentrated.

It is understood that military activities are not taking place in a geographical vacuum, hence the territory cannot be neglected; however, to put emphasis only on the territory and to neglect the activity in respect to the forces conducting the activity would not be in conformity with the intentions of the Stockholm document. Inspection of the territory might, however, become more important if an activity is believed to take place but had not been notified. Even in such cases on-site inspection is not intended to provide the inspectors with a pretext or a justification for military exploration or intelligence gathering related primarily to the territory, its military installations, and its combat value in military operations. Such a trend could become counterproductive and would undermine the confidence-building effect of inspection.

The CDE agreement contains no explicit reference to the *purpose of inspection*. Implicitly, inspections serve to dispel doubts, whether doubts arose as to the conformity of the activity with the notification or whether they had been substantiated otherwise. Generally it may be argued that in the overall concept of CSBMs verification by on site-inspection is designed to reduce the dangers of armed conflict and of misunderstanding or miscalculation of military activities. Verification ultimately has to ensure that implementation of the agreed CSBMs will contribute to these objectives (para 99).

PRACTICE OF VERIFICATION ACCORDING TO THE PROVISIONS OF THE STOCKHOLM DOCUMENT

Note the statistics in Figure 11.1.

Averages for involved troops 1987–88 were:

- Three activities below notifiable level (less than 13,000).
- Two activities involving one amphibious landing and one parachute assault by airborne forces at notifiable level (3,000).

Figure 11.1 Inspection statistics.

Number of inspections carried out to date	1987	1988
NATO	2	7
WAPA	3	6
NN	0	0
Total	5	13

1987		1988	
Inspecting states	Inspected states	Inspecting states	Inspected states
NATO		*NATO*	
USA (2)	SU, H	USA (4)	H, GDR, PL, USSR
UK (1)	GDR	UK (1)	USSR
		FRG (1)	GDR
WAPA		Turkey (1)	USSR
USSR (2)	Turkey, FRG		
GDR (1)	FRG	*WAPA*	
		USSR	Norway, FRG, UK
		Bulgaria	Italy
		Poland	FRG
		GDR	FRG

- Three activities between 20,000 and 30,000.
- Ten activities between 13,000 and 17,500. Thus there seems to be some validation for the presumption voiced already during the CDE negotiations according to which the gray area between the notification threshold (13,000) and the observation threshold (17,000) might become a preferred focus of interest for inspections.

Timewise, inspections during 1987–88 concentrated on activities conducted in the August to November (two-thirds of all inspections), in accordance with the density of notified activities during the same period. Fifteen inspections aimed at notified activities, and only three unnotifiable activities had been subject to inspection. This could be interpreted as a positive result of the entire confidence- and security-building process; such a conclusion might, however, turn out to be premature as the overall political climate in Europe during the last two years showed no signs of political or military tensions. Hence the agreement has not stood its acid test yet. Two inspections took place outside the exercise area indicated by the notification (IRON HAMMER in FRG, DRUSHBA in GDR). Four inspections related to military activities above observation−threshold (17,000 and more).

Geographically this leads to the overview shown in Figure 11.2. FRG (5), USSR (4), and GDR (3) were preferred territories for inspections (two-thirds of all inspections), whereby FRG showed obviously some reluctance in requesting as many inspections as it had to receive. In 1988 the USSR and FRG accepted three inspections each, the maximum number envisaged in the CDE Agreement for any one participating state per year.

Figure 11.2 Overview.

As inspected state		As inspecting state
Bulgaria:	–	once
FRG:	5 times (one activity almost exclusive UK participation, one activity almost exclusive U.S. participation)	once
GDR:	3 times (one activity almost exclusive USSR participation)	twice
Hungary:	once	–
Italy:	once	–
Norway:	once	–
Poland:	once (activity almost exclusive USSR participation)	–
Turkey:	once	once
UK:	once	twice
USA:	once (U.S. troops in FRG)	5 times
USSR:	4 times	5 times

Problems of Implementation

Inspection reports would suggest that the will to apply the verification provisions in conformity with the agreement prevailed in all 18 inspections. However, rumors that surfaced occasionally indicated that the way and the manner in which some inspections were conducted did not always reflect the spirit of the agreement.

It was claimed that inspectors had failed to listen to introductory briefings, directing their attention not to the exercising troops but to the civilian and military infrastructure instead. In one case this was reported to have led to a diplomatic intervention to the state conducting the inspection by the inspected state.

Attempts seem to have been undertaken to demand services not provided by the agreement, such as information on the designation of units and troops and peace-time locations.

In at least one (7.–9.9.88 on FRG-territory), possibly in two inspections (DRAKE'S DRUM, UK 5.–7.10.88), the USSR concluded that violations of the CDE agreement occurred. The USSR is reported to have considered a series of nine unnotified British military activities as one coherent exercise, comprising a total strength of 69,000 men and therefore subject to insertion in the annual calendar and subsequently to prior notification 42 days in advance.

On 13 October 1988 the USSR accused the FRG, and implicitly other NATO-states participating in the inspected military activity, of a violation of the CDE, agreement, on the basis of findings of the USSR inspection team, according to which the exercise(s) had involved over 170,000 U.S., French, and FRG troops. The USSR argued that activities of such dimensions had to be notified two years in advance in the annual calendar for 1987–88. "CERTAIN CHALLENGE 88," "LANDES-VERTEIDIGUNG 88," "GOLDEN CROWN 88," and "COLD FIRE 88," however, had been listed as independent activities in the annual calendar issued for 1988–89.

FRG, France, and the United States rejected the accusations and stressed the independent character of each of the four activities.

For the distant observer the quarrel looks like a cure inadequate to the illness. The Soviet Union appears to have chosen the instrument of on-site inspection to draw attention to an issue belonging rather to the complex of notification than to verification itself: the problems of large-scale military activities as such, of circumventions of agreed provisions by military activities close to each other in time and space, and of the definition of "a single operational command."

In another case, inspectors reported that a notified military activity took place partially outside the area of the activity defined by the prior notification.

Paragraph 95 states that an inspection report should be made available "without delay." Looking at the reporting practice, one has to learn of delays varying between 8 and 35 days (average delay in the first dozen inspections: 19 days).

From a point of view of confidence- and security-building, inspections are of particular interest to the participating states because they are tied to elements of suspicion. It is thus in the interests not just of the inspecting and the inspected state but of all participants of the CSCE process to be swiftly informed about the principal findings of an inspection. The sophisticated argument could be advanced that not only the report itself should be prepared without delay, but that a copy of that report should be provided to all pS without delay (i.e., as soon as the report was established). However, it had never been claimed that the provision on reporting should reflect such a degree of ambiguity.

Occasionally, inspectors complained about inadequate or insufficient radio communication systems rendering normal communication between two independently operating inspection teams impossible. Participating states had been recommended to devote particular attention to communication equipment used in inspections.

During the Vienna Follow-up Meeting, Switzerland (supported by Sweden and France) criticized off and on the fact that no requesting state indicated the reasons for a request as a contravention to the CDE-agreement. Though the relevant provisions are unambiguous, the United States and others argued that reasons need not be specified nor published, given the authorization to proceed to inspection on the basis of doubts; "the reasons are the doubts" is said to be a constructive ambiguity constituting the lowest common denominator for consensus in Stockholm.

U.S and FRG negotiators nowadays tend to stress that by now inspection had lost its trait of a suspecting, disreputable, and extraordinary measure and that it had developed into a kind of routine activity; doubts are reported to be no longer the justification of a request, hence no reasons at all would have to be given. The French representative did not share this view and Switzerland is not willing to accept an erosion of the document by contravening practices.

The mere fact that inspections take place should—and to a certain extent has already—become a matter of routine; inspections should, however, not be requested as a matter of routine, i.e. without reasons or doubts. Apart from confidence-damaging effects, such a perception of routine could also lead to downgrading observation of military activities.

Could not one also pretend that giving reasons would become more easy the less inspection is based on doubts? In any case, the current practice has either to conform with the agreement or the agreement has—through negotiations—to be adjusted to reality. Silence over the creation of precedents or of "derogating customary rules" would be detrimental to the interests particularly of smaller pS.

One exception, however, deserves mention: the German Democratic Republic, in its request dated 26 November 1988 relating to the FRG exercise "SACHSENTROSS 88" indicated as reason ". . . um sich von der Uebereinstimmung der in der Ankündigung der militärischen Aktivität Übermittelten Angaben mit den praktischen Handlungen überzeugen zu können."

Though the validity of reasons could be debated, we should recognize that the mere fact of going beyond the established practice constitutes a noticeable event, indicates a possible breakthrough and a change toward a more positive and wider accepted practice.

Until now NN-CSCE-pS did not get involved in the implementation of verification-procedures. Most of them apparently are quite satisfied about this situation. Whether they like it or not, in the interests of credible NNA negotiation positions—individually and collectively—NN states have to gain experience in that field, too, either by inspecting or by receiving inspections. Unless NN states become a part of the "inspection business" they might lose their know-how and expertise, and slowly also their legitimacy to participate as experienced partners in negotiations developing further the chapter on inspection.

NEGOTIATIONS TO BUILD UPON AND EXPAND THE SET OF CSBMs OF THE STOCKHOLM DOCUMENT

The chapter on verification of compliance constitutes in the field of multilateral security policy a major political breakthrough whose importance must not be underestimated nor belittled, despite certain shortcomings and deficiencies. The instrument of on site-inspections has so far proved to be a viable and useful tool to ensure compliance. It can be assumed that—on the premise of continuously though presumably slowly improving international relations—the oncoming negotiations on CSBMs in Vienna might deal also with further developing and tightening provisions on inspection.

Without going into the details and rather intending to animate discussion, let us identify the following issues deserving further consideration and/or deeper analysis:

- To clarify the provisions as to reasons/doubts (in order to get theory and practice coinciding).
- To specify the delay of reporting, perhaps to compel inspecting states to submit a summary with five days; to make reports more informative (militarily significant contents).
- To compel inspectors to accept/to listening to briefings before they start inspection, to limit the time for briefings, to hold briefings before the beginning of the inspection time period.
- To shorten the period of replying to a request (from 24 hours down to 12 hours).
- To shorten the period between issuing a request and granting permission to enter the territory of the receiving state (from 36 hours down to 24 hours).
- To concentrate inspection more on the ongoing military activity than on the territory and its infrastructure by defining the activity as the object of inspection.
- To establish special provisions as to the inspection of alert activities (shorter delays for all administrative procedures).
- To supplement on site-inspection by automatic verification systems (sensors).
- To extend verification beyond activities and to admit inspections of peacetime deployments.
- To widen the gap between/or to combine the threshold for notification and observation, so as to eliminate the small gray zone that gave rise to so many inspections.
- To increase the number of inspections a state is obliged to accept per calendar year on its territory (from three to . . .) and to increase the number of inspections a state is obliged to accept per calendar year from the same participating state (from one to . . .), so as to give expression of the conceptual change from "doubts" to "routine."

Chapter 12
RESPONSES

FIRST RESPONSE
Jean Desazars de Montgailhard

This response focuses on a single question: What is the role of confidence-building measures, or what should the role of confidence-building measures be today?

I raise this question from Adam-Daniel Rotfeld's remarks (Chapter 10) that when we were planning to launch the Conference on Disarmament in Europe in Madrid, we had in mind that it would not concentrate solely on confidence-building measures, but would ultimately turn to disarmament proper. Have we not now reached that moment, since negotiations on conventional disarmament are about to begin? What, then, is the role of confidence-building measures in that context?

In truth, I want to draw your attention to the fact – and I think this is the answer to the question posed by Rotfeld – that the two mandates adopted in Vienna in no way preclude the CDE from resuming its course, or the course that had been mapped out for it, nor do they preclude the Group of 35 from moving one day from confidence-building measures to disarmament proper. It is even stipulated in the mandate of the Group of 23, and alluded to in the mandate of the Group of 35, that the next CSCE follow-up meeting, to be held in Helsinki in 1992, should review progress in the Group of 23 and may consider the possibility of adding to the mandate adopted in Madrid; in other words, making that very move to the second phase of CDE on disarmament. This would mean that the Group of 23 exercise is in a sense no more than an initial stage, and that later on the Group of 35 might themselves embark on disarmament. This seems to be in line with the wishes or concerns expressed both by Ambassador Ekéus (Chapter 9) and by some of our colleagues earlier, Switzerland in particular.

Consequently, we too are going to embark on new negotiations on confidence-building measures, and we are in a kind of transition. We are no longer entirely in Stockholm; we already have the implementation of the Stockholm confidence-building measures behind us. Joseph Schärli (Chapter 11) has given us an outline, providing statistics and assessments concerning the implementation of those measures, but we have not yet fully reached the stage where constraints and reductions will go hand in hand, and may be decided on by all 35 states.

So the question that arises (to be found in Chapters 10 and 11) is: "What must be done today as far as confidence-building measures are concerned?" Must we content ourselves with ad hoc improvements to the Stockholm document—and Colonel Schärli has made a number of suggestions that I find very interesting and very welcome—or can we already go further? And if so, in which direction?

Let us review five or six avenues mentioned in both Schärli's and Rotfeld's reports and also in the reports from General Chervov (Chapter 7) and others.

One direction that could be followed at the present stage is that of information. In Stockholm we agreed on arrangements for the provision of information concerning military activities, but it is true that little has been done with regard to information on the organization of forces in Europe, and particularly peacetime replacements, etc. I am very encouraged by Rotfeld's comment that a few years ago, at the time of Stockholm, the Warsaw Pact countries were most unforthcoming in this field, but that today things had changed and that is a readiness to go further. In this regard Schärli talks of verification that could be applied to this new régime of information. I also note that Karpov, (Chapter 1) when we talked about data, told us that the 35 states might perhaps offer a framework by means of which the data issue, and thus exchanges of information of all kinds, could be studied in detail, without the talks in the Group of 23 being held up by disputes of the type encountered by the MBFR participants. Thus here we have in a sense a first brick in the new edifice, information accompanied by verification, including on-site verification, for example, by random sampling, and it seems that in the intermediate period we are in at the moment, that would be very appropriate.

But there are other avenues, indicated in particular by Rotfeld in his report.

The first is the issue of special status zones. I also note that when Chervov speaks of confidence-building measures, all but one of the measures he puts forward are measures relating to special status zones. The zone of contact between the two alliances, in which the level of armed forces and armaments would be reduced, from which the most dangerous weapons would be withdrawn, the nuclear weapon-free zones—250 kilometers wide on either side—or a chemical weapon-free zone, etc.—all this is explicitly presented by Chervov as confidence-building measures. Is this—and Rotfeld also refers to it, particularly when expanding on the Jaruzelski Plan—an avenue that corresponds to the current state of affairs in which we find ourselves, which as I said is in a sense intermediate? I am not completely sure. I would even be tempted to say that it is not, for I cannot see logically how we could articulate the idea of somehow favoring such small special status zones with the idea that we wish to deal with the entire area from the Atlantic to the Urals.

Second, I cannot see how we could reconcile this approach, which is essentially an alliance-to-alliance approach, since we are talking of the contact zone between the two blocs, with negotiations among 35 sovereign states.

Third, some of these measures deal in an explicit way with nuclear and chemical weapons; in other words, two types of armaments that do not fall within the scope of the negotiations, whether they be the Group of 23 negotiations based on the mandate adopted recently in Vienna or the Group of 35 negotiations based on the mandate adopted in Madrid earlier. Finally, it is clear that, in political as well as in military terms, such zones could have the opposite effect to that which we seek. In political terms, they would enhance the status of the alliances; they would, in a sense, crystallize the role of the alliances, since the states concerned, seeing their security diminished, would have a greater need than ever of guarantees on the part of their partners in the two alliances, and especially the most important of them. Similarly, in military terms, the extraordinary narrowness of these zones would make them artificial in character, as the withdrawal of the weapons could be nullified in a short time by their very mobility, which would enable them to be brought back to the zone in question very quickly.

A third direction to which reference is made is the question of constraints, constraining measures. For example, restriction of certain major activities, limitations of all kinds. Here, too, I wonder whether this approach fully corresponds to the moment in which we find ourselves in this process, after Stockholm but before cuts. I could well understand constraints being adopted at the moment when actual cuts are agreed upon. But in the current state of affairs, it is quite clear that as long as there is no stability—and we know that stability will be secured essentially through the cuts—flexibility in military activities is certainly a key concern for any European country. But at the same time I can clearly see the value of trying to go a little beyond the notifications that constitute the heart of the Stockholm package.

The question I raise in this regard is the following: Is there not an approach, also intermediate in a sense, that would bring out what is normal in Europe today in terms of military activities? In particular, if we look at Schärli's statistical table (Chapter 11), and if we imagine that it is to be added to from year to year through the implementation of the Stockholm document, we will in a sense have a photograph—or rather a series of photographs—in time that bring out what each party considers to be more or less normal, to provide no grounds for concern, to call for no explanations and require no particular emergency measures. And if, using a statistical indicator calculated on the basis of a table of the kind proposed by Schärli, on the basis of a statistical indicator, we managed to bring out what is normal and ordinary—in a sense the average behavior of the various European countries in military terms—we could then imagine inquiry procedures for cases where someone suddenly departed from this average, where the line went off the page for one country or another. Then, using communication links yet to be defined, we could ask questions inviting a country that had departed from its usual line of behavior to give the reason why it felt it had to do so.

The fourth avenue of research mentioned by Rotfeld is the question of communication links, which I combine with the idea of a risk prevention center, and the idea that in a sense underlies it, of a degree of institutionalization of arrangements that to date have been basically fluid, flexible. I can understand that the need is felt for communication links, Rotfeld refers to the existing "hot lines." I can understand that the *notes verbales* by means of which notifications have been exchanged so far are considered rather a cumbersome procedure, but I wonder nevertheless whether institutionalization is the best approach.

I think there is some confusion in the texts we have seen between risk prevention, crisis management, the exchange of ideas, and that there is a constant shifting from one to another. Rotfeld tells us, finally, that the center would be used to exchange information on the major politico-military questions of interest to Europe. Elsewhere, he tells us that what would be involved would be crisis management as with the "hot lines." In another place, mention is made of the existing Nuclear Risk Reduction Center between Washington and Moscow, which is not, either in its statutes or in the agreement that has been signed, a crisis management center.

Hence I think that we cannot envisage doing everything at once. Nor can we plan in a sense to sidestep the issue. We must know what we want to do. In this regard the CSCE tradition should lead us to steer clear of the idea of institutionalization in favor, perhaps, of automatic procedures for the exchange of notifications, which might also make it possible to raise questions if that famous average indicator of which I spoke earlier were to light up suddenly.

Rotfeld's fifth thought, or proposed line of thought, is the question of doctrines. It has already been brought up several times, notably by Karpov. Rotfeld is kind enough to say that this topic is of interest to France and also to West Germany. That is perfectly true, but it is also true of other countries. It is all the more true since we are all interested in what we have been told by Kaprov and Chervov concerning the evolution of Soviet military doctrine, the shift to a more defensive posture. Chervov said, "We have managed to change the mentalities of our officers and the commanders of our military academies." This is very interesting, and it would certainly be very beneficial to the 35 states as a whole to learn how one can succeed in changing the mentalities of officers. And in fact a seminar on military doctrines or instruction would be very valuable in that regard.

Taking up Chervov's idea, I think that exchanging among the 35 states the manuals used for the instruction of young officers would undoubtedly be very instructive, especially if it enabled us to check, for example, that Soviet military instruction has now abandoned not only the idea of offensives, but even the idea of counteroffensives. And in such a seminar, I myself would wish to ask General Chervov for clarification on what he said concerning a return to a counteroffensive following 20 days of exchanges of "military measures," in the event that the political authorities continued to consider that an attack was being prepared.

Another line of thought mentioned by Rotfeld deals naturally with the question of naval-related and air-related measures. This is an old and familiar debate, one we had in Madrid, which we had again in Stockholm, which recurs continuously. Is it possible to make an effort in the future to undertake notification measures, not to say constraining measures, concerning independent naval and air activities? Chervov, though he writes that the naval sphere should be the subject of the second phase of the negotiations in the Group of 23, has corrected his approach in a sense to say that the naval sphere should be set aside for confidence-building measures rather than actual cuts.

But I nevertheless wonder whether it is possible, whether it is justified to try to pursue this path in respect of confidence-building measures negotiated by 35 states for Europe. It seems that there is a certain contradiction in saying—as Rotfeld does when discussing naval measures, for example—that the Soviet Union needs to be compensated on the sea for the extension of the zone to the Urals. I thought that this debate had vanished with the "old thinking." And this also contradicts what Gyula Horn (Chapter 5) writes on the necessary recognition by the Warsaw Pact countries of geopolitical differences, and particularly of the need for the Atlantic allies to be reinforced by sea.

Second, as Rotfeld acknowledges, this raises the entire problem of freedom of the high seas, a difficult problem that I cannot imagine being dealt with regionally. Third, and here, too, Rotfeld underlines the point, nuclear weapons come immediately to mind, and in fact he speaks of nuclear submarines, ships carrying nuclear cruise missiles, etc. Consequently, here, too, we would be going beyond the mandate. Last, it is clear, when we read Rotfeld's words, that the measure would be addressed to the two alliances and would come under the interbloc talks. Space here does not permit me to cite the passages of his report in which this emerges clearly.

Consequently, I cannot at present see any reason for us to change what was in fact written in the Madrid mandate—on which the new Vienna mandate is based—which is that naval and air activities, the only naval and air activities that can definitely be said to affect the security of Europe, these are naval and air activities that have a functional link with military activities on land in Europe. Naturally this does not preclude seeking other measures relating to the naval sphere—for example as Rotfeld says himself, agreements on incidents on the high seas. He mentions two countries: he could also have mentioned France, which is in the process of reaching agreement in this field with the Soviet Union.

Last, there is a final area for reflection, namely "stabilization" measures, or the measures that would accompany the cuts, whether they will be verification measures in the strict sense or specific monitoring points, either with inspectors permanently assigned to a specific post in the European zone, or with recording devices installed permanently in the field. This is naturally a source of highly interesting reflection, but it is obviously closely connected with the arrangements for cuts that will be accepted, we hope, at least by the Group of 23.

I conclude with three observations. The first is that we are indeed at an intermediate stage, we are beyond Stockholm, beyond the falterings of Stockholm, but we are this side of an agreement on cuts and stability. In these circumstances, I think it is better to think about measures that are themselves intermediate in nature, which in a sense take stock, and the statistical stock-taking of the activity as it may be observed on the basis of the implementation of Stockholm, but without yielding immediately to the temptation to look for constraints that would not be justified as long as conventional stability does not exist. Second, the Group of 35's confidence-building measures remain of fundamental importance. They constitute a political message addressed to the 35 European states: the right for the 35 European states, for the neutrals and nonaligned in particular, as Ekéus said with great force and vigor, to have their full place in a discussion in Europe on security. Indeed, Karpov gave us an example of the synergy between the group of 35's measures and the Group of 23's measures when he said that a dispute on data in the Group of 23 could be avoided by conducting an effort on information in the Group of 35. But I am convinced that there are many other examples of possible synergy between the two fields. And of course, verification and inspection will clearly constitute a fundamental input by the 35 states to the implementation of the future agreement in the Group of 23. Indeed, one might wonder, since Schärli made some observations on the discriminatory aspect of the use of national technical means, whether we should not envisage means for the benefit of the 35 states as such. For example, mention has been made of a satellite agency that would operate for the benefit of the 35 states, and France has pursued some thoughts in this area, in the context of the United Nations.

I end with a third observation, which is in fact a question: What should we expect? Will the talks on confidence-building measures advance less or more rapidly than the stability talks? I think we must be prudent in this field, and that we must not neglect all the opportunities offered by the negotiations on confidence-building measures in the Group of 35, especially if the talks in the Group of 23 were to reach an impasse fairly rapidly. Concerning the dialectic between the unilateral and multilateral; I raised the question of whether there is not a risk of impasse, either on the data or on identification of the armaments to be taken into consideration, or even because of the fact that the Soviet Union might await a response in the nuclear area to the unilateral gesture it undertook to make in the conventional area. If this reading, which I hope is incorrect but cannot rule out, proved to be the right one, then we would perhaps have a 10-times greater interest in confidence-building measures. And that should be enough to make us embark enthusiastically on these negotiations.

SECOND RESPONSE

Ignac Golob

Confidence-building is an inherent element of the process of strengthening security and cooperation in Europe. It is not any more a new and experimental idea. In the course of last 14 years two sets of confidence- (and security-) building measures were developed — in Helsinki (1975) and in Stockholm (1986) — and implemented in practice. The meeting of CSCE to develop CSBMs will take place soon again. Its aim will be to improve the existing measures and have a try at the adoption of a new set of CSBMs, more ambitious and more far-reaching than the present one.

The record of implementation of the CSBMs has been analyzed by the participating states and military experts. They assessed the record positively and concluded that the measures have proven their validity and that the process of building security and confidence in the military field should be enhanced.

Although CSBMs apply, at least for the time being, only to the military sphere, it would be misleading to treat them as purely military-technical measures. Indeed, it would be wrong to treat them as "measures" only.

Confidence-building should be viewed as a political-security concept, and measures as an instrument to implement it.

Let us have a look at recent history.

At the time it was introduced, in the mid-1970s, the concept of confidence-building, which became part of the CSCE Final Act, was certainly something new. As an idea it had something unreal about it. It will be recalled that the fragile detente, after it had brought its first major achievements, came very nearly to a screeching halt due to interventionism and the renewed arms race. To speak about confidence-building when the lack of confidence among East and West was obvious seemed a fine and noble but distant aim.

In such circumstances to the surprise of no one the concept of confidence-building was, in terms of practical measures, narrowed down to the reduction of mistrust. This relatively modest purpose of the first-generation CBMs is expressed in the Final Act itself, which speaks about "the need to contribute to reducing the dangers of armed conflict and of misunderstanding or miscalculation of military activities which could give rise to apprehension, particularly in a situation when the participating States lack clear and timely information about the nature of such activities."

Some, especially the Western school of thought, used this formulation to claim that the prime purpose of the CBMs is to reduce or, ideally, eliminate the danger of surprise attack. Consequently, CBMs were conceived primarily as measures to increase transparency, i.e., as information-type measures.

This concept approaches the interstate relations as confrontational relations between political adversaries and not between partners that trust each other. Instead of making surprise attack an unimaginable and politically unacceptable event and "to outlaw it," it made it only less surprising.

Detente of the mid-1970s was short-lived and its shortcomings in Europe became most obvious in the military sphere. The late 1970s and early 1980s saw the deployment of advanced medium-range nuclear weapons in Europe by both super powers, the modernization of conventional armaments, and the increased level of military exercises. Show of military force was used for political purposes, also within the military alliances.

During all this period, the CBMs from Final Act were, by and large, implemented faithfully. Notifications of military maneuvers were given, the observers were exchanged, albeit on a relatively limited scale, and on a voluntary basis.

Some may argue that the uninterrupted implementation of CBMs in the midst of the crisis of detente proved their viability and relevance. However, it may be also argued, and in a more convincing way, that this shows the very limited relevance of modestly conceived CBMs and their scant influence on the trends in political and military sphere. First CBMs may have helped to start lifting the veil of secrecy over military activities, but they certainly did not succeed in making the picture or the situation less threatening.

A number of European countries, especially nonaligned and neutral ones, were aware of the limitations of information-type CBMs. Therefore, some of them, in particular Yugoslavia, argued in favor of a more ambitious approach. They wanted measures that would not only inform about but also regulate, and finally restrain behavior of the states in the military field. Their view came through only partially, mostly due to the reluctance of big powers and leading members of military alliances. However, it was generally agreed at the Madrid CSCE meeting that CBMs should be further developed and qualitatively improved, leading to politically binding, military significant, and verifiable measures.

In order to indicate qualitatively new and wider character of measures to be negotiated in Stockholm, Yugoslavia proposed that the security element be inserted in the name of new measures (CSBMs instead of CBMs). This proposal was adopted.

Stockholm measures, although marking the significant advance over Helsinki measures, did remain, however, largely within the existing concept of information-type measures. Still, their importance should not be underestimated. Ambitious and more elaborated parameters resulted in a wider system of notification and observation, which included not only military maneuvers, but also military movements. However, independent air and naval activities were not part of this system. Although real constraining measures were not adopted, the concept of constraining military activities, in its embrionyc form of "time constraints," was accepted in the Stockholm document.

The most important achievements of the Stockholm agreement was, no doubt, the adoption of the procedures for verification in the form of on-site inspection. This was not only an innovation for the CSCE, but also generally in the security field. Such a breakthrough actually reflected a change in the climate in international relations, the increased degree of openness, and even a degree of trust. It also confirmed the acceptance of a principle that major advances in the field of security and disarmament require an adequate system of verification. This example was soon to be followed by the U.S.-Soviet agreement on the elimination of intermediate and medium-range nuclear missiles.

The way in which the provisions of on-site inspection were used in the past two years also shows that contrary to earlier predictions, it is not only one side, but both of them, who have found clear interest in using this measure. This confirms that major steps in the security field can be made only when there is mutually shared interest in a given measure. The way in which on-site inspection was carried out also proved that it can serve not only as a means of control, but also an instrument to increase mutual confidence.

Still, it would be wrong to deduce from this that the most promising and most useful way to proceed in the field of confidence-building should lead solely to more control, more information, and more openness. We need more control, but it would be much better to have less need for control. In other words, the aim should not be only to regulate the military confrontation, but to reduce it. And that cannot be done only by military-technical confidence-building measures, but by measures where confidence is also a political notion.

One should make an effort to cease to consider confidence-building in an old, conventional way. A wider, more comprehensive approach is needed. Point of reference should be the present situation in Europe. The interdependence should be a true governing principle, and not the concept of a divided Europe where security rests on the military balance.

Balance is important, but if we are to remain in the conceptual framework of balance, as defined by the two military alliances, the scope for genuinely new confidence-building measures will remain limited. More courage and more imagination are needed. New measures should be devised in response to the requirements of time and situation in order to make a political investment in trust and to make it possible for the security in Europe to gain. If this would be the generally accepted point of departure, then it should be possible to find balanced and mutually beneficial measures in all fields.

In a way, the concept of confidence-building is at this moment at the crossroads, and future negotiations in Vienna have a particular significance. The fact that the parallel negotiation of 23 participating CSCE states on conventional armed forces in Europe will take place in the framework of the CSCE poses a challenge to the CSBMs negotiations, but also presents new opportunities.

The international environment for the negotiations has rarely been so good. This opportunity should be fully used to advance to such measures that would, in turn, reinforce present positive trends, giving them a firmer and more durable basis. No single proposed measure should be rejected outright, but all should be considered in good faith and judged upon their merits. Whereas for practical purposes, short-term priorities will inevitably emerge in the course of negotiations, long-term aims of confidence-building should be borne in mind.

Now that the issue of conventional disarmament in Europe is finally brought to the negotiating table, it is particularly relevant to recall the organic link between confidence-building and disarmament. This link has been recognized and operational in the Vienna Concluding Document. Therefore, in terms of substance of new CSBMs to be negotiated, the emphasis should be on those that have not only confidence-building potential but also security-building potential, and, indeed, sui generis disarmament potential.

In this sense, the genuine constraining measures naturally come to mind first. One should not shy away from these measures that may enter into a so-called gray zone between confidence-building and disarmament.

When designing constraining measures, it should be ensured that they cover both the military activities and deployment of forces and weapons, especially those situated near the borders and having an offensive purpose. Agreed ceilings could be put on the size, scope, and duration of military activities, especially those that have multinational character. Reduced concentration of forces and/or armaments in agreed areas ("thinning-out zones") would be an example of a constraining measure that is by its nature very close to a disarmament measure.

Whereas constraining measures, as well as other CSBMs, should apply to the military potentials of all the participating states, in negotiating specific parameters for those measures it should be borne in mind that in Europe the most destabilizing element is represented by large bloc exercises and by the presence of foreign troops and forces in the territories of some participating states.

It is worthwhile recalling that the function of CSBMs is to create confidence and increase the security of individual states and not of the blocs. They are not measures to apply between the blocs, but throughout Europe, including within the blocs. Gradual abolition of foreign military presence in Europe, although a disarmament measure, is also the measure with a tremendous confidence-building potential. The atmosphere created by the announced withdrawal of a part of Soviet troops and armaments from Eastern Europe is a case in point.

Similarly, it would seem that the improved international climate should alleviate the persistent objections of the states to the extension of CSBMs to independent naval and air activities. If this area should remain outside the negotiation of the 23 members of alliances, there is a reason more to tackle this subject at the negotiations of the 35 participating states on CSBMs.

Continued exclusive concentration on ground forces and on "central front issues" would certainly mean a disregard for security concerns of smaller, especially nonbloc countries situated at the flanks of Europe. Let me add that the issues we discuss are not only "East-West" or "Svaalbard-Sicily" issues. Nonaligned Malta, Cyprus, and Yugoslavia have rights and legitimate security interests as well.

Air and especially naval forces are today used for the demonstration of military power, and even for limited military strikes, against some states not far from Europe. This also has a destabilizing effect on the situation in Europe. Indeed, it is difficult to explain why naval and air forces should be exempt from any kind of control when all other components of armed forces, including strategic weapons, are subject of disarmament negotiations. In any case, development of CSBMs cannot proceed in a balanced way if increasingly important naval and air components are left largely untouched by the CSBMs regime. How can Europe feel safe if the seas and oceans adjacent to it, like the Mediterranean, remain an area of undiminished presence, and of occasional use of naval power of some major states?

Of course, along with constraints and extension of CSBMs to all military activities, further improvement of existing measures should not be neglected either. True, it would seem that the scope for change of present parameters, agreed only two years ago in Stockholm, is at present relatively small. However, one could explore possibilities for improving the regime of observation of military activities, consider reducing the threshold for applying this measure, and also examine the possibility of further improving the parameters for notification of military activities.

On the other hand, the new area of verification measures could clearly benefit further from the improved international situation. Verification procedures of a multilateral type, with a role for neutral and nonaligned countries, seem worth exploring. In the peace-keeping forces of the UN the contribution of neutral and nonaligned European countries has traditionally been prominent.

Similarly, the moment seems ripe for discussion and adjustment of military doctrines to a defensive nature. Whereas it is not yet clear whether this subject is more proper for negotiations on conventional disarmament or for the negotiations on CSBMs, it would seem that the latter, with the participation of 35, is more appropriate.

The idea of publishing and comparing military budgets, followed by reductions of military expenditures, seems particularly timely. These ideas have been advanced in the past, when it was clear that the atmosphere was not conducive to it. Paradoxically, in a new environment it is somehow forgotten. And it should not be. Indeed, if efforts are concentrated only on constraining or reducing certain types of weapons and forces while leaving military budgets largely untouched, who can guarantee that savings on some items will not be used to modernize in some others, more advanced and, in the long term, more destabilizing? The reduction of military budgets could also be helpful in order to diminish the role of the so-called military-industrial complex, to go further in efforts to demilitarize modern societies.

Indeed, one would feel that much more imagination is called for in order to gain real confidence and trust among nations and to do away with remaining Cold War fears and prejudices. Generations were raised in the Cold War mentality and in the Cold War atmosphere. Practically all of us were formed during this time. Prejudices and fears were created, maintained, and enhanced. Trust and confidence will be slow in coming if we do not do away with deep-seated prejudices.

Governments and negotiators, as their representatives, should be more open and more receptive to the public opinion and to ideas that are advanced by peace movements.

Unilateral steps also have an important confidence-building potential. The recent example of Gorbachev's announcement of unilateral Soviet army reductions shows this clearly, and it would be most welcome if such a move could be in some way reciprocated.

Along with reduction in the size of armies in Europe, a process of deprofessionalization of armies could also contribute to more confidence.

Furthermore, mutual trust would benefit from more developed and more diversified contacts between armies of different countries. The visits and contacts between military personnel are already recommended in the CSCE provisions. One could develop this and even consider international cooperation of army units in tasks of different civilian purposes, as in the field of environmental protection, in cases of natural disasters, etc.

The combination of all these measures, accompanied by corresponding progress in conventional disarmament in Europe, could generally improve confidence in the military and political fields. However, confidence is a much wider notion and therefore confidence-building should be enlarged to other areas as well.

One could even say that imbalance in technological and economic development is today a more destabilizing factor than military imbalance. The effects of technological and economic imbalance are felt in the everyday life of nations and individuals. They are a threat to security and confidence. On the other hand, if nations show a willingness not only to share knowledge and achievement, but also to engage in joint projects, it is clear that they view one another as real partners and not as competitors or, worse, potential adversaries.

Similarly, the field of environmental protection is another where countries and peoples should gather and work for the same cause, thereby increasing mutual trust.

Indeed, the notion of confidence is such that it does not allow for partial approaches in any sphere of international relations. Cooperation in all fields is the best code word for confidence.

Would not open frontiers and free human contacts serve the same prupose, but on a much larger scale and more effectively, as the exchange of military observers? But then again, mutual trust will be slow in coming if the governments that are champions of the free flow and circulation of peoples and ideas and of the right to leave one's own country make this effectively impossible. They are in the same breath championing these freedoms and introducing the new and ever more stringent visa requirements.

Trust in Europe cannot gain if new obstacles are created for the circulation of peoples. It would be indeed detrimental to confidence and security in Europe if the diminishing of secrecy over military affairs in Europe would not be accompanied by the efforts to bring down and prevent new barriers in economic, technological, or humanitarian fields.

All this shows that the building of confidence in Europe is a complex task that cannot be reduced to measures in the military or political field. Even if one proceeds very far in the military area, confidence will not gain unless there is more stability and less uncertainty in economic, technological, and other fields. In order to be safer, Europe needs to be not only less militarized, but also more prosperous in all its corners, and less divided than today.

And, finally, it is important that confidence and trust are enhanced among government, military, and other structures. However, it is confidence and trust among peoples of Europe that counts. Let us keep in mind that it is for the better and freer life of peoples that we are discussing these issues.

THIRD RESPONSE
Roger J. Hill

Canadians have taken a keen interest in verification, and also CSBMs, for some years, as many people know. Let us focus now on a few principal points.

Both reports (Chapters 10 and 11) indicated the importance of political context and pointed to the complexity of the verification process. One significant conclusion that can be drawn from both is that developing effective CSBMs, and effective verification systems for CSBMs, will not be a simple or easy matter. A lot of hard work lies ahead in these areas.

However, the two reports do not, of course, cover the whole of the field indicated by the title of this work. A report on the verification of *conventional force reductions and arms control* is also needed at some stage, to complement Joseph Schärli's assessment of the verification of CSBMs (Chapter 11). A report listing Western and NNA proposals and initiatives on CSBMs should also be added, to supplement Adam-Daniel Rotfeld's very interesting study (Chapter 10).

The key points are these. *Verification will be really critical to the pursuit of enhanced stability in Europe through conventional force reductions and arms control. In fact, it can be argued that verification will be at least as important as reductions themselves.*

Why is this so? Let me cite the following reasons.

Effective verification will be essential to countering the danger of *surprise attack* on the central front. The recently announced Soviet and East German unilateral reductions, plus some further cuts agreed in the forthcoming negotiations, may produce *common ceilings* and an *overall balance* of Warsaw Pact and NATO forces on the central front, but *verification systems* will also be required to *prevent undetected concentrations* of forces near the front line, such as would provide the local superiority needed for a *surprise attack*. Intelligence systems and confidence-building measures will also help in this regard, of course.

Robust verification systems will also be needed to help counter the danger of either side developing a capacity for initiating *large-scale military action*, i.e., by gaining an edge in mobilization and reinforcement and carrying out a massive build-up on the front line, especially on the Central Front. For example, for NATO, solid and reasonably intrusive verification systems are needed to provide early warning of any Warsaw Pact mobilization, and to give crystal-clear indicators of any major Soviet troop movements, for example, across the Polish border into Central Europe. NATO would know that it would have to respond to such developments; decision making about moving to higher states of alert or taking other necessary counter-measures would be made much more certain if such clear indicators were available.

This whole issue of reinforcement rates and early warning needs much more attention. It has not been addressed adequately so far, but it is vital to tackling the problem of geostrategic disparity between NATO and the Warsaw Pact forces in Central Europe and Soviet forces in the Western USSR, for example, and to studying time and space linkages. That is one way to address the difference between NATO and Warsaw Pact positions on the force reductions issue (where NATO wants the Soviet Union to make very heavy cuts in the forces stationed in the Western USSR, whereas the Warsaw Pact is mainly, at this stage, focusing on cuts in Central Europe).

Effective verification systems, backed up by intelligence systems and CSBMs, would help a great deal to address the early-warning problem and thus to strengthen security in Europe.

We should also pay attention to the special situations of the countries on the flanks and of the neutral and nonaligned countries, as others have mentioned. Maybe some reductions will be possible in northern Europe, in the southeast, and in the Caucasus area. Maybe they won't focus on tanks, but on other weapons systems, However, reductions seem more problematical in those areas than on the central front. Verification systems and CSBMs may be all the more important as a means of pursuing enhanced security in these regions.

Let us turn to a more general point, concerning *types* of verification systems. A lot of work is being done on technical and other requirements, for example in Canada, among other countries. Whatever systems are established, they must be *robust*. By this I mean solidly established, not easily brushed aside, fairly intrusive, with different levels and layers of density for different regions and different types of military activity. For example, there might be very intensive verification in the forward areas on the central front, but different levels in some other areas. There should be major checkpoints at the rail crossing points on the Soviet-Polish border. And so on. The details will have to be worked out in the negotiations.

Robustness is absolutely essential, because, after an arms control agreement, security in Europe will be heavily dependent on *institutional arrangements*, including the verification network. The military balance will continue to underpin the new system, but there will be a major new element in the security landscape of Europe. East, West, and the NNA will look to these institutional structures to contribute strongly to their security. So we must be sure that, in times of crisis, they will not crumble under pressure or prove inadequate in other ways.

In sum, verification systems and confidence-building measures will be critically important in the effort to reduce and control conventional forces in Europe. The task of creating effective systems will not be an easy one, but it should not be impossible if there is the political will to reach an accord.

FOURTH RESPONSE

Victor-Yves Ghebali

The reports introduced earlier call for two comments, one on inspection and the other on confidence-building measures.

With regard to *inspection*, it has to be admitted that the practice of 1987 and 1988 is in the process of making inspection into *obligatory observation on request*—which does not altogether correspond to the spirit of the régime agreed at Stockholm.

Furthermore, the issue dealt with by Colonel Schärli (Chapter 11), "problems of implementation," should be supplemented by an item concerning the implementation of paragraph 74 concerning *restricted areas* of the Stockholm document. In April 1988 during the inspection of an (unspecified) East German military activity, the U.S. inspectors were only able to gain access to the training area after long discussions with the Soviet liaison officers, who did not feel they could make a decision, positive or negative, in the absence of their superior officer. It is, however, clear, as the inspectors themselves pointed out, that "any significant delay in permitting inspectors access to an entire training area creates a *de facto* restricted area." The U.S. inspectors in the German Democratic Republic were also, after three hours of waiting, forbidden access to a point at which a Soviet Scud missile unit was deployed. Finally, another point in the training area was also declared—temporarily— a forbidden area merely because a parachute assault was to take place there. Since parachute assaults in excess of a certain level are subject to prior notification, it is to be hoped that that will not constitute a precedent—a precedent in flagrant contradiction with the sentence in paragraph 74 of the Stockholm document that states that restricted areas will not be employed in a way inconsistent with the agreed provisions on inspections.

With regard to *the future of confidence-building measures*, the following should be noted. Immediately after the adoption of the Stockholm document, in September 1986, it could justifiably be asked whether confidence-building measures had not, at least for a while, reached their natural political limits. There was, indeed, nothing from which it could reasonably be foreseen that the confidence-building measures rejected at Stockholm could shortly afterward, in phase II of CDE, become acceptable to one and all. In fact, two new elements have since seemed to provide grounds for tempering that opinion.

On the other hand, whereas the implementation of confidence-building measures has, on the whole, been satisfactory (for both East and West) in 1987 and 1988, it has (as is very clear from the report on inspection introduced by Schärli) revealed the need for improvements in many respects.

On the other hand, the Warsaw Pact countries have recently adopted—in the wake of the *aggiornamento* of Soviet foreign policy—a new attitude of openness toward the issue of confidence-building measures. This change of course with regard to a concept that was formerly suspected of serving as justification for a process of "legalized espionage" is illustrated by the Budapest statement of 28 October 1988.

What is to be found in that statement? Certainly a series of ideas that are hardly acceptable to the countries of the Atlantic alliance, namely constraining measures (for example, a limitation of the size and number of simultaneous military activities), extension of the system of confidence- and security-building measures to North America, or the inclusion of military activities other than land or combined activities (independent naval and air activities). But the statement also contains other ideas that go in the direction desired by the

Western countries. These are: improvement of the in situ inspection procedure; and two confidence-building measures proposed by the West during the first phase of CDE and rejected then by the Eastern countries, the exchange of structural military information and the establishment of a mechanism for rapid communication between the 35 participating states. In view of these points of convergence, the prospects for phase "1 *bis*" would not—a priori—seem altogether disheartening.

That having been said, it is nonetheless the case that the *prolongation* of the phase of CDE devoted exclusively to confidence-building measures may be thought regrettable. Such a prolongation is open to criticism from a conceptual and from a political point of view.

On the one hand, there is the fact that the Vienna Closing Document defines the link between CDE and the CAFE negotiations only in terms of general principles (two autonomous exercises conducted within the framework of CSCE) and of organization (periodic, joint information meetings, and consultations), but that there is not definition in conceptual terms. How will the confidence- and security-building measures of phase "1 *bis*" be linked to any measures adopted in the future within the framework of the CAFE negotiations? The terms of reference for those talks refer to the possibility of "reductions, limitations, redeployment, equal ceilings and *related measures*." By "related measures" is meant not CSBMs, but "stabilizing" measures. The problem, therefore, remains to be solved.

On the other hand—and although France has managed, by a hard struggle, to contain the damage, the dichotomy between the negotiations in the Group of 35 and the Group of 23 is a sign of political regression. It will be recalled that the confidence-building measures under the Helsinki régime were thought up, in 1975, as a sort of "gadget" intended to compensate the nonaligned countries for being left on the sidelines in what was for them a crucial area by the CSCE/MBFR dichotomy. The Madrid mandate (1983) had the great merit of heralding the supplanting of that dichotomy by providing for a 35-state exercise concerning in sequence CSBMs and disarmament. Qualitatively speaking, the situation in 1989 seems no different from that in 1975: phase "1 *bis*" of CDE, being exclusively devoted to confidence- and security-building measures, is, in the final analysis, serving merely to compensate the nonaligned countries (plus Ireland and a few micro-states) for the sidelining resulting from the CAFE negotiations.

Part V

Conventional Disarmament in Europe and Its Impact on the Rest of the World

This section broadens the perspective of the conference by introducing the idea of the interdependence of different regions of the world as well as of different issues. No significant development can take place in the world today without having an impact worldwide.

In discussing the stability that Europe has achieved since World War II, it is noted that Europe itself dissuaded other regions from adopting this model of stability based on military preparedness. Other regions of the world should therefore encourage Europe to achieve a stability that it would be proud to diffuse as a model. These reigons have a vested interest in European developments because a failure of self-restraint in Europe would have consequences for all. There is at last the beginning of a process leading to a significant reduction in the concentration of weapons in Europe—a concentration that has created problems for Europe itself and for other regions where basic causes for conflict have been complicated by East-West tensions.

On the link between disarmament and development, it is argued that expenditure on arms has caused internal problems and this is being openly acknowledged in the USSR. A shift of resources to areas in domestic economies is needed. The link between Third World debt and global arms expenditure is also noted.

In discussing proposals for a special UN security system for nonaligned countries, it is noted that whereas the West has NATO and the East has WTO, the nonaligned have no means to achieve security, without which there can be no disarmament. Such a system is not intended to be interventionist since there are other ways to halt conflicts such as through sanctions, great power pressures, and so on.

The view is expressed that although NATO and WTO countries have different perceptions of who has superiority in specific areas, these are two ends of the same problem that have to be tackled at the Vienna talks.

Chapter 13
THE PROSPECT OF CONVENTIONAL DISARMAMENT
Olu Adeniji

The prospect of conventional disarmament in Europe holds out great consequences not only for the continent but also for the entire world. The arms race both in its nuclear and conventional aspects has been the single most important element of the destabilizing factors in international relations since 1945. Though initially borne out of the ideological division of Europe and the consequent quest for strategic military superiority, it soon developed a technological momentum of its own, becoming more the cause than the effect of the distrust in the relationship of the two alliances. The issue of conventional weapons was raised for negotiations side by side with that of nuclear weapons when the United Nations took up the question of disarmament in 1946. Due, however, to the unforeseen and most dangerous advance in nuclear weaponry, the fear engendered shifted all attention at the multilateral level to nuclear weapons.

Except in Europe where the Mutual and Balanced Force Reduction Talks in Central Europe were initiated, conventional weapons disarmament did not attract multilateral attention again until the First Special Session of the United Nations General Assembly Devoted to Disarmament in 1978. The Final Document of the Special Session did accord highest priority to negotiations on nuclear weapons. However, it also affirmed that side by side with negotiations on nuclear weapons, the limitation and gradual reduction of armed forces and conventional weapons should be resolutely pursued within the framework of general and complete disarmament. States with the largest military arsenals, it was stated, had a special responsibility in pursuing conventional armaments reduction. Underscoring the central role of Europe further, the Final Document postulated that the achievement of a more stable situation at a lower level of military potential would contribute toward strengthening of security in Europe and constitute a significant step toward enhancing international peace and security.[1]

The increased attention given to conventional weapons at the multilateral forum was the result of a broader appreciation of the role of that category of weapons in the security situations not only in Europe (where it has always been considered very important) but also in other regions. The factors that hastened that broader appreciation can be summarized below.

1. The conventional arms race is closely related to the ideological and political rivalries between the East and West. The super powers that are the leaders in the nuclear arms

race are also responsible for propelling the conventional arms race. They and their allies are responsible for all technological innovations in conventional weaponry whose main focus is the arms race in Europe.
2. The increasing sophistication and destructive power of conventional weapons constitute an ever growing threat. Unlike nuclear weapons, conventional weapons are easily used, mostly in areas far removed from Europe.
3. Conventional arms transfer became a major foreign policy tool in the global lateral expansion of the East-West rivalry. It has therefore contributed in no small measure to the complications of Third World national and regional problems, creating instability and insecurity.
4. Conventional weapons are the drainpipe of the arms race, consuming 80 percent of military expenditure.
5. Conventional arms accumulation in the Third World has led to regional competition and arms races, some of which are independent of the central arms race.
6. Conventional arms purchase creates a financial burden on the developing countries, leading to economic difficulties that in turn provoke national instabilities.
7. The interlink of conventional and nuclear weapons in the arms race in Europe as contained in the theory of deterrrence whereby nuclear weapons can be used in response to an attack with conventional weapons.

The militarization of Europe, arising out of the bipolar alliance, encouraged militarization of the Third World as part of the means of creating spheres of influence for strategic advantage. Nuclear weapons remain the most spectacular aspect of the arms race as they pose a threat to the very existence of the human race. Nevertheless, the complimentary race in conventional weapons has had a more direct and proven impact on the Third World. Unlike Europe, which has escaped the outbreak of war and use of the awesome conventional weapons that have been developed by the two alliances, the Third World has had to endure the consequences of their use. More than 150 wars have been fought in about 70 countries since 1945, accounting for more than 20 million casualties.[2] Instability in the Third World has been further promoted by the requirement of many countries that have been subjected to acts of aggression, to embark upon the acquisition of military potentials that they certainly could ill afford and would have preferred to avoid.

Europe is today the region with the highest concentration of conventional and nuclear weapons. This is in keeping with its central role in the security considerations of the super powers and their alliances. In Europe the inextricable linkage of conventional and nuclear weapons is complete such that conventional weapons and forces are perceived in the context of the factor of nuclear weapons. The military situation in Europe therefore remains the greatest threat to international peace and security. In addition, the global requirements of the super powers and their two alliances have always demanded the extension of their influence and presence beyond Europe. Their defense strategies incorporate military presence either directly or by proxy in the Third World. These have combined with their defense concept based on an adversary model of reality to reinforce their propensity to view everything in the context of East and West.[3]

The central arms race of the super powers and the two alliances has replaced open armed conflict in Europe. However, there is a continuous war in the research laboratories in Europe and the United States. The number of scientists engaged in military research and development is estimated at half a million, representing about one-quarter of the number engaged in research and development in all sectors of human endeavors. The amount of $70–80 billion is expended annually on military research and development. The impact of the massive and expensive work of these scientists creates an unstable military perception that translates into a never-ending security dilemma fueled by ever more sophisticated and efficient weapons.

Any war in Europe, even if it starts with conventional weapons, is bound to escalate to the nuclear level. Nobody believes any longer in the theory of a limited nuclear war. Nobody also is any longer in doubt as to the consequences of such a war given that the arsenals of the nuclear weapon states, particularly of the super powers, contain enough to destroy the world several times over. Even the use of only a part of these arsenals is sufficient to provoke a nuclear winter from which no country anywhere in the globe can escape. The severe and prolonged low temperature that will follow a nuclear war will not be restricted to the Northern Hemisphere, which will be the center of the nuclear exhange. The Southern Hemisphere will within weeks experience a similar drastic drop in temperature. Thus the survival of countries having no part in the conflict and not belonging to either of the two alliances would be as much in jeopardy as those that launch the nuclear war. Countries as far apart as India, Brazil, Nigeria, and Saudi Arabia, and as far away from the center of a European-provoked nuclear war could be wiped out even though no nuclear weapon is dropped on their territories.[4]

Notwithstanding this overkill capacity, the race in nuclear weapons continues. According to the theory of deterrence, which is at the center of the military doctrine of NATO, nuclear disarmament is inconceivable without conventional disarmament in Europe. The controversy that the America/Soviet Agreement on Intermediate-Range Nuclear Weapons provoked within the NATO countries emphasized this point. Whereas the agreement affects the destruction of only 3 percent of the enormous nuclear arsenals of the two super powers, opposition was raised that it would result in weakening NATO's options of response to a Warsaw Pact attack. It was argued that the treaty had opened the floodgates for denuclearization of Europe and for decoupling Europe from the American nuclear umbrella, at a time when Warsaw's superiority in conventional weapons, it was argued, was intact.

Conventional disarmament in Europe therefore should lead to progress in nuclear disarmament, thus progressively reducing our race to self-extinction. Nuclear disarmament by the nuclear weapon states will also directly benefit other regions where pariah states taking advantage of the selective transfer of nuclear technology have been able to develop nuclear weapon capability with which they threaten the security of other states in the region. Nonproliferation can more forcefully be enforced in a situation that demonstrates the practical commitment of the super powers to nuclear disarmament. The basis of the indulgent treatment of states such as South Africa that have clandestinely developed nuclear weapon capability would have been removed. The presumed strategic usefulness of South Africa in NATO's defense planning was no doubt at the basis of the cooperation with that country in the nuclear field. Notwithstanding hard evidence to prove the point, including its preparation of the site for a nuclear test in the Kalahari Desert in 1977 and the flash of a nuclear test picked up by a U.S. satellite in 1979, there was extreme reluctance by the West to admit a South African nuclear weapon capability. African countries whose proposal for a regional nuclear weapon-free zone is being frustrated by South Africa were accused of being alarmist. Even when, finally, the South African foreign minister admitted at a press conference in Vienna in August 1988 that the Pretoria regime disposes of a nuclear weapon capability, the reaction of the nuclear weapon states has not been anywhere as forceful as their nonproliferation pretensions would have dictated. Political and strategic considerations continue to operate in shielding South Africa from the full effect of its manysided threats to the peace and security of Africa.

A likely result also for global security will be the abandonment of the dangerous military doctrines that have been developed to justify the arms race. Among these, the doctrine of nuclear deterrence has been the most controversial, as it foresees the early first use of nuclear weapons. Its rationale is rooted in the presumed inferiority of one alliance in conventional weapons. Such is the belief in deterrence by its advocates that it is credited with the absence of the outbreak of a nuclear war in Europe since 1945. Having no objective limit, however, deterrence feeds on the subjective assessment of the capabilities and intentions of the other side. It has resulted in the ever present danger of global nuclear annihilation by encouraging the continuous vertical proliferation of nuclear weapons. Moreover, it has encouraged horizontal nuclear proliferation certainly by South Africa whose untenable apartheid policies can, it believes, be sustained only by force.

EXTENSION OF IDEOLOGICAL CONFRONTATION AND THE ARMS RACE TO THE THIRD WORLD

The political changes that followed the end of World War II saw the loosening of imperial holdings and the beginning of disintegration of the old empires. Peoples in the colonial territories were asserting their right to self-determination and national independence. At the same time the smaller independent states were becoming, through their role in the United Nations, aware of the influence that they could have in international affairs. This situation provided the two European-based alliances with both a challenge and an opportunity. It was clear to the leaders of the two alliances, the Soviet Union and the United States, that their ideological rivalry could not be confined to Europe. Capitalism and communism were seen by each of the protagonists as ideas with universal appeal. However, since they were diametrically opposed to each other, each side quickly understood and portrayed the whole world as an arena in which the ideological quarrel could not be separated from power political advantage. Each super power, inspired by its universalist doctrine, had to struggle for support in the emerging Third World.[5] A new international security order based on alliances confronted the people in Asia, the Middle East, Africa, and Latin America with a fait accompli to which they were obliged to adjust.

The strategy of the two alliances to contain each other and widen their respective influence to all parts of the globe has played a major role in the destabilization of the security of the Third World. The main instrument has been the supply of conventional weapons, which became a vital instrument of foreign policy, employed as well to assist friendly Third World governments to uphold their security as to subvert and destabilize unfriendly governments. The interests of the two alliances became intertwined and often takes precedence over local conditions such that arms supply to a country or a region is often dictated more by the requirements of the maintenance of sphere of influence than the peace of the region.

The pattern of arms transfer to the Third World has always shown a correlation between the level of transfer and the competitiveness of the major powers in the area. Thus it is not surprising that the Middle East has remained the most militarized region, both quantitatively and qualitatively. Over 46 percent of all arms transfers to the Third World countries between 1971-85 went to the Middle East.[6] The extent of super power involvement in other regions can also be gleaned from the nature of arms support. Africa, whose share of arms transfer was very modest in the 1960s, saw a great jump in the 1970s. A major reason was the conflicting interests of the super powers in the Horn of Africa and in Southern Africa. The revolution in Ethiopia in 1974 and the war with Somalia in 1977 accentuated the East/West involvement in the Horn and witnessed a flood of weapons into the subregion. In Southern Africa, the independence of Angola and Mozambique in 1974 and 1975 saw a great step up of South Africa's policy of destabilization aimed at diverting the frontline states from being able to assist the South African and Namibian liberation movements. South Africa's support for insurgents in both Angola and Mozambique was countered by massive arms and military personnel supplies by the Soviet Union and Cuba to assist Angola defend its sovereignty. For East/West reasons, the United States supported with arms supply the Angolan rebels.

Arms supply to the Far East has also reflected a similar pattern. The Indo-China wars, which started as an issue of decolonization, became complicated by super power involvement until the United States withdrawal from Vietnam in 1975. Thereafter, distrusts between Vietnam, especially after its involvemment in Kampuchea, and the ASEAN states saw an ASEAN arms importation program. As in the Middle East, about 80 percent of the volume of weapons supplied to the region of the Far East between 1971–85 were from the two super powers.

There is no doubt that regional problems do exist that propel countries of the Third World to seek arms. National defense in an uncertain environment provides a legitimate reason. However, the encouragement to acquire weapons to a degree that provokes regional competition and tensions also arose out of the demonstration effect of the central arms race. Arms transfers as a feature of the lateral escalation of the Cold War from Europe into the Third World[7] encouraged the creation of regional centers of power. For the super powers, their global political and strategic requirements transform arms sales into "far more than an economic occurrence, a military relationship or an arms control challenge; arms sales are foreign policy writ large."[8]

Two developments propelled the process of arms transfer to the alarming level it attained in the 1970s and early 1980s. First, the arms market grew much wider over the years. Unlike the nuclear arms race, which is confined mainly to the super powers, the conventional arms race followed a great variety of initiatives arising from research and development. Apart from satisfying national and alliance requirements, surplus arms were available for sale. For suppliers other than the super powers, economic and financial necessities made the arms market in the Third World attractive. This was particularly so with the sharp increase in oil price in the 1970s and the consequent balance of trade problems. Second, the increased resources available to Third World countries, especially producers of oil, facilitated the acquisition of arms for a variety of reasons. Even those developing countries that could not afford to pay cash for arms procurement were nevertheless tempted with easy credit. Arms exports became a major tool of the so-called recycling of petrodollars, which enabled the major Western countries to preserve their dominance of the international financial and monetary system.[9] The period of the 1970s witnessed a gigantic increase in arms transfer to the Third World, to the tune of $286 billion, four times the value in the previous two decades. The average annual growth rate during much of the 1970s was 13 percent. Though there was a decline in the annual growth rate in the period 1978–84, the early 1980s saw the supply of more major weapons to the Third World than at any time in history.[10]

The economic consequences for the Third World of this massive transfer of arms is seen in the current debt burden. Arms-related credits, which were no more than $3 billion in the early 1970s, rose to $10 billion in the early 1980s. The total accumulated military debt for the period 1972–82 is estimated at $86 billion.[11] Of the total debt of the developing countries put at $1,217 billion as at 1987 by the International Monetary Fund, it can be inferred that between 15 to 20 percent is related to arms transfer. Thus arms importation has contributed to the current financial and economic crisis in many developing countries, perpetuating underdevelopment, which breeds insecurity.

Even more than in Europe there is need in the Third World for a rethinking on the requirements of security both national and regional so as to create conditions of greater stability and development. The economic crisis engulfing much of the Third World has set that process in motion. Increasingly, security is being perceived much beyond military preparedness. Military-based security in the Third World often ends up ignoring the social, economic, and cultural aspects of security. Development, aptly described as the constant improvement of the well-being of the whole of the population of any country, is a precondition for security. The current situation in most developing countries shows overall living standards well below the levels as at the beginning of the present decade. The gains made even by the oil-producing countries as a result of the last oil price increase in 1979–80 are said to have been completely reversed. For Africa the situation is alarming. Average living standards have fallen by more than 20 percent since 1981.[12]

Conventional disarmament in Europe will contribute to the process of greater security in other regions first by way of example. Though the conditions in different regions are not identical to Europe's, the possibilities for regional initiatives taking account of particular situations abound. The United Nations Study on Conventional Weapons identified conventional weapons as being most adaptable for regional actions. Since arms transfer from super power and European suppliers is the main source of the weapons used in other regions, greater rationalization of supplies will help the process of regional action. Seen in the context of the process of the Conference on Security and Cooperation in Europe, conventional disarmament in Europe will be the culmination of efforts to re-establish mutual trust and peaceful coexistence. If it signals an equally new approach to Third World security problems, devoid of East-West confrontational attitudes, then it will relieve Europe as well as other regions the burden of the present overemphasis on a state's military power, an approach that has proved to be expensive, dangerous, and even elusive.[13] Such is the involvement of the East/West dichotomy in issues worldwide that no important regional problem can now be resolved without the cooperation of the super powers. Afghanistan and Southern Africa are current examples of this all-pervasiveness of super power influence. Even regional initiatives aimed at promoting regional peace and security can be frustrated if it is perceived by a super power as a hindrance to its strategic planning. The long-standing proposal for a Zone of Peace in the Indian Ocean, though unanimously endorsed by all states in the region, has run into difficulties because of opposition based on East/West consideration. The same fate has befallen the more recent proposal for a Zone of Peace in the South Atlantic.

TOWARD COMMON SECURITY

In his analysis of postworld war disputes, Ernst Hass identified a total of 319, not all of which admittedly led to armed conflicts. According to the analysis, the Cold War is the single constant factor in most of the disputes. It directly accounted for 19 percent; it played an important role in the 20 percent that were the outgrowth of decolonization; it was also clearly noticeable in more than a quarter of the 31 percent that led to civil wars. The study also showed that of the disputes submitted to the United Nations, those that are free of Cold War complications were the most successfully managed; conversely, those Third World disputes where East/West rivalry became dominant were the most intractable.[14] Therefore, the lessening of ideological confrontation, the promotion of confidence arising from de-escalation of the arms race in Europe would be beneficial to the multilateral process in conflict resolution and peace-making. Collective security on which the maintenance of international peace and security by the United Nations was predicated fell victim to the Cold War. It can only be revived again by the determination of the super powers and their alliances to abandon their unilateral division of the world into armed camps and to encourage steps for a system of common security.

A new security system that will assure the security of all states will be an indispensable complement of the lessening of the ideological military confrontation in Europe. Disarmament in Europe will not resolve all intra-European problems, though it will create a very favorable condition in which those problems can be tackled. By the same token, the problems in other regions that have propelled states to acquire arms will remain. An efective system of international security will be necessary for reassuring all states in regions outside Europe. The massive transfer of arms from European producers to the Third World has been accompanied in some cases by the transfer of arms technology such that several developing countries are now counted among significant arms producers. The quality and sophistication of the arms technology transferred vary widely and have often tended to favor pariah states that constitute a threat to their regions. The apartheid regime of South Africa, whose policy of extreme racism is held in contempt in and outside Africa, has been able to develop almost total self-sufficiency in military requirements, notwithstanding the long-standing arms embargo imposed by the United Nations. Regional security under such circumstance will need to ensure that no regional hegemonic power develops. For international peace to be built on a commitment to joint survival rather than on certain initial destruction requires as a starting point a very drastic reduction of weapons now concentrated in and on Europe. Beyond this, however, there will have to be a renewed pledge by the major powers to respect the principles of the Charter of the United Nations and to rebuild the peace-making capacity of the organization. Among the major proposals that have emerged in this connection is that contained in the Report of the Olof Palme Commission, which unfortunately has not drawn much super power attention.

MILITARY COMPETITION AND INTERNATIONAL ECONOMIC COOPERATION

The ideological division of Europe and the accompanying arms race has its economic counterpart. The competition of economic systems dictated that political and economic contacts with each other be kept under very tight control. For the NATO countries that have an edge on technology, great constraint has been placed on exchange with the Eastern European countries of technology and capital flows, especially in critical technologies and strategic materials that are used in military industries. Studies have shown that the arms race has an impact not only on domestic economy but also on the balance of international trade and capital flows, in as much as military spending by the major military powers can engender imbalance, fluctuations, and bottlenecks in the world economy, and thus undermine its stability.[15]

Military expenditure has also been shown to retard growth since similar outlay in the civilian sector would have made greater contributions to growth and employment. Fewer jobs are created in the arms industry than in other sectors especially since the highly sophisticated technologies of the arms industry require large investments. A comparative analysis reveals the following number of jobs created by a $1 billion investment:[16]

1. Military production (aircraft, missiles, artillery)   76,000
2. Machinery production (farm, metalwork, industries)   86,000
3. Administration   87,000
4. Transport   92,000
5. Construction   100,000
6. Health sector   139,000
7. Education   187,000

The conversion of military industries to civilian sectors, which will follow conventional disarmament in Europe, would have not only domestic but international benefit. The amount released will be considerable. Conventional weapons and forces are responsible for about 80 percent of military expenditures, which currently approaches $1,000 billion. As stated in the Final Document of the International Conference on the Relationship between Disarmament and Development, held in September 1987, reduced world military spending could contribute significantly to development considering the present resource constraint of both developed and developing countries. The relationship between disarmament and development in part derives from the fact that the continuing global arms race and development compete for the same finite resources at both the national and international levels. The use of resources for military purposes amounts to a reduction of resources for civilian sector.[17]

As many developing countries have come to realise, a new international economic order will not be achieved easily. Developing countries will need to take individual and joint measures including internal structural adjustment of their economies. However, as experience has shown, structural adjustment has to be complemented by a stable international economic system permitting remunerative external trade as well as access to external resources. The East-West hindrance on free economic exhange is often extended to developing countries on political and ideological grounds. Thus international economic cooperation with some developing countries is subject not to the dictates of economic but political factors. For resons for which the current Euro-centered arms race is partly responsible, the distortions in the international economic system work in such a manner that many developing countries are currently net exporters of capital and are not able to realize their full economic potentials. In an interdependent world, a determined healthy rivalry in providing economic collaboration with the Third World has to be a fallout from the improved economic exchange between the alliances, which is bound to follow the lessening of tensions. Otherwise, the insecurity that has been induced in the Third World to a great extent by the bi-polar policies will continue to haunt the developed world.

Notes

1. Final Document, UNGA First Special Session Devoted to Disarmament 1978, paras, 81, 82.

2. U.N. Study on Economic and Social Consequences of the Arms Race and Military Expenditures, Doc. A/43/368, para. 33.

3. Krister Stendahl, Comments at the SIPRI Conference on Common Security, 2 September, 1983. SIPRI Yearbook 1984, 585.

4. Carl Sagan, Nuclear War and Climatic Catastrophe, *Foreign Affairs*, Winter 1983/84.

5. Paul Kennedy, *The Rise and Fall of the Great Powers* (New York: Random House, 1987), 380.

6. M. Brzoska and T. Ohlson, *Arms Transfer to the Third World* (New York: Oxford University Press, 1987), 15.

7. Kennedy, Rise, 379.

8. Andrew Pierre, Arms Sales; The New Diplomacy, *Foreign Affairs*. Winter 1981-2, 266.

9. Raimo Vayrynen, Economic and Political Consequences of Arms Transfers to the Third World. *Alternatives*, iv (1980), 131-155.

10. Brzoska and T. Ohlson, Arms, 1.

11. U.N. Study of Economic and Social Consequences of the Arms Race and Military Expenditure A/43/368 para. 112.

12. International Monetary Fund Annual Report 1988, 11.

13. *SIPRI: Strategic Disarmament, Verification and National Security*. (London: Taylor and Francis, 1977), 57.

14. Ernst Haas, The collective Management of International Conflict 1945-1989. UNITAR; The United Nations and the Maintenance of International Peace and Security. (Dordrecht: Martinus Nijhoff 1987), 1-18.

15. U.N. Study A/43/368, 67.

16. M. Rogalski and C. Yakubovich, *Strategies for Reconstruction of Armaments Industry. Disarmament and Development on Global Perspective*. (Westport, CT: Greenwood Press, 1984), 266-267.

17. Final Doc. International Conference on the Relationship between Disarmament and Development, paras. 10, 11, 25.

Chapter 14
SUPER POWER RELATIONS AS A KEY
Rikhi Jaipal

Although there may be good reason for optimism in regard to substantial reductions of nuclear and conventional arms in Europe in the near future, conventional disarmament itself is still a far cry. Negotiations at present appear aimed at arms control measures, such as lower levels of deterrence, equal security through mutual vulnerability, and nonoffensive defense systems and postures, subject to effective verification regimes. If these measures should lead to the desired political ends, one might look forward to a Europe in which the fear of surprise attack has been eliminated and there is a greater sense of security, despite retention by the two alliances of a sufficiency of nuclear and conventional arms for purposes of deterrence and defense. But it would still be "armed" peace, though more stable than now, and not conventional "disarmament."

Arms control negotiations have doubtless been strengthened by the parallel political process of negotiations designed to build mutual confidence by removing misperceptions about military hardware, exercises, and movements, and by restraining other actions that create fear and suspicion. From the Helsinki Accords of 1975 to the Stockholm Conference of 1986 the progress made in confidence-building, though modest, is nevertheless remarkable, because of the adverse political climate in which negotiations had to take place. The Stockholm experience has reinforced faith in the dual track to disarmament through arms control and confidence-building, despite the fundamentally different approaches of the two processes. It is conceivable that the winds of change now blowing within the Soviet Union may well have a beneficent impact on the Stockholm process, and hopefully breed greater self-confidence in all the European negotiating parties. In that event they may take bolder steps toward conventional disarmament and common security while retaining a declining nuclear deterrent and possibly replacing it by a conventional deterrent of equal lethality in the first instance on the way to conventional disarmament.

The key to world peace is in Europe, for war in Europe would engulf the whole world. The rivalry between the two super powers and the ideological divide in Europe underwritten by the two military alliances cause serious concern in the non-European world. Ever since Charlemagne, various powers and persons have tried again and again, fortunately without success, to establish one single authority over Europe, the last such attempt having been made by Hitler. This obsession with one law and one universal state persists to this day in the split heritage of Europe and the potential therein for war.

The Third World—nonaligned and neutral nations—are, in the event of war in Europe, entitled to immunity, which would be absent if there is nuclear war. They cannon accept such a consequence of East-West hostility, nor mutual nuclear deterrence as a stable pattern for world peace and security. The risks for them in it are as great as for European nations, and such a situation is unwarranted. Nonaligned nations have therefore strongly urged the initiation of a dialogue between East and West *inter alia* for the purpose of dispelling existing fogs of mutual distrust and suspicion. The importance of European peace and disarmament for Third World security and stability cannot be overemphasized.

It is axiomatic that whatever is happening in Europe is bound to have an impact for better or worse, sooner or later on the rest of the world. The present positive trends in European confidence-building and arms control have already begun to cause some amelioration of certain conflict situations in various parts of the world, e.g., Iran-Iraq, Afghanistan, Angola-Cuba-Namibia-South Africa, Korea, Kampuchea-Vietnam, and Israel-Palestine. Behind this process of amelioration is the hand of super power cooperation on the basis of some understanding between them. Though their relations are still adversarial, they are exerting their influence and pressure in their different ways to stop conflicts. But it is by no means certain that they are prepared to go further, or that they will be able to restore lasting peace between parties to disputes, without which there can be neither security nor disarmament in the Third World.

The nature of some of these disputes is so complex that even angels may decline to be peacemakers, not to speak of the two super powers currently far more concerned with putting their relations on an even keel. There are still major differences between the super powers, which, unless resolved quickly, could cause a serious setback in their relations. The rivalry between them in certain Third World areas continues. They are still engaged in an arms race to develop third-generation nuclear weapons and other exotic arms based on new physical principles, and to secure military dominance in outer space. They continue to supply arms to nonaligned countries in confrontation or conflict, though perhaps now on a slightly diminished scale. Unless international action is taken to restrain and control the application of new technology for military uses, the arms race is bound to continue, and its pervasive impact will be felt also in the Third World. The deterrence concept, however discriminate or discreet it may be in practice, has also a much wider appeal than is assumed. It stimulates derivative arms races in all parts of the world that are prone to tension and hostilities.

Mikhail Gorbachev, president of the Soviet Union, said earlier this year:

> If we start orienting ourselves to a minimal nuclear deterrence, I assure you that nuclear weapons will start spreading around the world, rendering worthless and undermining even what we can achieve at Soviet-American talks and at talks among the existing nuclear weapon States.

In the matter of nuclear deterrence there are already four countries—Israel, South Africa, Pakistan and India—that seem to be pursuing a so-called strategy of ambiguity, which is a sort of discreet deterrence, regardless of whether or not they have nuclear weapons. Their nuclear arms capability is assumed and that in itself is believed to have a deterrent effect on the perceived enemy. The visible effect of it, however, is to stimulate arms races in the regions concerned.

Security is the key to disarmament. The shape of emerging European security in the light of the direct talks between the two super powers will be of interest also to the rest of the world. Historically, European security has depended primarily on diplomatic, political and economic factors, for the countries of Europe do not have impenetrable borders, and being physically close together they have had to deal with each other. The advent on the European scene of the two super powers was a recent wartime necessity. As the shadows of the last war recede into history, European relationships may be expected to revive and assume the trappings of normalcy. The achievements of European diplomacy in the matter of security may well be sustained eventually by conventional arms, for the nuclear umbrella has not been without political holes. Its credibility has never been without doubt, and many Europeans have been in dread of it anyway.

In the circumstances conventional deterrence in Europe based on weapons born of emerging technologies and with the new-fangled strategies of "defensive defense" may well find favor with political leaders and even military planners. This, however, remains to be seen, for even drastic reductions of nuclear arsenals do not necessarily lead to replacement of the nuclear deterrent, desirable as it is for the future of humanity. Nevertheless, there is a growing compulsion—moral, political, and legal—caused by the widespread lethal consequences of nuclear explosions, to move into a nonnuclear era of common security. To recognize this imperative and to respond to it is the challenge that Europe will have to face in the years to come.

The modern inheritors of non-European civilizations that cohabit the same world have had to adjust and adapt themselves to Europeanization of international relations, law, and practice. They are obliged to judge the world of today by the values and norms of European civilization. It is ironical that the nuclear means of destroying humankind, a European invention, should exist at the same time when respect for human rights has never been greater in Europe. Paradoxically, the struggle for ideological victory in Europe continues in one form or other, when it is plain that it is the factors making for diversity that have contributed the vital force displayed in the artistic spirit, intellectual ingenuity, and scientific cum technological advance of Europeans.

For the majority of the peoples of the Third World, however, life is a daily struggle for survival against heavy odds, man-made and otherwise. It is surely appalling that their daily burden should be enhanced by the entirely unprovoked nuclear threat to them that arises from super power adversarial relations. They cannot but be baffled by the prospect of their becoming victims in a nuclear conflagration over the superiority of the American dream in relation to the Soviet paradise, or of free private enterprise in relation to public ownership of the means of production.

They have a right to express their concern that Europe should thus hold in its hands their fate and that of all humankind in the nuclear age. For them peace, security, development, and disarmament will remain a daydream until the nuclear albatross falls from the necks of the great powers. To experience the full irony of the situation, one should also be aware that despite the nuclear danger to them, Third World countries—mostly orphans of a colonial past—seek the same goals as modern industrial Europe, the creator of the nuclear danger.

Between the fulfillment of expectation and the reality of achievement falls the shadows of Europe's failures and the Third World's nightmares. Of grave concern to the nonaligned is the absence of security to states outside the military alliances of the super powers. Such states are militarily and economically weak and are denied the collective security to which they are entitled by reason of their membership of the UN. Those states that are within the perimeter of military alliances enjoy the security of bloc membership, and to the extent they are secure, there is hope for their disarmament, individually and collectively. There is not the same possibility for nonaligned and neutral states that are obliged to rely on their own military strength for self-defense and security.

When conflicts have broken out between nonaligned states, they have attracted the support of the two super powers on the opposing sides, without their becoming directly involved in the actual fighting. As a result, the wars have turned out to be scenarios of no-win situations or limited engagements, but without incentives or disincentives for the warring parties to settle the disputes peacefully. Where the UN has been brought in, temporary cease fires have been arranged only with the cooperation of the super powers in some cases. And in others wars have continued to be waged for years, as between Iran and Iraq, with both parties buying arms from countries that had actually called for ceasefires.

In the absence of an international security system for nonaligned states and bearing in mind the causes of wars between them, it is not surprising that they should feel that their disputes can only be settled by war as the last resort. There have been no attempts made to dissuade them from this tragic conclusion, such as by establishing institutional arrangements for mandatory settlement of disputes by peaceful methods, or by imposition of disincentives to make war. The general view toward such parties in conflict is the cynical one to the effect that if they must fight, they might as well be sold arms to do so.

Humans appear to have little capacity for compromise or mutual accommodation in times of peace, or even during indefinite ceasefires. The demands made in peacetime are usually for much less than what may in fact be surrendered after war. Nevertheless, the will to war remains much stronger than the nebulous yearnings for peace, and peace (such as it has been historically) is no more than the interregnum between wars. Prevention of war and peaceful settlement of disputes have therefore been extremely difficult.

It will continue to be so unless a third party like the UN is duly empowered to enforce the restoration and maintenance of peace. Having seen the worst and best in human nature in this century, perhaps in its closing stages it is the duty of those nations that have enjoyed the blessings of peace through the acquisition of enormous power, to define their role and responsibility in the preservation of peace in the Third World, whose security has so far been neglected. The example of military blocs in safeguarding their security and maintaining peace between themselves is clearly not to be recommended to Third World countries.

In terms of the UN Charter, the great powers have accepted primary responsibility for world peace and security and agreed to discharge it through their joint actions, and this includes the Third World. Security for Third World states should therefore be provided in conformity with the UN Charter, which is the basic international treaty of our times for regulating relations among sovereign states. There are two important obligations placed on all member states of the UN, namely, that they *shall* settle their disputes by peaceful means in such a manner that international peace and security, and justice, are not endangered, and second, that they *shall* refrain from the threat or use of force in their relations— vide articles 2(3) and (4) of the UN Charter. These obligations are obviously mandatory, and their violation could attract collective sanctions and enforcement actions, which is the key to effective maintenance of peace.

Unfortunately, the expectation that the UN would act in the above manner has not been fulfilled due to the failure of the great powers to act jointly. Consequently, responsibility for national security has devolved on individual states and they have been exercising their inherent right of self-defense according to the doctrine of natural law. This has led not only to the formation of super power military alliances, but also to individual preferences for safeguarding security through seeking more or less the open clientage of the two super powers. Whereas military alliances have been adequate for maintenance of peace between them, the system of clientage is surely a gross distortion of the international responsibility of the super powers under the UN Charter for the security of states.

This is a thoroughly unsatisfactory system for Third World nonaligned states, as long as security is perceived only in the military dimension. But now that super power relations are moving in non-confrontational directions, it should become possible for the super powers and their allies to fulfill jointly their legitimate responsibilities for maintenance of international peace and security at least in the Third World in the manner prescribed by the UN Charter. Specifically, the permanent members of the Security Council should take the initiative and devise in terms of the UN Charter a special collective security force and system for countries outside their military alliances. Second, they should also devise a special machinery for peaceful settlement of conflicts and disputes in the Third World, not excluding as a last resort compulsory arbitration, which should be accepted as the positive alternative to war.

When Third World states try to settle their disputes by nonpeaceful means, they are clearly in violation of the Charter of the UN. That is at the root of their insecurity, for it exposes them to exploitation by outside forces in the event of conflicts. However, external circumstances alone cannot be blamed for such situations. The absence of internal strength and stability has also a great deal to do with vulnerability and external dependence. The most vulnerable of these states are those at the peripheries of super power security perimeters, or with strategic importance to super power rivalry, or with resources vital for super powers' defense or economy. They come under greater pressures to compromise their independence to the required limits in favor of one or other super power.

For their part, the super powers have tended to behave as if their security interests are paramount and override others' interests. The main preoccupation of the super powers, common to both, has been to avoid a war between themselves and to protect and promote their own interests. As a result, international relations have come to reflect the actual state of the power balance between the two super powers. It is not easy to predict whether this equation will stabilize at the present level. Nor does one know whether their balance of power will be affected in the remote event of the nuclear deterrent being substituted by a conventional alternative.

At any rate, super power relations are entering a new phase characterized by a certain degree of openness in arms control and arms reductions as well as multifaceted cooperation for mutual benefit in other areas. It is unwise, however, on that basis alone to leap to optimistic conclusions about disarmament in Europe—nuclear or conventional—for super power relationships are extremely complex and beset with problems that do not lend themselves to predictable solutions.

Where do Third World nonaligned states fit into the balance of the power and threat system of the super powers? They fall outside it but are nevertheless subject to its centrifugal forces, regardless of whether the super powers are in a state of mutual hate or mutual bliss. The system's saving grace lies in the fact that it co-exists with the UN. However, it functions within the framework of the UN Charter in such a manner that whereas it does not supersede the UN, it does render it impotent in certain situations, and in other circumstances it reduces its effectiveness. The potential has always been there for the super power balance of power system to strengthen the UN through joint cooperation, especially in the matter of safeguarding the security of Third World states that are outside the super power alliances.

It is to be hoped that this potential for security will increasingly manifest itself in the third world.

At the end of 1986 there were 35 armed conflicts in the Third World—four in South Asia, eight in the Far East, six in the Middle East, 11 in Africa, and six in Latin America. Most of them were local insurrections, and in four of them some external powers were involved. However interstate conflicts were only three, namely, Iran-Iraq, Vietnam-China, and Ethiopia-Somalia.

The causes of conflicts are as numerous as the conflicts themselves; there is no one dominant cause for them. Religious and ethnic rivalries, struggles for political power, border disputes, and the factor of nationalism have motivated them. In spite of their local nature and origin, foreign countries, especially the United States and the USSR, have become involved in one way or other in virtually every conflict. This is the view of SIPRI, which has further stated in its yearbook of 1987, "The superpowers see many of these conflicts as proxy wars. USA is a major supplier to 16 governments engaged in conflict, and the Soviet Union to 14."

Another authoritative view is expressed by the Olof Palme Commission in its Report of 1982 and the following excerpts from it are relevant:

> We live in a milieu in which each State feels obliged to wage war in defense of its vital national interests. Military strength is seen as a symbol of this resolve, but the expansion of national arsenals is in turn interpreted by other nations as evidence of hostile intent, a cycle which undermines the security of the international community as a whole. The hopes expressed in 1945 for a world order in which the United Nations would be the guarantor of international peace and act as protector of States against aggression recede by the year. . . . The more we strive for security from external threats by building up armed forces, the more vulnerable we become to the internal threats of economic failure and social disruption. . . . When nations resort to arms, international society must isolate the conflict and resolve it by peaceful means.
> . . . Common security must begin with relations between the USA and the Soviet Union and between their two alliances, NATO and WTO. The developing world is neither immune to the consequences of East-West conflict, nor is it without fault as a contributor to the risk of war. Increasingly, political tensions between East and West affect the developing world, aggravating conflicts between nations in particular regions. In some instances developing nations have sought the political and diplomatic support of one of the Great Powers. . . . Involvement of the Great Powers on opposing sides of regional conflicts could result in a dangerous escalation. . . . If East-West relations are to be stabilized and sustained, then regional conflicts in the developing world also must be resolved and the opportunities for competitive Great Power involvement thus reduced. . . . Indeed, we would go further and urge international agreement in support of collective security operations for all Third World disputes likely to cause breaches of the peace, a sort of concordat among the permanent members of the UN Security Council.

The extent of European trade in arms with countries in conflict is a sad commentary on how European states, both West and East, view their responsibility toward maintenance of peace in the Third World. What should they do to help parties resolve their disputes peacefully or stop their conflicts? In point of fact they seem to do neither, because the parties refuse to respond and insist on fighting. Under the circumstances the arms-supplying states presumably feel they cannot refuse arms to either party to defend itself on being attacked and prevent being overwhelmed. Although that is a laudable feeling, the consequence is an arms race between the parties, whereas the conflict continues indefinitely, or becomes stalemated in a no-win situation with unstable ceasefires.

The losers are the warring parties both in economic and other terms, and the beneficiaries are the arms supplier countries in commercial and political terms. An obvious alternative is the self-denying act of refusing to sell arms to countries engaged in conflict. The argument against it is that in any case arms would flow unavoidably to countries in need of them from those that have a surplus of them for money or other considerations. The possibility of exerting combined political and economic pressures on the parties in conflict so as to compel them to settle their disputes peacefully is considered impractical, except when the super powers and their allies agree to do so. This dilemma is not beyond resolution, and the key to it, as it is to so many other problems, is the state of relations between the super powers.

Following are some recent examples of the equivocal behavior of arms supplier countries. The United States had covertly supplied arms to Iran in contravention of its own regulations. Some industrial companies of the Federal Republic of Germany had sold submarine blueprints to South Africa, violating UN sanctions and their own government's laws. A Swedish arms manufacturer had supplied weapons to Middle Eastern countries in breach of Swedish government restrictions. It has been estimated by experts in the field that no less than 27 countries had supplied both Iran and Iraq with weapons since the war began in 1980. The same 27 countries had also joined the general chorus of criticism against the belligerents for carrying on their war for eight long years.

Tensions and conflicts are good for the profitable international arms trade, and arms supplier countries readily opt for short-term economic incentives or political gain in preference to complying with arms export restrictions. The arms market has become commercialized and privatized, and commercial considerations often outweigh sound political judgment. Even so, there has been a sneaking suspicion that arms trade cannot flourish without governmental connivance, though the trade is in the hands of private arms dealers, obscure shipping companies, and middlemen. Whatever the truth of this may be, there is no doubt that supplier countries should be required to display their political will by demonstrating greater ability to control the arms flow in the interests of international peace and security.

According to the SIPRI Yearbook of 1987, the United States accounted for 34 percent of worldwide arms exports during 1982–86, and the USSR for 31 percent. The leading arms supplier to the Third World was the USSR with a share of 34 percent; the U.S. share was 26 percent; the share of the major West European suppliers—France, FRG, Italy, and UK—was 28 per cent. The Third World share of arms imports has been 65–70 percent, half of which goes to the Middle East. South Asian arms imports are beginning to rise dramatically. A new feature in some Third World countries is the importation of military technology, which is likely to continue to be attractive even after tensions are defused, crises controlled, and conflicts stopped.

Arms supplier countries are beginning to recognize the uncertain political benefits of the arms trade, although for some of them commercial incentives will always predominate political considerations. Though unreliable as an effective instrument of foreign policy, arms transfers appear to be indispensable. Conversion of arms industries to civilian uses and alternative ways of disposing of surplus stockpiles of arms would have to go hand in hand with efforts to reduce and regulate transfers including transfer of military technology, as well as efforts to resolve disputes peacefully through collective mandatory actions under the UN Charter. But the generation of adequate political will among all governments for these measures would not be easy unless strong leadership is forthcoming from the super powers and their principal allies.

The member states of the UN have always regarded conventional disarmament as an integral part of a comprehensive program of disarmament. The ultimate objective of the program is seen as "general and complete disarmament under effective international control" in a world in which international peace and security would prevail. The process is perceived as progressive reduction of armaments and armed forces until their final elimination. An immediate objective is the strengthening of international peace and security, as well as the security of individual states, in accordance with the Charter of the UN. This is viewed as directly related to peaceful settlement of disputes through building confidence, relaxation of tensions, and strengthening institutions for maintaining peace and for peaceful resolution of disputes. The UN, it is agreed, should have a central role and primary responsibility in the sphere of disarmament.

Negotiations on limitation and gradual reduction of armed forces and conventional weapons are to be pursued together with negotiations on nuclear disarmament measures. This has in fact been taking place in relation to Europe and the super powers at the bilateral, regional, and multilateral levels. The principle to be followed is that at each stage of disarmament there should be undiminished security for the negotiating parties at the lowest possible level of armaments and military forces, and no individual state or group of states may obtain advantages over others. The negotiations should cover other measures, such as progressive reduction of military budgets, establishment of zones of peace in various parts of the world, confidence-building measures, etc. The form and modalities of verification measures to be provided for in any specific agreement depend upon and should be determined by the purposes, scope, and nature of that agreement. The Conference on Disarmament, which has been negotiating a comprehensive program of disarmament envisages three stages—the first, the intermediate and the last. There has been no consensus, however, for undertaking negotiations within the framework of a timeframe, fixed or flexible.

The negotiations at the bilateral and multilateral levels clearly indicate that there is a link between nuclear and conventional disarmament. It is also clear from recent developments in super powers' relations that they set the trend for the arms race as well as for relaxation of tensions. The impact of the latter trend has already been felt both in Europe and the Third World. And conventional disarmament among the states belonging to NATO and WTO is very likely to trigger similar developments in the Third World.

But the word "disarmament" needs to be precisely defined. It is evidently not a condition of existence without arms of any kind. Does it mean disarming to levels of arms required only for maintenance of domestic law and order? Or, does it mean disarming to levels of arms required for individual self-defense, or collective self-defense? Presumably the answer is the latter definition in the first instance, and the former definition if and when there is a UN system of collective security functioning effectively. It may also be necessary to clarify the meaning of "self-defense" so as to exclude from the scope of definition what are known as "offensive defense" and "deterrence."

In the Third World, disarmament measures can be undertaken by states only when enduring peace is restored between parties to disputes. For that purpose, there should be established in the UN a special machinery for disputes settlement through exclusively peaceful means including compulsory arbitration, and a special security system especially for the security of nonaligned and neutral states. These special institutions would serve to reduce and eliminate super power rivalries, contribute to the preservation of international peace, help stabilize East-West relations, and promote conventional disarmament in the Third World.

Chapter 15
RESPONSES

FIRST RESPONSE
Marcos Castrioto de Azambuja

In response to Ambassador Adeniji (Chapter 13), when he says that the arms race both in its nuclear and conventional aspects has been the single most important element of the destabilizing factors in international relations since 1945, I could not agree more. I would only wonder whether the perspectives for this trend being curbed are not still very blurred and still have to be assessed very cautiously. Adeniji says that we have always, in the neutral and nonaligned world, attached absolute priority to the nuclear dimensions of disarmament, although since the first SSOD, conventional disarmament questions were there very much in relief. I agree also.

When he says that he believes that conventional disarmament should lead to progress in nuclear disarmament, thus progressively reducing humankind's race to self-extinction and when he mentions the period of deterrence, which is the center of the military doctrine of NATO and which says that nuclear disarmament is inconceivable without conventional disarmament in Europe, I agree that all of this would be excellent, but I unhappily do not know of any statement by any of the main nuclear weapon states that adhere to the deterrence theory that they are prepared to give up the nuclear weaponry as an ultimate antidote to conventional or "geopolitical" supposed superiority of the other side, even in the event of considerable progress in conventional disarmament, which we feel is still a far cry from where we are now.

Ambassador Adeniji mentions that the pattern of arms transfers to the Third World has always, he says, shown a correlation between the level of transfer and the competitiveness of the major powers in the area. Apart from satisfying national and alliance requirements, surplus arms were available for sale.

This is a provocative question; one of the major questions we pose to ourselves about the prospect of conventional disarmament in Europe is what will occur with the hardware. What is going to happen with the immense amounts of equipment that in a sense would be deactivated? Are we dealing here with physical destruction of equipment? Are we having to deal with huge surpluses that will have to be sold or transferred to other areas? This question is crucial to the interests of countries in and outside Europe. Is there a danger—to put it bluntly and in a very oversimplified manner—should the European market for conventional weapons shrink, that the Third World could become a considerably more attractive market for these weapons?

Adeniji's point about the correlation between the Third World debt and massive arms transfers and the cost that a lot of countries incurred by buying such military equipment is very relevant. A number of significant debtor countries were not significant buyers of military conventional equipment, with Brazil very much a case in point.

Adeniji then says that conventional disarmament in Europe will contribute to the process of greater security in other regions first by way of example; although the conditions in different regions are not identical to Europe's, the possibilities of regional initiatives taking into account particular situations abound. The UN Study on Conventional Weapons identified conventional weapons as being most adaptable for regional action.

I would like to take issue, first, with the idea of Europe as a model. Taking into account the present and past military expenditures of the super powers and the members of the military alliances, they still have to go a long way to be presented as models for other regions of the world; South America, for instance, has one of the lowest rates of military spending in the world. This is not to say that South Americans are envious or in any way nongenerous. The idea of the model quality of the European situation is somewhat irksome to regions that have been far more exemplary for a much longer period.

Second, I doubt very much that in a world dominated by global technologies, such as the nuclear, space, and aerospace, to speak about regional disarmament makes a great deal of sense. We must not forget that for Europe to be envisaging some kind of arms reduction process, it has to rely mainly on the global strategic balance and on the improved dialogue between the super powers.

I am in agreement with Ambassador Jaipal (Chapter 14) when he says that conventional disarmament is still a far cry in Europe, that negotiations at present appear aimed at arms control measures and at lower levels of deterrence, when he speaks about armed peace, though more stable than now and at lower risks, and that he rejects to some extent the idea of conventional disarmament. I agree about the limits of the exercise in reducing nuclear and conventional arms in Europe.

I think we should not mistake the hope and real possibility with regard to some progress in reducing the huge stockpiles of nuclear and conventional weapons when either the end of the Cold War, albeit in its milder neo-détente forms, or with conventional disarmament—disarmament understood as a process that would ultimately and hopefully lead to zero arms. The issues are complex, and therefore there is a long road still ahead of us.

Jaipal struck the right note of caution in the sort of moderation in expectations. He says that the key to world peace is in Europe, for war in Europe would engulf the whole world.

Although this is true, its reverse is not automatically true. There is no guarantee that peace in Europe would mean peace for the rest of the world, even if we recognize the role of East-West rivalries, which are not only European, the real centers of power being Washington and Moscow, in igniting conflicts in the Third World in the past.

Jaipal indicates that whatever is happening is bound to have an impact for better or worse, sooner or later on the rest of the world. He says that the present positive trends in European confidence-building and arms control have already begun to cause some amelioration of certain conflict situations in various parts of the world, and he quotes as examples Iran-Iraq and Afghanistan. It is not, I believe, the process of confidence-building measures and arms control in Europe that causes the real evolution we saw in 1988 as far as regional conflicts are concerned, but the changes in super power relations, in which Europe obviously plays a rather crucial role, but more as an object of rivalry than as its main actor. I do not underplay the central role of Europe, but I think the centers lie elsewhere and should be seen as such.

In another point, Jaipal says that when conflicts have broken out between nonaligned states, they have attracted the support of the two super powers on the opposing sides, without their becoming directly involved in the actual fighting. Although I agree, I have certain doubts when he suggests a new role for the Security Council permanent members. He assumes that the Security Council would generate more permanent cooperation between the super powers regarding conflicts in the Third World. As a second and more provocative question, are we sure that this will always be in the best interest of the Third World countries involved? In a sense do we assume that super power understanding is good, constantly, permanently, and as a matter almost dogma to Third World countries?

We are perhaps presupposing as evident something that is not necessarily true – that there is a direct effect or direct linkage with the rest of the world of eventual progress in conventional arms reductions in Europe. It is likely, but it should not be assumed. We should be very cautious so as not to mistake our deeply held hopes for a more peaceful world with reality, at least before talks and negotiations begin to show concrete results. It may be stimulating but somewhat disturbing that professional groups are being contaminated in a very delightful way by optimism. I share this, but perhaps we are getting carried away by the promise of the future more than by the awareness of what actually has happened or is in the course of happening.

We are concerned here with conventional arms reductions and not conventional arms disarmament, and even less than that, about East-West, the end of East-West rivalry or competition. Language here also has to be very, very carefully used.

Another point concerns the so-called levels of reasonably sufficient defense between the two military alliances, which would still be very high if compared with other regions of the world, and, for that reason, very threatening to the adjoining and even more remote regions not involved in the future negotiations. Even countries in Europe not directly involved with the two military alliances, with our concern with the Atlantic to the Urals are sort of waving their hands and saying they should be brought more into this picture. So perhaps the center in Europe is being overplayed. If a certain amount of noise comes from elsewhere, we must remember that there is a lot of world outside Europe.

This being a process of accommodation of interests between two groups of countries, it is not very clear yet if this accommodation, at a certain stage, will not be made at the expense of other groups or states or regions of the world, which would be expected simply to accept and subscribe to a new order conceived and negotiated in the horizontal dimension of the East-West relations. We must remember that the NPT, a clearly discriminatory and unequal treaty, was elaborated when we had the other détante, the earlier one, the simpler one, the narrower one. Some indications make some of us fear that the same oligarchical forms of regulating the world problems could be tried again in the framework of the new thinking. So we are not totally reassured. We must look into this far more carefully.

We are facing some modest progress in the shorter range level of weaponry. But the developing world, the neutral, nonaligned world would be far better off if we saw progress in all the weapons and systems that involve the longer range nuclear weapons, missiles, strategic bombers, and naval power in all its forms, including long-range submarines, naval bases, aircraft carriers (all of these carry a formidable power of intervention abroad), the question of rapid intervention forces, and the military applications of space technology. The rest of the world hopes, although we accept that there is no automatic linkage, that in conventional arms reduction in Europe some part will be given to liberating resources for the rest of the world development.

SECOND RESPONSE

Fan Guoxiang

Conventional disarmament, especially conventional disarmament in Europe, has always been at the center of international attention. We emphasize that nuclear disarmament and the prevention of a nuclear war should be given top priority among all areas of disarmament. At the same time, however, all countries in the world are becoming increasingly conscious of the grave threats posed by the wars and conflicts conducted with conventional armaments to the international peace and security, as affirmed by the Final Document of the First special Session of the General Assembly devoted to disarmament in 1978. The importance of the conventional disarmament has further been underlined by the repeated unanimous adoption by the UN General Assembly for the past couple of years of the relevant resolutions sponsored by the Chinese delegation.

It is well known that more than 100 wars and conflicts have been conductad with conventional weapons since World War II. In carrying out armed invasions and occupations of other countries, a few countries have also relied exclusively on conventional weapons. Meanwhile, new types of conventional weapons are becoming increasingly lethal and destructive. Most of the yearly $1,000 billion military expenditures in the world goes to conventional armaments. To maintain and enlarge their conventional forces, some countries have depleted an enormous amount of human, material, and financial resources. Europe, the battleground for two world wars, is now not only a continent with a large number of nuclear weapons in deployment, but also an area with the highest concentration of conventional weapons and forces in the world as a result of the direct confrontation between the two military blocs. A conventional war in Europe will very likely escalate into a nuclear war, bringing untold sufferings to the people of that continent and to the rest of the world as a whole. No wonder that the conventional disarmament in Europe should arouse such a keen interest on the part of the international community.

European conventional disarmament holds a significant place in maintaining European as well as international security. In the climate of prolonged tension in East-West relations, however, the MBFR has long lapsed into a stalemate without any substantive progress ever since it took off in 1973. The past few years have witnessed a gradual relaxation in the international situation, with confrontation giving way to dialogue. Encouraging signs have also emerged in the negotiations on the conventional disarmament in Europe. In 1986 the Stockholm meeting of CSCE reached an agreement on confidence- and security-building measures in Europe, exerting a positive impact on promoting the process of conventional disarmament in this continent. Over the past year European countries have been conducting explorations and consultations on new fora of negotiations on European conventional disarmament. Just a week before, an agreement was reached on the mandate of the Conventional Armed Forces Negotiation Talks. Soviet president Gorbachev not long ago announced the decision for an unilateral reduction of half a million troops in the next two years coupled with a substantial cut in its conventional armaments. Before 1991 the Soviet Union would also pull out six tank divisions from East European countries and dismantle related military installations. The combat forces and military equipment deployed in the European part of the Soviet Union would also be trimmed. The West European countries also forwarded specific proposals. The international community widely acclaim these developments and ardently hope that the parties concerned will reach an early agreement on the conventional disarmament in Europe and put it into effect.

The ease of the international situation has contributed to the progress in disarmament negotiations, and vice versa. These are mutually complementary processes. The apparent improvement of the international situation over the past years should be attributed to the sustained joint efforts of all peoples and peace-loving countries of the world. The postwar history has borne witness to the futility and repeated defeat of hegemonism and power politics that seek to subjugate small and weak nations by dint of military force. Most countries, developing and developed alike, are opposed to the scourge of another world war and have consequently engaged in the search for peace and development. The super powers, for their part, have also come to recognize that neither of them could emerge victorious from a nuclear war and have thus publicly announced that "a nuclear war cannot be won and must never be fought." Over the years, the strong demand of the world's people for the cessation of the arms race and for the maintenance of world peace and the practical actions taken to this end have been playing an increasing role. All these factors conducive to safeguarding peace and preventing war cannot but contribute positively to the process of disarmament. It is within this general international context that promising signs emerged with regard to the European conventional disarmament negotiations.

If drastic conventional disarmament could be realized in Europe, where the two blocs have long been locked in a confrontation with massive troops and various kinds of sophisticated weapons deployed on both sides, its impact on the world would undoubtedly be significant. It would considerably consolidate peace in Europe, strengthen European security and stability, promote confidence and cooperation among countries concerned both inside and outside Europe, and reduce the risk of the outbreak of a war in Europe. Under the new circumstances, can the countries concerned start as early as possible earnest negotiations on conventional disarmament in Europe? Within what time-frame and scope will substantive agreement be reached? This will have far-reaching consequences for East-West relations and for the world situation as a whole.

As for the specific impact of conventional disarmament in Europe on other regions of the world, various regions will face some common problems in conventional disarmament and the moves in one region will influence those in other regions. In this connection, I raise the following points.

First, within NATO and the Warsaw Pact, the two super powers that possess the largest arsenals have a special responsibility for conventional disarmament. In regions outside Europe, they should also stop their rivalry for spheres of influence and military intervention, to facilitate the cooling down and reasonable political settlement of regional hot spots.

Second, the military forces of all countries should serve exclusively the purpose of self-defense. Taking into account the security need for keeping necessary defense capabilities, countries should be encouraged to step up efforts and take appropriate actions individually or within regional framework to promote conventional disarmament. It should be noted that the troops and equipment cut down from one region must not be redeployed elsewhere.

Third, armed aggression committed by one country against another should be opposed. Foreign military occupation should be terminated without exception and all occupying forces withdrawn from foreign territories.

Fourth, the arms race should be checked not only in terms of quantity but also in terms of quality.

Fifth, the enormous manpower and resources released from conventional disarmament should be devoted to social and economic development. This is applicable not only to developing countries but also to developed countries.

At the same time, we should note that conditions are different in various regions. Efforts for conventional disarmament can be effective only if specific regional conditions are taken into account. Experience of one region should not be copied mechanically in other regions. For example, in Asia, including the Middle East, in Africa, Central America, and some other places, no final solution to the hot spots has been found so far, and there still exists the problem of foreign aggression and occupation. Different situations require different approaches. As regards many small and medium-size countries, to keep a limited defense force is entirely justified by their need for self-defense and security. It is evidently unreasonable to argue for equal responsibilities for all countries in the field of conventional disarmament.

Much has been said about the relationship between confidence-building measures and conventional disarmament. Confidence-building measures do play a positive role under many circumstances. At the same time, the satisfactory handling of international relations in conformity with the purposes and principles of the UN Charter will cast far-reaching and fundamental impacts on conventional disarmament. Countries in the Asian-Pacific region differ from one another greatly in their own conditions, such as history, geography, social systems, and culture as well as economic development. The question is how to create and maintain a sustained peaceful international environment so as to avoid overarmament and armed conflicts. The Five Principles of Peaceful Coexistence, initiated by the leaders of China, India, and Burma in 1954 and reaffirmed by both China and India during the visit of the Indian prime minister, Rajiv Gandhi, to China in December, represent the correct and effective ways for the development of normal interstate relations and for the maintenance of international peace and security as well as for disarmament including conventional disarmament. The Five Principles are mutual respect for sovereignty and territorial integrity, mutual non-aggression, noninterference in each other's internal affairs, equality, and mutual benefit, and peaceful coexistence. The Ten Principles of the Bandung Conference in 1955 reflected the same spirit. Later on, during the visits by Chinese leaders to countries in the Middle East, South Asia, ASEAN, and Oceania, it was reiterated that China together with those countries would abide by the Five Principles. The normalization of Sino-Japanese and Sino-American relations were realized in accordance with these Five Principles. It is certain that the normalization of Sino-Soviet relations will also be based on the same principles.

Whether they have identical or different social systems and ideologies, all countries should build confidence among themselves so as to settle international disputes peacefully. Gone are the days when might is right. Setting up and strengthening military blocs contribute only to the increase of international tension, whereas the Five Principles of Peaceful Coexistence constitute a solid basis for the development of normal relations between independent and sovereign states.

To abide by the Five Principles is beneficial to conventional disarmament, not only in Europe but also in the Asian-Pacific and other regions.

THIRD RESPONSE

Pierre Morel

Three essentially shared elements should be noted in the two reports by Ambassador Adeniji (Chapter 13) and Ambassador Jaipal (Chapter 14).

First, it is instructive to note that the nonaligned states, or, more broadly, representatives of countries from regions outside Europe, remain relatively alarmist concerning the *nuclear threat*, and in all event more alarmist than East and West. Certainly there is the problem of principle, the problem of deterrence as such. This is a major international debate that we must continue, and that is one of the realities of the modern world. There is also, notably in the context of the references that have been made to the topic of the nuclear winter, the question of the actual risk of such weapons being used.

We must not, of course, trivialize a major risk, which remains a major risk, nor must we ignore the fact that the risk of an outbreak of a nuclear conflict has diminished in relative terms in recent years.

As far as perceptions in Europe are concerned, we should remember, on the one hand, that 1988 saw the entry into force of the first nuclear disarmament treaty, which covers nuclear forces directly linked with the situation in Europe. Moreover—and this is no small matter—it was concluded after a long and intense political debate, which was a feature of elections in all the West European countries over the past ten years. The outcome of the major debate on Soviet and American intermediate-range missiles reflects fundamental choices on the part of societies, peoples, and—in the first place—governments, which moved ahead of electorates with relatively unpopular positions on these matters. These governments went through an electoral ordeal by fire at the time of deployment, and then a parliamentary ordeal by fire at the time of ratification of the treaty. In terms of deterrence and in terms of perception of the nuclear threat, there is an element here that cannot be ignored. The simultaneous confirmation of the specific role of deterrence in the organization of security and of the first nuclear disarmament treaty was not the work of a few foreign ministries, but truly the result of a profound commitment by the countries concerned.

Finally, recall another fact: we are embarking on negotiations on conventional disarmament in Vienna. Everyone knows that any outbreak of a nuclear conflict in Europe, or from Europe, would be associated with the initial use of conventional forces. Here too, above and beyond the conventional forces element itself, we have an exercise aimed at reducing in a very concrete way the risk of the outbreak of a nuclear conflict.

The second element in the reports (Chapters 13 and 14) was the reference to the *role of the United Nations*, and more generally, perhaps a profound yearning for a return to collective security, to the Charter. As Europeans, we cannot but subscribe to this idea. How important a direction this seems to be for shared reflection in this phase of the evolution of international society. Even if collective security as such, as a major organizational undertaking launched almost a century ago, is not attainable in the immediate future, the role of the United Nations is now growing again, regaining its true perspective, and this is not without importance for the future of conventional disarmament.

The third element is more critical. I noted (in Chapters 13 and 14) a certain tendency to leave aside the *specific aspects* of conventional overarmament in the other regions of the world. Yet we have to talk about them sooner or later. Where regional conflicts are concerned, these two reports tend to highlight external factors, vis-à-vis internal factors.

Of course, there is often an element of ideological confrontation, but we know that its influence is very small; there is also the question of arms transfers, but these do not occur only from north to south. As for the role of new military technologies, it should be remembered that it may not be the most advanced technologies that generate most conflict in the Third World.

As against these external aspects, it would seem that internal factors deserve greater attention in the current phase. True, the role of regional powers was mentioned, but it was not really dealt with in the two reports. That is a pity, because we all have an interest in better evaluating the consequences of the emergence of the regional powers, which today is an indisputable fact. I am also thinking—to return to the idea that arms transfers should be taken into consideration—of the profoundly destabilizing role played by the fact that countries that are passing through a crisis may possess considerable quantities of conventional arms, which are relatively unsophisticated by European standards, but whose sturdiness, ease of production, and wide distribution undoubtedly help to fuel conflicts, independently of north-south transfers. Situations of regional overarmament are increasingly arising and developing.

Here, then, are a number of aspects that we should try to address in more concrete terms. To sum up, what overall demand could we put forward in the field of conventional disarmament?

In the past there has been a general tendency to downgrade the importance of conventional disarmament for a variety of understandable reasons. They are linked to positions of principle on nuclear weapons, which have been discussed at length in the international community over recent decades. Recently again, the tense phase of East-West relations at the beginning of the 1980s encouraged the parties to fall back on such positions of principle. But given that 80 percent of military expenditure goes on conventional weapons, it is impossible not to see in them a real priority: the facts demand it.

Also despite this tendency to downgrade the relative importance of conventional disarmament, and despite this tense period in East-West relations, it was possible to embark on negotiations on conventional disarmament in Europe. One must not underestimate the importance of the fact that the talks in Madrid, and then those in Stockholm on confidence-building measures, succeeded in negotiating the period of crisis in East-West relations without being diverted from their path, without being broken off at any time. This is a signal, an indication that made it possible to gauge the importance of this chapter and the degree of interest of the European countries, which showed themselves capable of refusing to be swept along by the overall political context. It is also a useful indication, for countries outside Europe, of the strength of the commitment entered into by the Europeans and the lesson that may also be drawn concerning the chances of continuing negotiations in a difficult context.

There are, of course, objective reasons that may lead one to separate the situation in Europe from that obtaining in the other regions of the world. But it seems that at present interaction is tending to prevail. It is this idea that I would expand upon to say that the process leading to conventional disarmament is now under way starting from Europe. This first stage is necessary, but it is not sufficient to tackle all the urgent tasks in the conventional field. If a difference remains between what has been started in Europe and what might be started in other regions, it is not so much a difference of kind as of degree. We must, in fact, endeavor to achieve a parallel and complementary approach in this area. I am thinking in particular of the concerns or warnings put forward by Ambassador Azambuja (see under First Response earlier in this chapter). It is, of course, not possible to re-establish hierarchical or oligarchical relations, in his words. But it is necessary to sketch out what this parallel approach might consist of.

I begin from a *political* point of view. One of the lessons we have been able to draw from the work already accomplished in the field of conventional disarmament concerns the importance of the context, the political framework, as a factor promoting movement toward the initiation of effective negotiations on conventional weapons. In that regard, the experience in CSCE leading to the Vienna talks is a very important element, and everyone knows how much France is attached to it and values that link. Naturally, direct transposition is not possible. But in recent years the growing awareness, within the United Nations, of the importance of conventional disarmament has also been quite tangible.

In that connection, recall the role that France played, both immediately following the Stockholm negotiations in the autumn of 1986 and this year, when the work in Vienna was drawing to a close. Two years ago, in the First Committee, then in the General Assembly, France proposed the adoption of a resolution welcoming the results achieved in Stockholm, and on the latter occasion encouraging the achievement of the results that were on the point of being reached in Vienna. This support was not expressed in a formal and procedural manner, as in many resolutions, but by trying to retain the political essence of the exercise and underlining in passing that these negotiations had an impact and a significance for other regions of the world.

It is true that matters were not easy in 1986, when we put this text forward: a number of countries abstained, and it was rather striking to see that among them were twenty or so countries that were engaged in conventional conflicts. Their response was to say in a way that the confidence-building measures drawn up in Stockholm were an unattainable luxury, and this reaction was highly instructive. But this year, on the perfectly comparable resolution on the future negotiations on conventional stability, it was possible to secure consensus. This shift that we prompted went hand in hand with a broader effort, launched by China, concerning the principles of conventional disarmament, and there, too, the Chinese resolution was adopted by consensus.

The issue of conventional disarmament is thus gathering growing support, which has a political meaning. In that context the last paragraph of the resolution adopted in New York concerning the Vienna talks invites all states to consider the possibility of taking appropriate measures with a view to reducing the risk of confrontation and strengthening security, taking due account of their specific regional conditions. The wording is admittedly very broad, but it is necessary to proceed from such a political framework in order to achieve concrete results.

More generally, it is time to emphasize that the United Nations offers an appropriate framework and regains its real function in the task of political preparations for conventional disarmament. That begins with the settlement of conflicts, of course, but may more generally cover possible "confidence-building measures," even if they are to be put into effect at the regional level. The extraordinary year we witnessed in 1988, with that succession of settlements under the auspices of the United Nations, demonstrated incontestably the need for a political framework to be in place in advance of actions in the field of conventional disarmament in various regions of the world.

I would like to end with a word on the *practical* aspects and the parallelism between Europe and the other regions. What has happened in recent years on the European continent? We have witnessed an effort in the direction of political stabilization, and at the same time a qualitative and quantitative growth in armaments, in such a way that the two trends tended to cancel each other out in an unsatisfactory status quo. The very aim of the effort undertaken more recently was to transform this zero-sum game into a positive-sum game, by trying to curb this build-up. But it is important to prevent the reverse from happening at the same time in the other regions of the world, where political instability would go hand in hand with growth in arsenals and would lead to a negative-sum game, in which everyone would be a loser. Thus it is indispensable to forestall this serious risk of divergence, by working simultaneously at the political level and in very concrete terms. As regards political stabilization, I have said something about the role of the United Nations. Regional confidence-building and security-building measures also have an important role to play. It is not possible to decide on everything at once, but it is possible to move forward by stages, and that is indeed the role of such measures.

In that regard, the idea of preventing surprise attacks does not only fit in with a European logic: it can be of interest in many theaters. There is also a need—and this is a major point, emphasized in the reports—to address the question of arms transfers. This year, for the first time, a resolution sponsored by Italy and Colombia on this subject was adopted at the United Nations, and that is an important sign. For our part we are quite ready to discuss it; we simply wish to underline the extent of the methodological work that will have to be accomplished, particularly as regards transparency. How can we control arms transfers if we do not possess at the outset an objective basis for ascertaining the real state of affairs, in other words; military budgets? Let us begin by fully applying what has been stipulated— the notification of military expenditure by each state to the United Nations—and then we will be able to start serious work on controlling arms transfers.

In conclusion, we can identify certain elements of agreement: a parallel approach in conventional disarmament should be encouraged both in Europe and in the rest of the world, while fully respecting specific regional conditions. The movement that has begun recently in Europe and to a certain extent in the United Nations is still slow, necessarily gradual, and perhaps fragile. But it is real; it reflects a new attitude on the part of states, and has already opened up many new prospects. That is why all the opportunities for forward movement must be grasped, even if they appear modest at first sight.

FOURTH RESPONSE
John Edwin Mroz

The subject under discussion is, of course, a very difficult one. It has been referred to by a European colleague as "a mosquito in a tent" of East-West relations. The question of how north-south issues impact on the possibility for a fundamental change in the relationship between the East and the West had tended to result in very general, abstract, or theoretical responses. Here I formulate specific issues that must be addressed by the policy communities both in the north and the south. The first is the relationship of European disarmament talks to the issue of the export of arms to Third World countries. It is no secret that military research and development costs together with the high per unit production costs have been and continue to be a key factor in the sale of arms by both the East and West. Whether we talk about the enormous UK sales to Saudi Arabia or the Soviet Union sales to Libya, the United States sales to Korea, it is a fact that such sales do lower the unit cost of weapons. There is the serious prospect for an agreement for massive cuts in conventional weapons in Europe; we have to take into account the financial effect. This is not an abstract question for military contractors or for ministries in governments in both alliances.

The second issue deals with scientific research. Unless we balance proposed cutbacks in R&D with new funding for civilian research programs, there will be major problems in terms of remaining competitive in the high technology areas. This is one of the problems with conversion. This is an issue that is increasingly being discussed, but has not been seriously researched. We must look at the increases. A successfully researched program of conversion would have to deal not just with the curtailment of funding for military R&D, but equally where the increases will come in civilian R&D. I think this issue can be linked to that of technological transfer and scientific cooperation with the rest of the world.

A third point is the necessity for the Third World not to have unrealistic expectations of the amount, if any, of direct development aid that will result from European disarmament agreements. There has been a great deal of speculation, but it is not clear whether a negotiated reduction (or unilateral reductions) will in fact lead to any significant resources being made available for the Third World. The odds are overwhelming that this money is going to be used for domestic needs. Significant progress on reducing defense expenditures in both alliances could, however, enable bold action on issues such as the Third World debt. There are today a number of proposals that could be looked at much more seriously if the economies were healthier. Gorbachev has discussed this issue publicly as have some Western officials. But we should not delude ourselves with the idea that there could be massive sums of new development assistance from the East or West. This is an illusion.

A fourth point is the regional implication of the major disarmament agreement in Europe. For example, the second largest army in NATO is Turkey. This region is fraught with tension. One can ask, as some are beginning to do in the Balkans, what effect would a major conventional arms reduction in Central Europe have on the Balkan region with military forces of this size? This is a sensitive question, but the east-east, west-west, east-west, and north-south tensions in the southern flank give reason to pause for reflection.

A fifth point deals with the implications of the re-emergence of Europe and Japan as powers of global significance. There is a careful need for a re-examination, a thoughtful re-examination, of the role of these larger powers in conflict. Those of us who are involved in U.S./Soviet relations frequently note that when the United States and the Soviet Union have tense relations, everyone worries, but when they improve their relations there is a great deal of concern that reminds me of the "grass-suffering" stories. I know two of them. One is of Swahili origin—when two elephants fight, the grass suffers. But there is another one that the prime minister of Singapore contributed—when two elephants make love, the grass also suffers. It is very interesting to observe the reaction of some of the major powers in the world to the increasing cooperation between the United States and the Soviet Union in regional areas. For example, recently in a major Western European capital I was castigated as an American by a senior politician who had read the Brazzaville papers regarding the Angola negotiations. He was quite upset that whereas the Soviet Union was admitted as a fifth member of that agreement, Europe was not even mentioned. This kind of an attitude reflects something important about the growing desire of other major powers, many of whom are going to be involved in the reduction of arms agreement, about their role in regional conflicts. Of course, the progress in the Security Council and the cooperation between the five permanent members are things to be welcomed, but it does require some serious rethinking about what we are prepared to do and who should do it.

Sixth, Ambassador Jaipai (Chapter 14) proposes the idea of an aggressive peacekeeping policy for the United Nations—an intervention force under UN auspices and compulsory arbitration. We have to look carefully at the tension that will exist over the so-called national sovereignty argument. We all know of the cases where Third World states do not want immediate resolutions of conflicts.

A seventh point deals with deterrence for nuclear, chemical, and biological weapons. We are unlikely to see, at least in my lifetime, an elimination of nuclear weapons. Although a massive reduction of nuclear weapons, perhaps a 90 percent reduction of the existing stock is possible, there are trends that should make us give pause as to whether we want to abolish nuclear weapons. Take, for example, the spread of ballistic missile technology in the Third World. It is already happening and it does provide a reason why nuclear deterrence should in fact remain. The issue of chemical and biological weapons comes about, of course, for reasons unconnected with the East-West conflict or the Cold War. A radical change or transformation of East-West relations will *not* resolve the issue of chemical and biological weapons. Until the international system is able to agree to a collective security system with sanctions perhaps chemical weapons will be used as a last resort.

An eighth point is the need to have a much more serious study of the issue of how CSBMs, the experience in the European context, can be modified for use in other regions. In the academic world several modest studies have been undertaken. But this subject has certainly not received the amount of attention it should be given.

My final point is on research and development in the Third World. It is no secret that most of the R&D that does go on in the Third World is military-related. There is very little R&D assistance from the north into the south that is not in some way military-related. I think it is interesting for us to ask, if one considers the possibility of a major arms reduction agreement in Europe, whether there could be specific efforts by the United States, Japan, the European Community, and the CMEA states to help stimulate civilian research and development investment, especially in the states that are called "technological desert" states. We must, of course, ask the question whether the costs of Third World R&D outweighs the benefits as long as the Third World economies are structured in a way that does not make them receptive to major civilian R&D efforts. There are, however, practical efforts that could be undertaken by those in the north. In the 1960s there was created an international center for theoretical physics, which was established to advise Third World scientists on important scientific developments in R&D areas. Unfortunately it has had less practical effect than hoped, in large measure due to the brain drain to the north. One can see even in the list of scientists dealing with SDI contracts a very large percentage of Third World scientists under contract. The reasons are because the laboratories and scientific establishments and the scientific opportunities for research are much greater in the north in the military-related areas than they are anywhere else.

Let me add a final word about a subject that stands out from the two reports (Chapters 13 and 14). A very negative trend that we should deal with in parallel with the issue of super power and great power transfers of arms is the trend in the Third World, especially among the so-called threshold countries, to increasingly become major exporters of arms.

The horizontal proliferation of arms, including the higher technological ends of the business such as ballistic missiles technology, is a most worrisome development. It is ironic that while the United States and the Soviet Union sign an INF agreement to eliminate a class of missiles, similar technologies are spreading and are being helped by certain Third World arms producers. The list is very significant, but whether we look at Asia, North and South Korea, or in South America at Argentina and Brazil, or Egypt and Israel or South Africa, we see an imposing and a very strong list of states that are increasingly able to manufacture and to sell very sophisticated weapons. In the 1990s the regional conflicts will not be as familiar as in the past, e.g., stemming from the legacies of the decolonization process. If we look at the 1990s as sources of regional conflicts, we are going to find an increasing number of transnational phenomena at the cone, including resource shortages, ecologically based reasons, demographic and migration problems.

FIFTH RESPONSE

Hennig Wegener

These reports (Chapters 13 and 14) have opened many fascinating perspectives. Let me contribute to some of the issues raised by offering basically three thoughts. The first is about stability and its prospects in a global perspective, the second about the future role of nuclear arms in preserving stability, and finally, a comment on the Vienna negotiations.

The reports have been almost unanimous in condemning the undesirable features that have characterized the East-West relationship over the past four decades. I would rather like to point—despite all its unsatisfactory traits—to the great contribution it has, paradoxically, also made: that is, stability. The highly sophisticated power equation between East and West has been the backbone of stable developments in the world, at a price, to be sure. The eagerness of the two alliances to avoid any real danger of war between them has brought their protagonists to transplant their deep antagonism to the outside, thus exacerbating, and ideologizing existing conflicts in the third world. It is unnecessary to cite the list; yet the fact that there was no major turmoil affecting the East-West relationship has provided at least the countries of the Western alliance, as the leading economic players in the world, with a degree of internal reassurance and an opportunity for wealth generation without which the development of the third world, however unsatisfactory, would not have been conceivable.

Now the task, of course, is to cut out the undesirable, unsatisfactory features of this influence of the East-West relationship on the other regions of the world, but at the same time to preserve its stability. I think that is a major challenge: to preserve stability in times of such rapid change as we see, change that does create new apprehensions.

Jerome Paolini's report (Chapter 8) betrays some of the nervousness that unavoidably accompanies change. But change, before all, provides us with unique opportunities for the topic with which we are dealing. There is the prospect of a major receding of the military factor in the East-West relationship and beyond that, in international relations at large. The fact that the East-West partners face the prospect of being less preoccupied over time with the mutual threat and with the military factor in their own relationship, and the fact that they may arrive at a new basis for their competition in the remaining situation of secular antagonism potentially have beneficial features for the other regions of the world.

The first one of these likely features is undoubtedly the growing disenchantment of the two major military powers with global interventionism and, connected with that, their willingness to contribute increasingly to cooperative conflict solution. While the prospect of military East-West conflict recedes even further and the consciousness of the futility of war becomes more widely spread, the growing cooperative features of this new East-West relationship could very well spill over to more cooperative relationships worldwide.

That could lead, as we already witness, to a progressive reinstatement of the United Nations. It would allow the two major military alliances jointly and increasingly to focus on common global issues and global threats. These certainly include the new global military threats, but also the—no doubt security-related—threats of economic disparities and ecology. I set great hope in the increasing integration of the Soviet Union into the larger multilateral world system by way of what some have called the "deabnormalization" of Soviet policies. The time may come when the members of the two military alliances and the community of free developed democracies outside of NATO will contribute more strongly to global stability in a better division of labor.

The fulfillment of such promises will hinge on whether stability in Europe really comes about; stability in a higher sense. In other words, if we go back to our topic, whether the CAFE talks in Vienna will turn out to be successful. Success must be measured, of course, in terms of realism. Whereas the Soviet conventional superiority in Europe has been the central factor of East-West relationship as we know it, and whereas there is now the chance that the shadow of a vast Soviet superiority may cease to hang over Western Europe, there is, of course, no prospect of a permanent demilitarization of Europe.

There will be an attenuation of the military threat but the Soviet Union will remain, and one should be careful not to characterize this in entirely negative terms, a major military power commensurate with its world power role. But while the military factor recedes, a new relationship, broader, multidimensional, may result, gradually overcoming the division of Europe and stressing more strongly the dimension of liberty and human rights.

The conditions for this development to come about are twofold in military terms: first, a degree of parity of conventional forces, but also an increasing emphasis on the defensive features, which deprive the forces on either side, but mainly, of course (from NATO's view), the Warsaw Treaty Organization of its invasion capability, at least reducing this capability decisively. But conventional stability, even if underpinned by new, defensive force structures, is not enough, and it is perhaps not even entirely feasible. Conventional stability is a relative term; it can be achieved only to a point. A second component is essential: the nuclear factor.

Here we have to take a clearer view of the role of nuclear weapons in the East-West relationship. Too often it has been argued that nuclear weapons were there to make up for conventional deficiencies. They can fulfill that role but only in the sense that they make the entire option of conflict unacceptable, thus neutralizing a conventional superiority, making it pointless. They are not weapons of warfare in competition with conventional armament. Under conditions of parity and beyond this equalizing function, nuclear weapons have an even more important stabilizing role as—to use a nutshell term—the ultimate guarantor of peace. In the view of NATO nations, nuclear weapons must therefore be a complement to a more stable conventional balance and to a durable East-West relationship. To be most effective, they must retain the features along which the Western system of deterrence has been conceptualized: a highly stratified arsenal with as many stabilizing elements as possible. Today we see the prospect of strategic stability achieved at much lower levels of strategic nuclear weapons in the START Agreement, with additional inherent incentives for further stabilizing unilateral measures, which the START Agreement may entail as an expression of the shared responsibility of the two major powers in the nuclear age. To this stable strategic order must also correspond a highly stratified system of nuclear weapons down to the theater arena, in lower numbers but with their generic presence unaffected.

One could even say that under terms of conventional parity at lower levels and under more defensive circumstances, nuclear weapons become *relatively* more important for the preservation of peace and stability. That means, of course, that the nuclear arsenal in Europe has to be restructured in a major way; we can already clearly conceive how. But one thing is certain: that these weapons need to be up-to-date, i.e., modernized. Without belaboring General Chervov's point (Chapter 7) it is quite certain that modernization and the maintenance of effective arsenals at lower levels must be a right of both sides. It is not possible that one side conducts, at high numbers, a major modernization move and then stops and cries "Wolf" if the other side, at much lower and modest levels, attempts the same.

My third comment refers back to the impending CAFE talks and the way in which the alliances prepare for these negotiations. Properly speaking, these are not alliance-to-alliance negotiations. I cannot speak for the NATO countries that participate; they will negotiate as sovereign nations. Still I would stress that in their joint preparations they have devoted a heavy amount of work to the conceptual basis of these negotiations.

The whole way in which these negotiations appear to take off—with a concentration on capabilities for surprise attack and invasion, for holding and keeping land, on the very key weapon systems, highly mechanized, that confer high mobility and high fire power—is largely a result of our conceptual effort. It is pleasing to see that this conceptual approach has not only found its reflection in the mandate for the negotiations but that Gorbachev's and Honecker's first unilateral steps prior to these negotiations have reflected this very conceptual approach by concentrating on the key weapon systems that we have identified as the ones on which the stability of the military relationship will hinge.

Our proposals have now been worked out in detail. Again, it is gratifying that they are in large part compatible with those that are now entertained by the other side. In that respect, I would particularly mention Minister Karpov's report (Chapter 1). A large part of his ideas are interesting and possibly acceptable to the other side. NATO has already given a glimpse of its negotiating approach last December, with a good deal of concrete indications, even with numbers; regrettably, this has not been given enough credit here. General Chervov asks, "Where is the reply to proposals from the WTO?" I argue that we have given more than a reply, that we have taken the initiative, set the scene. Of course, further details are there for the negotiating table. We are preparing to divulge them.

We are also encouraged by the view clearly conveyed in Karpov's report that we should not be bogged down by a struggle about data. The data issues will be difficult, but it should be our common endeavor to harness them. Approximate agreement on the dimension, on the order of magnitude, of existing forces are enough to move toward lower ceilings and then construct the verification régimes that we need to keep the participants to these lower residual, equal levels. It is important that unilateral steps have been taken, but it would be dramatic and fatal if they were considered to be all. We must not becloud the need for further reductions in the course of negotiations.

The significance of CSBMs for the entirety of Europe, especially involving the states not participating in these reduction negotiations, and as a support for the conventional arms talks has been stated amply. What we probably need is two CSBM régimes; one of confidence-building measures between the 23, which will be legally binding within their treaty relationship, and then a partly overlapping régime among the 35 under political auspices, which govern the larger relationship of all 35 CSCE participants. There is a package of transparency measures and predictability measures, which we have worked out in detail in NATO and which we want to introduce into the CSBM talks at 35.

There will also be new categories of proposals. I am particularly intrigued by an exchange of views on military doctrines, in their relationship to present capabilities and force structures in Europe. NATO countries agree that they need to be studied. I would even go further and think that one important element of the confidence-building measures talks here in Europe, and later perhaps elsewhere in the world, should be proposals for a joint education for peace where states would not only compare individual elements of their strategic thinking but would work broadly among their military colleges, among their general staffs, among political and military decision makers, in checking and devising their force structures, their exercise manuals and training courses, thus learning to structure their military for the preservation of peace, learning this jointly. There would be a vast and promising field for study by future conferences!

LIST OF CONFERENCE PARTICIPANTS*
(in alphabetical order)

---

* Benoît d'ABOVILLE, Deputy Director of Political Affairs, Paris, France
* Oluyemi ADENIJI, Ambassador of Nigeria in France
  Ednan AGAEV, Ministry of Foreign Affairs, Moscow, USSR
  Herbert von ARX, Head of the Office for Special Political Affairs, Federal Department of Foreign Affairs, Bern, Switzerland
* Marcos Castrioto de AZAMBUJA, Ambassador, Representative of Brazil to the Conference on Disarmament, Geneva
  Vicente BERASATEGUI, Director, United Nations Department for Disarmament Affairs, Geneva
* Arne Olav BRUNDTLAND, Senior Research Fellow, Norwegian Institute of International Affairs, Oslo, Norway
  Mario CAMPORA, Ambassador, Representative of Argentina to the Conference on Disarmament, Geneva
* Nikolai CHERVOV, General-Colonel, Ministry of Defense, Moscow, USSR
* Jean DESAZARS de MONTGAILHARD, Office of Strategic and Disarmament Affairs, Ministry for Foreign Affairs, Paris, France
  Gheorge DOLGU, Ambassador, Permanent Representative of Romania to the United Nations at Geneva
* Rolf EKEUS, Ambassador of Sweden in Vienna
* FAN Guoxiang, Ambassador, Head of the Delegation of the People's Republic of China to the Conference on Disarmament, Geneva
  Curt GASTEYGER, Director, Program for Strategic and International Security Studies, The Graduate Institute of International Studies, Geneva, Switzerland
* Victor-Yves GHEBALI, Geneva International Peace Research Institute (GIPRI), and Graduate Institute of International Studies, Geneva
* Ignac GOLOB, Ambassador, Ministry of Foreign Affairs, Belgrade, Yugoslavia
* Jon GUNDERSEN, Division Chief of European Security Negotiations, Division for Multilateral Affairs, United States Arms Control and Disarmament Agency (USACDA), Washington, DC, USA
* Roger HILL, Director of Studies, Canadian Institute for Peace and International Security, Ottawa, Ontario, Canada
* William HOPKINSON, Head, Defense Arms Control Unit, Ministry of Defense, London, UK
* Gyula HORN, Secretary of State, Ministry for Foreign Affairs, Budapest, Hungary
  Carl Magnus HYLTENIUS, Ambassador, Representative of Sweden to the Conference on Disarmament, Geneva
* Rikhi JAIPAL, Ambassador, New Delhi, India
* Victor KARPOV, Vice-Minister for Foreign Affairs, Moscow, USSR
  Miljan KOMATINA, Secretary general of the Conference on Disarmament and Personal Representative of the Secretary-General, United Nations, Geneva
  Dimitar KOSTOV, Ambassador, Permanent Representative of Bulgaria to the United Nations at Geneva

Boris **KRASULIN**, First Deputy Director, Department of International Organizations, Ministry of Foreign Affairs, Moscow, USSR
*Joachim **KRAUSE**, Advisor, Delegation of the Federal Republic of Germany to the Conference on Disarmament, Geneva
Paul **LEVER**, Head of the Security Policy Department, Foreign and Commonwealth Office, London, UK
Sten **LUNDBO**, Minister (Disarmament), Deputy Permanent Representative of Norway to the United Nations, Geneva
Ahmed **MAHIOU**, National Institute for Global Strategic Studies, INESG, Algiers, Algeria
*Pierre **MOREL**, Ambassador, Representative of France to the Conference on Disarmament, Geneva
*Kari **MÖTTÖLÄ**, Special Advisor for Disarmament and Security Policy Affairs, Political Department, Ministry of Foreign Affairs, Helsinki, Finland
*John Edwin **MROZ**, President, Institute for East-West Security Studies, IEWSS, New York, USA
*Manfred **MÜLLER**, Institut für Internationale Beziehungen, Potsdam, German Democratic Republic
*Hans-Peter **NEUHOLD**, Director, Austrian Institute for International Affairs, Vienna, Austria
*John van **OUDENAREN**, Policy Analyst, Political Department, The Rand Corporation, Washington DC, USA
*Zdeněk **PAGÁČ**, Senior Foreign Policy Advisor, Central Committee of the Communist Party, Prague, Czechoslovakia
Aldo **PUGLIESE**, Ambassador, Representative of Italy to the Conference on Disarmament, Geneva
Luc **REYCHLER**, Director, Centre for Strategic Studies, Catholic University of Leuven, Leuven, Belgium
Oswaldo de **RIVERO**, Ambassador, Representative of Peru to the Conference on Disarmament, Geneva
Anton **ROSBACH**, Deputy Commissioner for Arms Control and Disarmament, Ministry of Foreign Affairs, Bonn, Federal Republic of Germany
*Adam-Daniel **ROTFELD**, Polish Institute of International Affairs (PISM), Warsaw, Poland
*Joseph **SCHÄRLI**, Head of the Office for Security Policy, Federal Military Department, Bern, Switzerland
Alioune **SENE**, Ambassador, Permanent Representative of Senegal to the United Nations, Geneva
Stefano **SILVESTRI**, Deputy Director, International Affairs Institute (IAI), Rome, Italy
Marisol **TOURAINE**, Chargée de Mission, Office of the Prime Minister, Paris, France
*Hennig **WEGENER**, Deputy Secretary-General for Political Affairs NATO, Brussels
*Théodore **WINKLER**, Representative for Special Politico-Military Affairs, Federal Military Department, Bern, Switzerland
Chusei **YAMADA**, Ambassador, Representative of Japan to the Conference on Disarmament, Geneva
Juan A. **YANEZ BARNUEVO**, Director, International Department, Office of the Presidency of the Government, Madrid, Spain

UNIDIR
*Jayantha **DHANAPALA**, Director
Serge **SUR**, Deputy Director

IFRI
Thierry de **MONTBRIAL**, Director
Dominique **MOÏSI**, Deputy Director
Jean **KLEIN**, Director of Studies
*Jerôme **PAOLINI**, Researcher

---

*Names preceded by an asterisk indicate those whose reports are included in this book.

UNIDIR PUBLICATIONS
PUBLICATIONS RÉCENTES DE L'UNIDIR
(FROM 1987/DEPUIS 1987)

Research Reports/Rapports de Recherche

La guerre des satellites : enjeux pour la communauté internationale, par Pierre Lellouche, éd. (IFRI), Genève, UNIDIR, 1987, 42 p. Publication des Nations Unies, numéro de vente: GV.F.87.0.1. Also in English: *Satellite Warfare: A Challenge for the International Community.*

The International Non-Proliferation Régime 1987, by David A. V. Fischer, Geneva, UNIDIR, 1987, 81 p. United Nations publication, Sales No. GV.E.87.0.2.

La question de la vérification dans les négociations sur le désarmement aux Nations Unies, par Ellis Morris, Genève, UNIDIR, 1987, 228 p. Publication des Nations Unies, numéro de vente: GV.F.87.0.4. Also in English: *The Verification Issues in United Nations Disarmament Negotiations.*

Confidence-Building Measures in Africa, by Augustine P. Mahiga and Fidelis Nji, Geneva, UNIDIR, 1987, 16 p. United Nations publication, Sales No. GV.E.87.0.5.

Désarmement : problèmes relatifs à l'espace extra-atmosphérique, Genève, UNIDIR, 1987, 190 p. Publication des Nations Unies, numéro de vente: GV.F.87.0.7. Also in English: *Disarmament: Problems related to Outer Space.*

Interrelationship of Bilateral and Multilateral Disarmament Negotiations/Les relations entre les négociations bilatérales et multilatérales sur le désarmement, Proceedings of the Baku Conference, 2-4 June 1987/Actes de la Conférence de Bakou, 2-4 juin 1987, Geneva, UNIDIR, 1988, 258 p. United Nations Publication, Sales No. GV.E./F.88.0.1.

Disarmament Research: Agenda for the 1990s/La recherche sur le désarmement : Programme pour les années 90, Proceedings of the Sochi Conference, 22-24 March 1988/Actes de la Conférence de Sotchi, 22-24 mars 1988, Geneva, UNIDIR, 1988, 164 p. United Nations publication, Sales No. GV.E/F.88.0.3.

Le désarmement classique en Europe, par André Brie (IIB), Andrezej Karkoszka (PISM), Manfred Müller (IIB), Helga Schirmeister (IIB), Genève, UNIDIR, 1988, 63 p. Publication des Nations Unies, numéro de vente: GV.F.88.06. Also in English: *Conventional Disarmament in Europe.*

Arms Transfers and Dependence, by Christian Catrina, published for UNIDIR by Taylor & Francis (New York, London), 1988, 409 p.

Les forces classiques en Europe et la maîtrise des armements, par Pierre Lellouche et Jerôme Paolini, éds. (IFRI), Genève, UNIDIR, 1989, 100 p. Publication des Nations Unies, numéro de vente: GV.F.89.0.6. Also in English: *Conventional Disarmament and the Future of the European Security System.*

National Security Concepts of States: New Zealand, by Kennedy Graham, published for UNIDIR by Taylor & Francis (New York, London), 1989, 198 p.

Problems and Perspectives of Conventional Disarmament in Europe: Proceedings of the Geneva Conference 23–25 January 1989.

Forthcoming/A paraître

Verification by Airborne Means, by Allan Banner and Andrew Young.

Research Papers/Travaux de Recherche

No. 1. *Une approche juridique de la vérification en matière de désarmement ou de limitation des armements*, par Serge Sur, septembre 1988, 68 p. Publication des Nations Unies, numéro de vente: GV.F.88.0.5. Also in English: *A Legal Approach to Verification in Disarmament or Arms Limitation.*

No. 2. *Problèmes de vérification du Traité de Washington du 8 décembre 1987 sur l'élimination des missiles à portée intermédiaire*, par Serge Sur, octobre 1988, 62 p. Publication des Nations Unies, numéro de vente: GV.F.88.0.7. Also in English: *Verification problems of the Washington Treaty on the elimination of intermediate-range missiles.*

No. 3. *Les mesures de confiance du processus de la CSCE. Analyse paragraphe par paragraphe des régimes d'Helsinki et de Stockholm*, par Victor-Yves Ghebali, mars 1989, 114 p. Publication des Nations Unies, numéro de vente: GV.F.89.0.5 (forthcoming in English).

No. 4. *The Prevention of Geographical Proliferation of Nuclear Weapons: Nuclear Weapon Free-Zones and Zones of Peace in the Southern Hemisphere*, by Edmundo Fujita, April 1989, 53 p. United Nations publication, Sales No. GV.E.89.0.8. Existe aussi en français: *La prévention de la proliferation géographique des armes nucléaires: Zones exemptes d'armes nucléaires et zones de paix dans l'hémisphère sud.*

No. 5. *The Future Chemical Weapons Convention and its Organization: The Executive Council*, by Thomas Bernauer, May 1989, 37 p. United Nations publication, Sales No. GV.E.89.0.7. (à paraître également en français).

UNIDIR Newsletter/Lettre de L'UNIDIR — Quarterly/Trimestrielle

Vol. 1 No. 1, March/Mars 1988: "Disarmament-Development"/"Désarmement-Développement," 16 p.

No. 2, June/Juin 1988: "Research in Africa"/"La recherche en Afrique," 28 p.

No. 3, September/Septembre 1988: "Confidence-Building Measures and Limitation of Conventional Armaments in Europe"/"Mesures de confiance et limitation des armements classiques en Europe," 32 p.

No. 4, December/Décembre 1988: "Research in Asia and the Pacific"/"La recherche en Asie et dans le Pacifique," 40 p.

Vol. 2   No. 1, March/Mars 1989: "Chemical Weapons: Research Projects and Publications"/ "Armes chimiques : Projets de recherche et publications," 24 p.

No. 2. June/Juin 1989: "Research in Latin American and the Caribbean"/"La recherche en Amérique Latine et dans le Caribbean," 3 p.

For Product Safety Concerns and Information please contact our EU
representative GPSR@taylorandfrancis.com
Taylor & Francis Verlag GmbH, Kaufingerstraße 24, 80331 München, Germany